Governing after Communism

Governance in Europe

Series Editor: Gary Marks

Governing after Communism

Institutions and Policymaking

Vesselin Dimitrov, Klaus H. Goetz,
and Hellmut Wollmann

With Contributions by
Radoslaw Zubek and Martin Brusis

ROWMAN & LITTLEFIELD PUBLISHERS, INC.
Lanham • Boulder • New York • Toronto • Oxford

ROWMAN & LITTLEFIELD PUBLISHERS, INC.

Published in the United States of America
by Rowman & Littlefield Publishers, Inc.
A wholly owned subsidiary of The Rowman & Littlefield Publishing Group, Inc.
4501 Forbes Boulevard, Suite 200, Lanham, Maryland 20706
www.rowmanlittlefield.com

P.O. Box 317, Oxford OX2 9RU, UK

British Library Cataloguing in Publication Information Available

Library of Congress Cataloging-in-Publication Data

Dimitrov, Vesselin, 1974–
     Governing after communism : institutions and policymaking / Vesselin
Dimitrov, Klaus H. Goetz, and Hellmut Wollmann ; with contributions by Radoslaw
Zubek and Martin Brusis.
        p.   cm. — (Governance in Europe)
Investigates the processes and outcomes of more than a decade of institution
building at the center of government in Hungary, Poland, the Czech Republic and
Bulgaria.
     Includes bibliographical references and index.
     ISBN-13: 978-0-7425-4008-8 (cloth : alk. paper)
     ISBN-10: 0-7425-4008-1 (cloth : alk. paper)
     ISBN-13: 978-0-7425-4009-5 (pbk. : alk. paper)
     ISBN-10: 0-7425-4009-X (pbk. : alk. paper)
    1. Administrative agencies—Europe, Eastern.   2. Europe, Eastern—Politics and
government—1989–   3. Post-communism—Europe, Eastern.   I. Goetz, Klaus H.,
1961–   II. Wollmann, Hellmut, 1936–   III. Title.   IV. Series.
     JN96.A58D56 2005
     352.3′094′091717—dc22   2005018857

Printed in the United States of America

⊗™ The paper used in this publication meets the minimum requirements of
American National Standard for Information Sciences—Permanence of Paper for
Printed Library Materials, ANSI/NISO Z39.48-1992.

Contents

List of Tables and Figures

LIST OF TABLES

LIST OF FIGURES

Preface

This book examines the development of the institutions of central government and public policy–making in Bulgaria, the Czech Republic, Hungary, and Poland between the late 1980s and the early twenty-first century. The initial cutoff point for our empirical study was 2001, but, where possible, we have updated the information, albeit selectively, up to 2003. We trace and explain the trajectories of executive development with a focus on types of government, types of core executives, and types of centers of government—the two latter dimensions, in particular, have rarely been studied systematically and comparatively in postcommunist settings. We investigate the effects of executive institutions on policymaking through a detailed longitudinal analysis of budgetary policy. At heart, this book is about the processes and the consequences of initiatives aimed at filling the "hollow crown" (Weller and Bakvis 1997) at the level of the central state institutions, which had been created by the demise of the ruling communist parties. Our findings point to the precariousness of the institutional foundations of the power of chief executives (with the exception of Hungary); demonstrate the obstacles to effective cabinet government; provide many instances of "institutionalization for reversibility" under conditions of intense political conflict over institutional choices and sometimes sustained attempts at their external direction; and underline the decisive impact of party development and party system consolidation on executive development.

As Central and Eastern Europe is integrated ever more closely with "the West," postcommunist "transitology" is increasingly being replaced by mainstream approaches developed in the context of studying mature democracies. One of the key contributions of this book lies in the systematic application of the core-executive framework drawn from the West European literature, to four countries of Central and Eastern Europe, three of which have recently become members of the European Union, while the fourth can be expected to join soon. At the same time, we have sought to advance the discussion of the core executive by making a clear analytical distinction between types of government, types of core executives, and types of centers of government. This distinction can generate valuable insights not only with respect to the evolving government institutions of Central and Eastern Europe but also with regard to the more stable West European systems. Finally, with their focus on domestic institutions and the specific conditions under which they operate, our analysis of executive development and our attempt to account for executive trajectories over time engage with debates about the impact of EU enlargement, Europeanization, and, more broadly, the evolving patterns of European governance.

We offered anonymity to our interviewees. The list of interviewees toward the end of the book does, however, give an indication of the positions that our interviewees held at the time of our meetings.

Acknowledgments

This book could not have been written without the help and assistance of many individuals and institutions. Our biggest debt of gratitude is owed to the Volkswagen Foundation and especially Dr. Alfred Schmidt, who supported our work through a generous research grant. We could not have wished for more encouraging, helpful, and flexible sponsors. We hope that this book vindicates the foundation's trust in our ability to carry out a challenging project involving a team of five academics from three different institutions located in two countries carrying out research in four states.

At the time of approaching the Volkswagen Foundation, the three applicants—Dimitrov, Goetz, and Wollmann—took the decision to dispense with "country correspondents," that is, hired hands (and brains) in the countries to be studied, in favor of building a tightly integrated research team. Yet, in gathering and, in particular, interpreting our data, we did rely critically on the willingness of politicians, officials, and fellow researchers in Bulgaria, the Czech Republic, Hungary, and Poland to submit to interviews and to share their insights into the executive process with us (a list of interviewees can be found toward the end of the book). While we tried to base our findings as far as possible on documentary evidence, these interviews—lasting, on average, one to two hours but sometimes considerably longer—were invaluable when it came to the task of making sense of what, at first sight, often seemed incompatible or even contradictory information. We also wish to acknowledge the assistance of Tereza Vajdova in the Czech Republic and the Economic Policy Institute in Bulgaria.

Jeremy Richardson, the editor of the *Journal of European Public Policy*, offered us an opportunity to present some early findings of our work—along with several other commissioned pieces—in a thematic issue on executive governance in Central and Eastern Europe published in December 2001. This chance to publish preliminary findings encouraged us to reassess aspects of our approach while the research was still very much going on, and, thus, it proved enormously beneficial to the project overall.

Finally, we should like to thank Susan McEachern of Rowman & Littlefield and Gary Marks, who responded so positively to our initial proposal to place our book in the Governance in Europe series.

Abbreviations

AWS	Solidarity Electoral Action (Poland)
BCP	Bulgarian Communist Party
BSP	Bulgarian Socialist Party
COG	Center of Government
CSSD	Czech Social Democratic Party
DPM	Deputy Prime Minister
EU	European Union
FIDESZ	Alliance of Young Democrats (Hungary)
FIDESZ-MPP	Alliance of Young Democrats–Hungarian Civic Party
FKGP	Independent Smallholders' Party (Hungary)
GO	Government Office
IMF	International Monetary Fund
KDNP	Christian Democratic People's Party (Hungary)
KDS	Christian Democratic Party (Czech Republic)
KDU-CSL	Christian Democratic Union–Czechoslovak People's Party
KERM	Economic Affairs Committee of the Council of Ministers (Poland)
LPR	League of Polish Families
MDF	Hungarian Democratic Forum
MIÉP	Hungarian Truth and Life Party
MRF	Movement for Rights and Freedoms (Bulgaria)
MSZP	Hungarian Socialist Party
NMSII	National Movement for Simeon II (Bulgaria)
ODA	Civic Democratic Alliance (Czech Republic)
ODS	Civic Democratic Party (Czech Republic)

OECD	Organization for Economic Co-operation and Development
PiS	Law and Justice Party (Poland)
PMO	Prime Minister's Office
PO	Civic Platform (Poland)
PSL	Polish Peasant Party
PZPR	Polish United Workers' Party
SD	Democratic Party (Poland)
SLD	Democratic Left Alliance (Poland)
SZDSZ	Alliance of Free Democrats (Hungary)
UD	Democratic Union (Poland)
UDF	Union of Democratic Forces (Bulgaria)
UP	Labor Union (Poland)
URM	Office of the Council of Ministers (Poland)
UW	Freedom Union (Poland)
ZSL	United Peasants' Party (Poland)

I

THE STUDY OF
POSTCOMMUNIST EXECUTIVES

1

Core Executives after Communism

CREATING CORE EXECUTIVES

This book analyzes the development of core executive institutions and policymaking in Central and Eastern Europe (CEE) between the late 1980s and the early twenty-first century. It investigates the processes and outcomes of more than a decade of institution building at the center of government in Hungary, Poland, the Czech Republic, and Bulgaria. The empirical focus is on the emergence of coordinating institutions in central state executives and their impact on public policy, specifically budgetary policy. Thus, our analysis is concerned with what in the Western literature has become known as the "core executive," that is, those organizations and structures that "serve to pull together and integrate" government policies (Dunleavy and Rhodes 1990, 4). Our comparative investigation covers eight closely interlinked aspects of executive development, including the location of the executive in the political system; the outlines of the executive terrain; the powers of the prime minister; the powers of the finance minister; patterns of cabinet decision making; party-based political coordination devices; the organization and powers of the "center of government," that is, the Prime Minister's Office, the Cabinet Office, or the Government Office; and, finally, the politics–administration nexus, with a special emphasis on the tensions between professionalization, depoliticization, and politicization. The study explores the linkages between institutions and policymaking through a longitudinal comparative analysis of budgetary policy. At heart, this book is concerned with the processes and, in particular, the outcomes of initiatives aimed at filling the "hollow crown" (Weller and Bakvis 1997) that had been created by the disappearance of the ruling communist parties, which had served as the chief integrative institutions before 1989. It had been the leading party that strove to hold together an organizationally highly fragmented central executive system and provided the glue between the political and administrative parts of the central executive.

The study of the formation of postcommunist core executives casts new light on key concerns raised in the Western literature on executive development. Most notably, it engages with the debate on the "hollowing out" of the state, initiated by the work of Rhodes in the 1990s (1994). The notion of hollowing out suggests "a loss of capacity at the heart of the state—in the core executive" (Saward 1997, 17). In a recent summary of his writings, Rhodes (2003, 69) has briefly restated the argument about the erosion of core executive capacity, with specific reference to the British case: "The state has been hollowed out from above (e.g., by international interdependence), from below (by marketization and networks) and sideways (by agencies)." All of the processes noted by Rhodes could be observed in CEE in the course of the decline and collapse of communism. In terms of international interdependence, there was an abrupt shift from virtual autarchy under socialism (which was not fundamentally affected by cooperation within the Soviet bloc) to a rapid integration into European markets and international frameworks of political, economic, and military cooperation. With regard to marketization, a transition took place from a centrally planned, socially owned economy to market capitalism, on a scale vastly exceeding privatization in Western Europe. The last years of communism also saw the proliferation of agencies mainly concerned with economic reform, which were at best partially under the control of the executive. The collapse of communism may be seen, therefore, as an extreme variant of the hollowing out of the state.

The CEE experience is of interest not only because it provides examples of hollowing out in a radical form but also because the postcommunist countries witnessed its partial reversal. The Western European literature tends to perceive the hollowing out of the state as a unilinear process, and while many commentators have voiced deep normative concern over its consequences, they have rarely been able to observe determined and successful efforts at its reversal. In CEE, by contrast, we can study the re-creation of coordination capacity. Although by no means complete, this process has established core executives that, by the early twenty-first century, possessed coordinating capacities that in many respects resembled those of Western European democracies. This book traces the related processes on institution building and inquires into their chief determinants.

THE EXECUTIVE UNDER COMMUNISM

In trying to understand how and why the hollowing out of the state in CEE first took a radical form and was then partially reversed, we need to engage with another key debate in the study of executives that is concerned with the relationship between government and governing parties. This topic has been explored most systematically in the work of Blondel and Cotta (1996, 2000). The communist system was characterized by an unusually close relationship between party and government. This relationship has typically been conceived as one of subordination of the government to the party or, to use Blondel and Cotta's terminology, the existence of a "party" government in an extreme form. What has largely escaped comment is that this close relationship also made it possible for influence to flow in the opposite direction, from the government to the party, leading to the "governmentalization" of the party, a possibility hinted at by Andeweg (2000, 48). This process saw the transformation of the Communist Party from an agency of ideological revolution to an organ concerned primarily with technocratic policymaking. It gathered pace from the 1960s onward, in the context of a shift in the manner in which the communist parties sought to legitimize their rule. Instead of the creation of a perfect utopia, emphasis was placed on the rational administration of an increasingly complex society (Schopflin 1993). This shift proceeded to different degrees in the CEE countries, with Hungary and Poland going furthest in that direction. Yet, it affected all CEE regimes, including those of Czechoslovakia and Bulgaria, even though the reformulation of the party's legitimization claim was never made explicit (indeed, in Czechoslovakia, there was a deliberate reassertion of the ideological claim following the suppression of the Prague Spring of 1968).

The shift to technocratic governance was never fully completed; even in the most advanced countries, the Communist Party retained its claim to a monopoly of political power, on the grounds that it was the ultimate guarantor of the "people's will." There was, nevertheless, a major transformation in the functions of top-level party executive bodies, such as the Politburo and the Secretariat of the Central Committee. They became less concerned with the interpretation and imposition of Marxist-Leninist ideology and found themselves increasingly absorbed in the day-to-day tasks of government. Schopflin (1993, 133) goes so far as to argue that this functional shift led to the serious erosion of the parties' political skills, given that there was little occasion for their exercise: "There were few internal political challenges, only external ones from society, and these were fairly easily met. In effect, communist politics were more to do with administration than political decision-making."

The refocusing of party executive institutions toward governmental tasks meant that they operated, in effect, as part of the government. Indeed, to the extent that government involves the capacity for policy formation, they largely were the government. It is, accordingly, misleading to conceive of the communist executive as being confined to formal state institutions, using models derived from the study of Western democracies. The state executive institutions—the council of ministers, the ministerial administration, and other central state agencies—were primarily administrative bodies focused on implementation. Although the council of ministers was formally the government, it largely lacked essential qualities typically associated with this term in a Western context. The discussion of policy alternatives, arbitration among contending interests, and authoritative decision making were mostly the preserve of the party bureaucracy. Whereas in Western democracies the state executive combines governmental and administrative functions, under communism it was largely restricted to the latter.

The party executive not only performed policymaking functions for the state executive; it also took responsibility for holding the state executive together. The state executive was so highly fragmented that it could not have functioned in the absence of party coordination. Governments consisted of a large number of ministries (including the sectoral ministries charged with administering the various branches of the economy) and other central agencies. Many of the latter were formally attached to the Office of the Council of Ministers but operated with great degrees of autonomy. Since the ultimate center of power was the party and implementation was largely delegated to the individual ministries, there were few effective coordinating mechanisms within the government itself. In formal terms, the government was collective and collegiate, and its chairman had few prerogatives vis-à-vis his ministerial colleagues. Finance ministries, which, in Western systems, are seen as paramount policy shapers and coordinators, were weak. The "center of government," in the form of the Office of the Council of Ministers, exercised little control over the activities of ministries and other central agencies. It was largely restricted to providing administrative-technical assistance to the council of ministers (consisting of the prime minister and the ministers) but did not act as political gatekeeper and had few, in any, hierarchical powers.

The partial shift of Communist Party legitimization from ideology to technocratic competence also had implications for personnel policy in the public service. According to the typology provided by the Wasilewski (1990), one can distinguish three successive patterns of recruitment in the course of the development of the communist systems after the World War II. During the communist seizure of power in the mid- and late 1940s, the dominant pattern was one of "communist-combatant," based on active service in the war or in the struggle against opposition parties. The second pattern, established during the period of Stalinist industrialization, has been termed "communist-combatant-proletarian." It broadened the privileged group to include people of the "correct" class origin, involving the massive upward promotion of individuals from the urban and rural proletariat. The third pattern, which began to emerge after 1956, laid greater stress on administrative competence, corresponding to the shift in party legitimization toward rational technocratic management. This pattern of the "party expert" was an attempt to reconcile political and professional requirements. To satisfy the first provision, state officials had to be party members; to meet the second, a university education was required (Wasilewski 1990, 744). The balance between the two criteria was never fully clarified, although, over time, professional criteria gained growing importance. With the massive rise of Communist Party membership in the 1970s and the relaxation of entry requirements, party membership became a largely formal criterion, a process that advanced furthest in Hungary, spurred by the adoption of far-reaching economic reforms in the 1960s (György 1999; Meyer-Sahling 2003). The main problem of communist state administration was not, therefore, "politicized incompetence" (Derlien 1993) but rather the restricted nature of that competence. Reflecting an instrumental view of state administration as the executive organ for the will of the party, state officials, even at the highest levels, were perceived (and perceived of themselves) as administrators who were not routinely engaged in the formulation of and arbitration among policy alternatives. That capacity was concentrated in party bodies formally operating outside state structures, such as the Communist Party's Politburo and Central Committee and, as regards the generation of policy ideas, to a growing extent in academies and research institutes (this explains why the latter institutions became the favorite recruiting grounds of early postcommunist governments). The limited competence of senior state officials under communism reinforced the trend toward the ossification of the state apparatus, which was further encouraged by the absence of periodic political reshuffles of the type commonplace in most democratic systems.

BREAKING AND REESTABLISHING THE GOVERNMENT–PARTY NEXUS

The concentration of policymaking functions in Communist Party institutions meant that the gradual party withdrawal from the state during the last years of communism, as part of the Gorbachev-inspired reforms, led to a hollowing out of the state in that it created a "shell" of formal state institutions that possessed little, if any, coordinating capacity. The breaking of the link between the state and the party also had a reciprocal impact on the party—or rather, parties—since the Communist Party's abdication of its claim to be the sole representative of the people's will created conditions for the emergence of a competitive multiparty system. The parties developing within that system were primarily concerned with the representation of social interests rather than with the management of the state. In Blondel and Cotta's terminology (1996, 2000), parties became less "governmental"; that is, the influence of the government on the party diminished. It is useful here to remember Blondel and Cotta's distinction between the party-in-government, the parliamentary party, and the extraparliamentary party. The party-in-government consists of government ministers with the same party affiliation; the parliamentary party is composed of members of parliament sharing the same party identity; and the extraparliamentary party refers to the party organization outside parliament (Cotta 2000a, 2000b). In the context of the demise of communism, the influence of the party-in-government over the parliamentary and the extraparliamentary parties diminished. This reduction in "governmental" quality affected all parties, although it hit the new noncommunist parties especially strongly, since they had no governmental experience and often defined their identities primarily in terms of opposition to the government. In the former communist parties, the reduction in the "governmental" quality also occurred but was restrained by the legacies of the past.

The early years of postcommunism thus witnessed the growing apart of governments and parties. Governments that had previously relied critically on the contribution of the Communist Party to public policymaking saw themselves confronted with parliamentary and extraparliamentary parties that either tried to distance themselves from their previous record in government—in the case of the reformed communist parties—or had grown in opposition to the government. Within the executive a vacuum of policy leadership emerged, and few, in any, mechanisms were in place to hold together, let alone effectively coordinate, organizationally fragmented executives. At the same time, political parties either had no experience of being parties in government or deemphasized this role at the expense of their identities as parties in parliament or extraparliamentary parties. This led to a situation where the parties in government frequently found that their supposed supporters in parliament conducted themselves as if they were members of the opposition.

Against this background, the central challenge of postcommunist executive development has been to endow state executive institutions with political and governing functions and capabilities and to establish a political and administrative core executive capable of coordinating, integrating, and steering the activities of the government. Such a core executive could only emerge if supported by changes in political parties on the one hand and the public service on the other. As far as political parties were concerned, it was necessary to establish a mutually reinforcing relationship between state executive institutions and political parties. State institutions had to be shaped in a way that allowed them to be effectively directed by political parties in government; at the same time, parties in parliament and extraparliamentary parties that participated in the government needed to be molded so as to be responsive to the demands of exercising executive power. The development of the core executive also required changes in public administration. The key requirement in this area was the development of policymaking capacity at the top-level of the administration, the lack of which was arguably the most problematic inheritance from communism.

THE CHALLENGE OF COORDINATION

It is clear that the re-creation of executive coordination capacity was going to be a highly demanding process that would be affected critically by developments taking place outside the executive itself. Moreover, a powerful argument can be made that, in comparison to the mature democracies of Western Europe, the coordination requirements faced by the executives in postcommunist Europe have been especially demanding; the political, institutional, and financial conditions under which they have had to be addressed have been highly inauspicious; and the range of coordination options available in the short term has been severely restricted. Each set—coordination requirements, conditions, and options—deserves brief elaboration.

Like all governments, the postcommunist executives are faced with the consequences of their dual nature as political and administrative entities and of functional specialization and institutional differentiation, which are the defining characteristics of modern organizations. Accordingly, executive coordination can be understood on the one hand as a response to the need for authoritative political decision taking under the conditions of party government, coalition government, and parliamentary government and, on the other, as a response to organizational specialization, decentralization, departmentalism, and hierarchy as the hallmarks of modern bureaucracies. These challenges have long been present, but, as Peters and colleagues (2000, 8ff) point out, pressures for effective coordination have become more acute in recent decades, not least because of the increased sectorization of policymaking, growing budgetary constraints that force prioritization, and an evolving public policy agenda in which cross-cutting issues that do not fit neatly into existing departmental structures have gained in salience. As regards Western Europe, European Union (EU) membership is frequently identified as a further powerful force behind growing coordination requirements: "as Europe has grown in importance and complexity as a policy arena, it has become more important to 'get Europe right.' . . . The need for co-ordination on the part of governments has grown increasingly urgent" (Kassim, Peters, and Wright 2000, 3).

In the case of postcommunist executives, most of these standard coordination requirements apply with equal, if not greater force. For example, governing coalitions, in particular during the early transition years, were often disparate and loose alliances with little, if any, inbuilt stability; the relationships between government and legislatures were, at best tense and at worst openly hostile; central executives were characterized by a proliferation of ministries and specialized agencies; and budgetary pressures were chronic and, as discussed in chapter 8, sometimes dramatic. Moreover, although none of the countries we examined were EU members during the years covered by this study, accession negotiations and preparations for the full adoption and implementation of the *acquis communautaire* confronted Hungary, Poland, the Czech Republic, and Bulgaria with the need for a coordinated approach (Lippert, Umbach, and Wessels 2001).

The political, institutional, and financial conditions under which these challenges had to be addressed could scarcely have been less auspicious. At least during the first years of transition and, in the Bulgarian case, until well into the mid-1990s, the political environment in which executives operated was marked by instability and turbulence, the most visible expressions of which were high turnover of political executive personnel and frequent clashes between governments, presidents, and legislatures. The new democratic institutions had yet to consolidate, and their capacity to channel political competition was, accordingly, limited. Institutional legacies often hampered governments' ability to respond to the new policy exigencies: the helplessness of finance ministries with few directive powers in the face of spiraling budgetary deficits in the first transition years provides but one illustration.

More fundamentally, efforts to replenish the hollowed-out crown of the central executive were affected by the same "basic risks" that characterized postcommunist institutional transformation in general. They included, according to Wiesenthal (2001, 12ff.), the complexity of the tasks involved, combined with a lack of legal, cultural, and informational preconditions required for their solution; "decisionism," which is associated with the creation of institutions that appear as highly contingent, if not arbitrary, constructs; appropriateness, or rather inappropriateness, "because of the historical character of many of the institutions that serve as models" (15); and coevolution, where successful institutional innovation in one sphere relies critically on advances in another.

Chapters 3 to 6 provide many illustrations of how these risks affected the reshaping of central executives in Hungary, Poland, the Czech Republic, and Bulgaria. For example, administrative law needed to be established more or less from scratch; the new incoming democratic elites tended to distrust state officials appointed under the previous regime; and even basic information about the size and the structure of the public personnel system was lacking during the first transition years. "Decisionism" and "consequentialist" institution building followed a logic of "imitating, importing and transplanting" (Offe 1996, 212). Fostered by international institutions that operated with organizational blueprints, this encouraged a succession of short-lived institutional "fixes." Finally, the development of central coordination capacities was critically affected by other institutional arenas, most notably, legislatures and political party development (see chapter 2).

When it comes to the range of executive coordination options available in postcommunist settings, the trajectories of core executives in the countries under discussion appear closely resemblant to the general trend often noted in the West: "over the last thirty to forty years there has been a steady movement towards the reinforcement of the political core executive in most advanced industrial countries and...within the core executive, there has been an increasing centralisation of authority around the person of the chief executive—President, Prime Minister or both (as in France)" (Peters, Rhodes, and Wright 2000, 7). While in Hungary and Poland, this process can broadly be defined as "prime ministerialization," persistent ambiguities in the division of heads of state and prime ministers on the one hand and, more important, less-secure institutional foundations of prime ministerial authority on the other make the Czech and Bulgarian cases less straightforward to classify.

Part II documents the core executive trajectories in detail. It is important to stress that centralization in the form of a centralized prime ministerial core executive is not the only option to achieve coordination. As Peters and colleagues (2000) suggest, strong prime ministers often dominate core executives, but the emergence of core executives with substantial coordination capacities need not necessarily be associated with hierarchical coordination centered on the prime minister's authority. There is no shortage of typologies of both coordination tasks and devices (for recent surveys see Hayward 2002; Wright and Hayward 2000). Among the more frequently used are political versus administrative coordination; vertical (hierarchical) versus horizontal (nonhierarchical); imposed versus negotiated; positive versus negative; active versus reactive; and personalized versus institutionalized. The important point to note here is that a prime ministerial type of government— supported by a centralized prime ministerial core executive and a center of government directly subordinated to the chief executive—is arguably easier to attain and sustain than more contingent coordination systems, notably, cabinet governments. Put differently, faced with the "basic risks" of postcommunist institutionalization noted earlier, centralization around the prime minister offered a relatively straightforward answer to coordination requirements compared to more contingent coordination patterns that prioritize collegiality, collectivity, and inclusiveness. In particular, it appears less contingent or, put positively, more amenable to short-term institutional "engineering" than coordination based on policy networks, which take considerable time to emerge and require relatively high levels of trust among the participants.

THE EMPIRICAL SCOPE

Research on the core executive faces a problem all too familiar to the empirically minded social scientist, namely, that rigor and clarity in defining terms and concepts easily conflict with an untidy reality. Summarizing the findings of a major comparative study on policy coordination in six Western countries, Wright and Hayward (2000, 29) note that "the concept of the core executive proved to be more elastic in empirical practice than...anticipated"; that "it was not always easy to draw a distinction between co-ordination and decision-making in general" (30); and that "core executives everywhere are locked into a plurality of interdependent forms of coordinative exchange, mixing both processes of unilateral adjustment and interactive modalities of co-ordination, of hierarchy and network" (31). Accordingly, determining the empirical coverage of our investigation into the developmental trajectories of postcommunist core executives in a comparative—cross-country and longitudinal—design involved pragmatic choices. Each of the eight aspects of core executive development that are traced in chapters 3 to 6 deserves brief discussion.

The Location of the Executive in the Political System

The "external" dimension of molding a core executive concerns the position of the executive within the broader ensemble of state institutions and its interaction with political parties. In terms of its institutional position, two relationships have been of critical importance: first, the relationships between governments headed by the prime minister on the one hand and the presidency on the other; and, second, executive-legislative relationships. In each of these cases, the guiding question has been to what extent governmental functions have, over time, come to be concentrated within the executive headed by the prime minister. The executive's interaction with political parties is analyzed in terms of the party composition of the government, where we distinguish between one-party governments, coalition governments in which the partners can expect to stay together in future elections, and coalition governments in which the parties can expect to run against each other in future contests (Hallerberg 2000).

The Outlines of the Executive Terrain

Just as the distinction between coordination and decision making in general may be blurred, there are no fixed boundaries between the central executive in general and the core executive, which focuses on the business of coordination. At the same time, the dynamics of core executive development cannot be properly understood without appreciation of the overall executive terrain. The guiding intention here has been, therefore, to set out the overall executive terrain in terms of the main ministerial structures and, where appropriate, key nonministerial agencies.

The Powers of the Head of Government (the Prime Minister)

As already noted, prime ministerialization has often been regarded as a key feature of core executive development in the West. Against this background, our guiding question has been how the formal and informal powers of the prime minister have evolved over time.

The Powers of the Minister of Finance

Ministries in charge of planning and executing the overall state budget are regularly seen as an integral part of the core executive, as budgeting is perhaps the most complex and contentious coordination activity in which governments regularly engage. Our guiding question has been how the powers and coordination prerogatives of the finance ministries have evolved over time.

Patterns of Cabinet Decision Making

The cabinet is traditionally seen as the focus, if not the actual locus, of much coordinative activity in government. As Blondel (Blondel and Müller-Rommel 1997, 14–15) has argued in his comparative survey of Western European cabinets, even in countries where non-cabinet-based coordination devices are used extensively, the council of ministers "remains an arena in which final appeals can be and are made, as well as (at least in some countries) a place where ideas are discussed." Our guiding question has been how cabinets have evolved in terms of their collegiality (i.e., the degree of equality among cabinet ministers) and their collectivity (i.e., the degree to which decisions are taken collectively).

Party-Based Political Coordination Devices

Recent work on political coordination in Western governments has documented the extent to which executive-based coordination mechanisms, such as cabinet committees, have been supplemented by party-based devices. A prime minister may, for instance, be able to coordinate the work of his colleagues by virtue not so much of his state executive position but of his role as party leader. In coalition governments, we can expect to see the use of instruments such as written coalition agreements, coalition committees, coalition working groups, or party summits (Müller and Strom 2000). We have sought, first, to trace the evolution of such coordination devices and, second, to assess the pattern of their interaction with executive-based mechanisms. The two sets of mechanisms do not always operate in parallel. The effectiveness of one set of mechanisms may compensate for the weakness of the other; but it is also possible that the presence of one set of mechanisms may inhibit the development of the other.

The Powers and Organization of the "Center of Government"

Centers of government are generally understood to comprise the institutions that provide direct support and advice to the head of government and/or the cabinet. In an article published some years ago, Goetz and Margetts (1999) argued that, while in formal terms, centers of government in CEE might be at the heart of the executive process, their coordinating capacity had remained strictly limited. The empirical evidence on which this assessment was based was impressionistic and illustrative rather than systematic and comparative. The guiding question has been how the powers and organization of the center have evolved.

The Politics–Administration Nexus

The relationships between the political and administrative parts of the executive and, in particular, the role of nonelected officials in coordination are regularly regarded as being key to understanding core executives. Against the background of a legacy of a public service with a virtually exclusive focus on implementation, our guiding questions have been twofold: What steps were taken for the professionalization and depoliticization of the low- and middle-level civil service as a basis for long-term administrative competence? And what provisions have been developed for a legally regulated politicization of a layer of the top civil service, which would allow the executive to exercise its political-governmental functions?

FROM MAPPING TO EXPLANATION

The first objective of this book is unashamedly empirical: it seeks to trace the evolution of core executives across countries and across time. Judged by the demands of textbook approaches to comparative political inquiry, this is, of course, a modest ambition, for it is commonly held that "the goal is inference" (King, Keohane, and Verba 1994, 7; emphasis in the original), as scientific "activities always imply the quest for explanations" (Pennings, Keman, and Kleinnijenhuis 1999, 6). The holy grail of explanation is, however, unreachable without systematic data, and the first key objective of our research has been to gather such data, which is primarily qualitative. There is, of course, a large literature on postcommunist institution building in general, but comparative empirical enquiries into the workings of postcommunist governments have been few and far between (Blondel and Müller-Rommel 2001; Goetz 2001a, 2001b; Nunberg 2000; Nunberg, Barbone, and Derlien 1999; for studies on individual countries, see the references in chapters 3 to 6), among which Blondel and Müller-Rommel's work (2001) stands out for its rigorous analysis. The politics of macroinstitutional choices—between parliamentarism and presidentialism and between majoritarian and consensual democracies—which refer to the location of the executive in the wider political system, are quite well understood. Accordingly, as regards the first point of our empirical agenda, we have been able to rely very much on existing studies. But the central executives themselves—their organization and internal workings—have, in important respects, remained "black boxes" into which the searching light of academic research has rarely shone. In fact, much of what has been published on the executives in the region has been produced by international organizations (Nunberg 2000; Nunberg, Barbone, and Derlien 1999) or has arisen out of the work of consultants active in the region (Verheijen 1999a, 2001). We note this not to belittle their contributions to the stock of our empirical knowledge. But, inevitably, such investigations are driven by practical rather than scientific concerns, and it can be difficult to distinguish analysis from evaluation and prescription.

The second objective is to get a typological handle on the emergent executives. As chapter 2 sets out in greater detail in framing our empirical guiding questions, we employ mainstream typologies used in the literature on comparative executives so as to be able to classify our empirical findings. There is a danger here that is too well known to require much comment: it is to mistake ideal types for templates that institution builders ought to emulate. As Hellmut Wiesenthal (2001, 10) has observed, writing on postcommunist transformations is replete with "calamity diagnoses" that "concentrate on the discrepancy between official optimism and results that are identified as unsatisfactory." Confusing (or perhaps rather fusing) ideal types with templates, which themselves are idealized versions of supposed Western practice, encourages this misdiagnosis. Our use of typologies has been inspired by the aim to make our findings contribute to the literature on comparative government and public administration by trying to classify what we have found in terms that are used in mainstream studies.

The third and fourth objectives are then, indeed, essentially concerned with problems of explanation. As has often been noted (Egeberg 1999; Goetz 2003), there is a remarkable reticence on the part of students of the inner workings of executives to link particular arrangements to specific outputs. While much is known about how executive configurations vary in Western democracies, the importance of these variations for the quality of policy outputs is not well understood. As far as patterns of coordination in particular are concerned, this point is underscored by the findings of major recent comparative studies focusing on Western Europe. Thus, Wright and Hayward's summary (2000, 44–45) of the key findings of their six-country study of executive coordination concludes that "'optimal' coordination will depend on a host of variables, such as the nature of coordination ambitions and constitutional, institutional, political and administrative opportunity structures." Similarly, Wright's comparative analysis of the national coordination of EU policymaking (Wright 1996, 165; quoted in Kassim 2000) is extremely cautious about linking institutions and effects, noting that "the effectiveness of a country's domestic EU co-ordination capacity must be judged according to the issue, the policy types, the policy requirements and the policy objectives. Merely to examine the machinery of co-ordination is to confuse the means and the outcomes." The conclusions of a more recent comparative effort on the same subject are equally modest as regards the effectiveness of different national coordination systems: "The question of effectiveness—what it means in an EU context and whether there is a recipe for success in the form of a particular national strategy— though undoubtedly an important concern, is extremely problematic" (Kassim 2000, 254).

We seek to make a contribution to advancing this debate by focusing, in particular, on the effects of centralization on the outputs of budgetary processes. Building on the work of von Hagen (1998) and Hallerberg (2000; see also, Hallerberg and von Hagen 1999; von Hagen and Harden 1994), in particular, chapter 8 explores the hypothesis that centralized executive institutions lead to better budget performance, defined in terms of the level of the general government fiscal deficit, than do decentralized institutions.

Finally, in truly reaching our holy grail, our study seeks to account for cross-country variation in core executive trajectories. The literature on postcommunist institutional transformations is no different from analyses in comparative government and public administration more generally in that it operates with a bewildering array of explanatory schemes, with the common distinction between institutional and actor-centered approaches, in their many variants and mixtures. But a number of specific, although by no means unique, themes characterize many of the contributions (see, e.g., Wiesenthal 2001): an emphasis on the decisive role of organizational, institutional, cultural, and mental legacies in shaping postcommunist trajectories; the significance of "path-dependencies"; the critical role that political and bureaucratic "entrepreneurs" can assume under conditions when inherited institutions have been delegitimized or have disintegrated altogether but when new institutions exist only in rudimentary form and do not (yet) act as effective constraints on individual actions; the importance of "critical junctures" fairly early on in the transition process; the impact of generalized resource shortages—human, financial, organizational, informational, physical—that is, institutionalization under conditions of pronounced scarcity; the critical influence of time, timing, and sequence; and, finally, the often decisive contribution that external actors—notably, international financial institutions and the EU—have made in shaping institutional development.

While recognizing the contributions of these studies, we go beyond the analysis of the impact of isolated variables and attempt to construct a coherent explanatory framework. As set out in chapter 2, historical institutionalism (Checkel 1999; Featherstone and Kazamias 2001; Hay and Wincott 1998) can offer a basis for such a framework. We recognize the importance of structural factors, in particular, the powerful effect of inherited institutions in constraining the choices of actors and, to some extent, in shaping their identity; and the significance of critical junctures at which institutions are remolded and a new institutional "path" is potentially established. We also recognize that at the critical junctures, actors may be able to make choices that are less driven by the effect of existing institutions than by the actors' own power calculations. Having made these choices, actors find themselves increasingly bound by them, and both their pursuit of self-interest and even their identities are shaped by the institutions that they have created.

In the analysis of the development trajectories of postcommunist core executives, the most important structural factor is the impact of the institutional legacy of communism, although the choices made at critical junctures may establish new path dependencies. Two critical junctures can be identified in the development of CEE core executives: the fall of communism in 1989, and the mid-1990s "crisis of governance." The latter crisis was mainly expressed in the form of a severe fiscal imbalance, indicating the inability of governments to match their policy choices to available resources. In analyzing the role of actors, we focus on political parties. Based on the development of the institutional choice model put forward by Hallerberg and von Hagen (Hallerberg 2000; Hallerberg and von Hagen 1999; von Hagen 1998), we attempt to explain the choices made by political parties at the critical junctures for centralized or decentralized types executive institutions.

UNDERSTANDING INSTITUTIONS

The manner in which we approach the study of postcommunist core executive development warrants some comment, as it deviates in some respects from most of the work in this area. The first point to note here is that any approach needs to take account of the importance of institutional legacies; it must be process oriented and not conceive of change in the executive as a one-time event; but it should not privilege change in accounts of executive development. As regards legacies, it is still sometimes assumed that the implosion of communism left an institutional vacuum or tabula rasa from

which a new set of institutional arrangements has grown. Yet, as far as the
executive has been concerned, no such tabula rasa has ever existed. Postcommunist executive development has been, therefore, in the main about
reinstitutionalization rather than the creation of new institutions *ab ovo*. Our
longitudinal project design sought to bring out the emergence of core executives as a process.

It is also worth recalling that, given the impressive list of potential sources
of change, elements of continuity and inertia might easily be overlooked.
Thus, early writing on postcommunist reform construed "democratic cen-
tralism" as the antithesis or mirror image of a classical modern public administration. It concluded, accordingly, that only a radical—that is, root and
branch—reform of the executive would be compatible with full democratization. More recently, similar arguments have been made within the context
of the discussion about the EU compatibility of CEE administrations. Here,
the emphasis on accession criteria and the capacity to implement the *acquis
communautaire* goes hand in hand with calls for fundamental reform. In
the light of such change requirements, it is easy to lose sight of continuities
and to overemphasize change.

It should have become clear by now that our analysis of core executive
trajectories is strongly institutionalist and, what is more, at least in some
respects decidedly "old" institutionalist, in that we are, to a large extent,
interested in formal institutions. This institutionalist orientation is expressed
in the way in which the eight key aspects of executive development that
we have explored through empirical analysis are defined; it influences our
focus on types of government, types of core executives, and types of centers
of government; it is apparent in the causal linkages we seek to establish
between the configurations of budgetary institutions and budgetary outputs;
and it is also evident in the choice of factors that we consider in accounting
for divergence in core executive trajectories in the region.

There is no need here to rehearse the general arguments about the potential of, and limits to, institutionalist analysis; but two particular points
deserve some comment. They concern, first, the nature of institutionalization in transitional settings and, second, the specific nature of executive
institutions, characterized by the duality of political and administrative ratio-
nalities and an often very close connection between office and officeholder.
In respect of the first point, Wiesenthal's analysis (2001) of "basic risks" in
postcommunist transformation provides a reminder of the precariousness
of institutionalization; there are certainly good theoretical reasons for one
to expect the institutionalization of postcommunist core executives to be
slow and uncertain. The influence of pre-1989 institutional legacies features
prominently among them. There is disagreement over how this legacy can be
characterized in general terms, notably, as regards the absence of coordinating institutions within the formal executive. Thus, Lepsius (1997) has written

of a "politically enforced under-institutionalization" as a consequence of the dominance of political rationality criteria over all others. Under communism, "the fusion of institutions led to the omnipotence of one institution, the party line, which was determined by the politburo." Because of "deinstitutionalization and institutional fusion" under communism, the postcommunist creation of new institutions has been likely to face particular difficulties, not least because "although the West provides models, they have to be implemented endogenously" (68). While we do not fully agree with the argument that the communist executive as a whole—that is, including both the formal institutions of government and the policymaking party bodies—was underinstitutionalized, there is no doubt that the government institutions on their own lacked coordinating capacity and that the development of such capacity after 1989 presented formidable challenges. By contrast, Nielsen, Jessop, and Hausner (1995, 4) have argued that the fall of communism created no institutional vacuum but "what one can reasonably term a 'systemic vacuum,' i.e., a situation where there was no overall systemic logic, no dominant axis of societalisation secured through the conduct of key societal agents in a regularized, elaborate, and interconnected set of institutions." In either case, rebuilding executive institutions must be expected to be protracted process.

Second, the emphasis put on the enactment, internalization, and habitualization of institutional norms and values, which is typical of sociologically inspired institutional theory, draws attention to the potential incongruence between formal institutions and the people who bring them alive. Offe (1996) has stressed this aspect in his account of institutional design in CEE transitions. "Consequentialist" institution building raises the prospects of a scenario where "the new institutions are in place, but they fail to perform in anticipated ways, and thus become subject to ever more hectic cycles of renewed institutional engineering and concomitant efforts to 'reeducate' people so as to make them fit for their roles in the new institutions" (212). Put differently, the capacity of institutions to guide individual behavior is likely to be strictly limited.

However, it is misleading to equate obstacles to "deep" institutionalization with failed institutionalization. First, as the Hungarian case (chapter 3) in particular demonstrates, core executives with substantial coordination capacities have indeed emerged, despite "basic risks," which, as our empirical findings suggest, have in some cases been successfully overcome. Equally as important, evidence of frequent executive reorganizations (as provided by the Polish case, chapter 4), considerable turnover in personnel, and even a degree of incongruence between institutional norms and individual behavior must not in itself be taken as confirmation of a failure of institution building. The decisive point here is that under conditions of considerable uncertainty, resource shortages, and attempts at external direction, "institutionalization for reversibility" may be a more rational and appropriate strategy for institution building than one that deliberately seeks to foreclose future options. In other words, it may at times be more advisable to build tents rather than castles. Such patterns of "light" or "shallow" institutionalization are more evident in some countries than in others, and they are to be expected, in particular, in cases where political conflicts over institutional choices and external direction play a powerful role.

How the first wave of Eastern countries participating in EU enlargement sought to adapt their executives to the twin challenge of negotiating accession and creating institutional capacity for implementing the *acquis communautaire* provides an illustration of the dynamics at play (Goetz 2005). As long as the accession countries are in the position of being policy *takers* rather than policymakers, there are good grounds for keeping "sunk costs" low and for minimizing the thresholds for further institutional reform (i.e., to limit path dependencies) when accession can be expected to be accompanied by a major rebalancing of the power relations between the EU and CEE countries. Frequent changes in the domestic machineries for accession negotiations (Ágh 2002; Lippert, Umbach, and Wessels 2001; Lippert and Umbach 2005), legal harmonization (Zubek 2005a; 2005b), or the administration of EU funds (van Stolk 2005) are then not indications of a generalized institutional malaise but of provisional institution building.

Part II of this book and chapter 7 offer plentiful evidence for the difficulties involved in "governmentalizing" postcommunist executives, which both the specific institutional legacy and the "basic risks" to postcommunist institutional transformation help to explain. But, as the preceding remarks should have made clear, recurrent organizational changes and evidence of personalist institution building—where institutions are molded around key individuals and remolded as they leave the scene—must not be in themselves taken as proof for the lack of core executive capacity.

Reflecting on the nature of the institutional specificities of executives also helps to caution against exaggerated notions of stability and the capacity of executive institutions to govern individual action. Two characteristics of executives are of particular relevance—namely, their duality as political and administrative entities and the often very close connection between office and officeholder, especially at the level of executive politicians (for a more detailed discussion, see Goetz 2003). As political institutions, executives are oriented toward acquiring, securing, and exercising political power, a function that often predominates at the center of government. At the same time, executives are, of course, administrative institutions associated, at least in the West European context, with a bureaucratic rationality that stresses impartiality, objectivity, regularity, and legality. These principles and, in particular, the identification of a permanent civil service with the public good remain central to the self-image of ministerial public services in Western Europe.

At the same time, at the top levels of the political executive, in particular, office and officeholder may become difficult to separate analytically (Göhler 1994). Certainly mainstream executive studies, notably, of chief executives and ministers, regularly note the importance of the personal qualities, dispositions, and motives of incumbents and their capacity to shape the offices that they occupy. As regards administrators, rational choice accounts of public bureaucracy in particular stress the intention and capacity of officials to shape at least in part the offices they hold, whether they are understood as "budget maximisers" or "bureau-shapers" (Niskanen 1971; Dunleavy 1991).

What are the analytical implications of the dual nature of executives and the proximity of office and officeholder for the present study? First, at a most practical level, we have sought to bridge the divide between comparative government and comparative public administration in analyzing the executive. Thus, our study is placed at the interface of two subdisciplines of political science. The first—comparative government—typically focuses on the primarily political and governmental aspects of the executive. It deals, for example, with the role of prime ministers in government; cabinets and cabinet committees; coalition governments, including how they are formed and terminated, how portfolios are allocated, and how political decisions made; and the relationships between governments and political parties. By contrast, accounts from the perspective of comparative public administration are interested, first and foremost, in the bureaucratic parts of the executive that extend beneath its thin political veneer. Such studies concentrate on the executive "machinery," in particular, the ministerial administration and other types of central agencies; the status, organization, and role of non-elected executive personnel, notably, the civil service; and, increasingly, the importance of administrative law in governing executive action. On the basis of these two perspectives, the government can be seen as occupying the top level of two parallel pillars of power, one rooted in political parties and focused on political leadership and the other representing the bureaucratic foundations of executive power, with the government acting as the supreme authority of a multilevel and wide-ranging administrative machine. The government not only draws power from each of these pillars but is also affected by them. By its location at the top of both pillars, it has a uniquely advantageous position, enabling it not only to link the two but also to play one against the other (Blondel and Cotta 2000).

This subdisciplinary division of labor also influences the way in which problems of executive coordination are typically approached. Thus, accounts from a comparative government perspective tend to revolve around the notions of party government, coalition government, and parliamentary government. Such accounts stress the interwoveness of executives, governing parties, and parliamentary parties in the modern governing process and point to their consequences for executive coordination (Blondel and

Cotta 1996, 2000). Viewed from this perspective, executive coordination is principally understood as a consequence of the overriding need for political compromise in increasingly differentiated and complex policymaking frameworks. It is a means of resolving conflicts over political preferences and priorities, both within the executive and between the executive and the political forces and institutions with which it must cooperate. Cross-national variations in coordination mechanisms are, accordingly, chiefly to be explained with reference to political variables, such as the party-political makeup of government, the nature of executive-legislative relations, the dynamics of party composition, and/or the degree of centralization in the political system.

By contrast, discussions from the perspective of comparative public administration take the organizational features of the executive system as their point of departure. Thus, coordination is the attempt to cope with the tensions between specialization, decentralization, departmentalism, and hierarchy on the one hand and the real-life interdependence of policy issues on the other. Careful institutional design can help to minimize the need for interinstitutional coordination, but it cannot eliminate it altogether. Accordingly, comparative public administration is interested in the principles underlying the interministerial division of labor and the internal organization of ministerial departments and other central agencies; it analyzes how these affect coordination requirements; and it studies administrative coordination devices, such as task-specific working groups staffed by officials or formal procedural guidelines governing the preparation and interministerial coordination of legislative initiatives within the executive. In discussing coordination, we have attempted to bring the two perspectives together and, as far as possible, to situate our account within both subdisciplines.

A second implication of executive duality relates to the issue of stability. With reference to classical modernization theory, Lepsius (1997, 59), for example, has argued that "if under typical circumstances one finds a 'syncretism' of guiding ideas, then one cannot assume that behavior will become regular, predictable and typical." Without pushing this point too far, the duality of executives seems to imply that a measure of instability is inbuilt, more so than in purely political or purely administrative institutions. Dynamism is further enhanced by the capacity of executive politicians and senior officials to fashion the offices they occupy.

None of these remarks do, in our view, detract from the value of an institutionalist perspective. But they highlight the need to be sensitive to the specifics of core executives and the postcommunist settings in which they have begun to emerge, and they caution against overplaying the significance of stabilization and depersonalization in understanding core executive development.

THE DOMESTIC SETTING AND EUROPEAN GOVERNANCE

Early studies of postcommunist government and administration were strongly inspired by modernization theory in both its sociological and its political science variants (Hesse 1993; Hesse and Goetz 1993a, 1993b, 1993c; König 1992). Since then, however, two perspectives have come to predominate: enlargement and Europeanization (e.g., Ágh 1999, 2002, 2003; Dimitrova 2002; Fink Hafner and Lajh 2003; Grabbe 2001; Laffan 2003; Lippert, Umbach, and Wessels 2001). Both are closely related but tend to address somewhat different concerns. Enlargement studies have sought to ascertain whether the executives of CEE are "ready for Europe," in the sense of guaranteeing the effective and efficient implementation of the *acquis communautaire* of the EU; Europeanization studies have a broader interest in the consequences of EU accession for the governmental and administrative systems of new EU member states. Both perspectives share a concern with external determinants of change in domestic institutions in that they focus on EU accession as the driver or at least the catalyst of domestic change.

Our study, with its explanatory emphasis on domestic institutions and actor constellations, does not seek to offer a "rival" account. Rather, it directs attention to what the Europeanization literature typically labels domestic "intervening variables" (Radaelli 2003) or "facilitating factors" (Börzel and Risse 2003). As chapter 9 explores in greater depth, such a focus on domestic settings helps to understand how postcommunist institutions and policies fit into a broader comparative picture of developments in European governance. Thus, our evidence on the depletion, and subsequent replenishing, of the hollow crown in CEE shows important similarities with the West European experience with respect to the weakening of the state's coordinating capacity; but it also indicates, more optimistically, that the hollowing-out process could be reversed. It thus helps to identify the domestic conditions for rebuilding executive capacity.

COMPARATIVE DESIGN AND SOURCES

The golden rule of comparative research is to let "variables vary" and to base the selection on the variation in the explanatory variables rather than in the dependent variable. The four countries in our study—Hungary, Poland, the Czech Republic, and Bulgaria—have been chosen on the basis of variation in their structural conditions, actor constellations, and critical junctures. A number of more practical considerations also pointed to this choice. Each member of the research team had previous experience of empirical research in one or more of the four countries, and, with the exception of the Czech

Republic, at least one team member commanded the languages of the countries studied as a native speaker or with close to native-speaker standard. Thus, only in the Czech Republic did we have to rely on local interpreters and translators.

The research methods employed consisted principally of documentary analysis and open-ended interviews that were oriented toward the empirical guiding questions set out here. Much of the information collected was qualitative, with quantitative data being of some importance in the analysis of the civil service and budgetary policymaking. It is worth highlighting that even fairly basic data of the kind usually readily available for mature Western democracies—such as public personnel figures—often needed to be gathered in a fairly laborious manner. This proved a special challenge when it came to reconstructing the recent past of the early transition years. We conducted several interview rounds with high-ranking politicians and officials in each of the four countries, paying particular attention to the centers of government and finance ministries. The main types of documents consulted included official publications of national governments and international organizations and their websites; parliamentary papers; and newspaper reports. The study has also profited greatly from other work carried out by members of the team in the countries concerned, including Brusis's research (1999, 2002) on regionalization in CEE; Dimitrov's work (2001) on the Bulgarian political system; Goetz's involvement in a study funded by the British Economic and Social Research Council on the transfer of "good governance" to emergent democracies (Goetz, Panizza, and Philip 2004); Wollmann's work (1997) on postcommunist local government reform; and Zubek's doctoral research (2005a, 2005b) on the transposition of European Community legislation in Poland.

PREVIEW

The organization of the book reflects the four main objectives set out here. We start by explaining in greater detail our framework of analysis for the comparative inquiry (chapter 2). Part II then presents the empirical evidence of core executive development from the four countries under investigation. The chapters on Hungary (chapter 3), Poland (chapter 4), the Czech Republic (chapter 5), and Bulgaria (chapter 6), respectively, follow a common outline. Each surveys the main political developments during the time under investigation; charts the evolving location of the executive in the political system; provides an overview of the main executive institutions; examines the development of the center of government; considers the practices of cabinet decision making and political coordination; and explores the changing status of the public service, with a focus on senior officials. Part III is devoted to comparative assessments. Chapter 7 summarizes the main empirical findings by comparing and contrasting country trajectories and outcomes; it classifies the emergent executive systems with reference to type of government, type of core executive, and type of center of government; and it seeks to account for the cross-country differences found. Chapter 8 explores institutional effects through the analysis of executive arrangements for budgetary policymaking. This chapter, too, is concerned with explanation in that it discusses the link between the configuration of the core budgetary institutions and budgetary performance. Chapter 9 offers comparative conclusions that set our findings within the context of debates about the future of European governance.

2

Executive Institutions and Policy: A Framework of Analysis

MAPPING THE CORE EXECUTIVE

In line with Rhodes and Dunleavy's definition (1995), we understand "core executive" to mean "all those organisations and procedures which coordinate central government policies, and act as final arbiters of conflict between different parts of the government machine." These coordinating mechanisms include "the complex web of institutions, networks and practices surrounding the prime minister, cabinet, cabinet committees and their official counterparts, less formalized ministerial 'clubs' or meetings, bilateral negotiations and interdepartmental committees." They also include coordinating departments, such as the Prime Minister's Office, the Cabinet Office and the Finance Ministry (Rhodes and Dunleavy 1995, 12).

The concept of "core executive" has a number of analytical advantages. First, it recognizes that empirical analysis needs to go beyond the formal allocations of power in government and examine the coordinating institutions that support—or undermine—them. As Rhodes and Dunleavy put it, "'Who coordinates?' is an empirical question. It is quite possible that the prime minister and/or the cabinet play this role, but the point must be documented, not asserted." Second, the concept of "core executive" extends the analysis beyond the prime minister and the cabinet and considers the roles of coordinating institutions such as the Finance Ministry. Third, the concept places the focus on the critical issues of fragmentation and coordination in government. It links with the debate on the "hollow crown," which examines the capacity of governments to provide coherent policies and follow consistent procedures (Weller, Bakvis, and Rhodes 1997). As Rhodes (1994, 149) points out, "Fragmentation constrains the centre's administrative ability

27

to coordinate and plan. Diminished accountability constrains the centre's ability to exercise political control. In sum, current trends erode the centre's capacity to steer the system—its capacity for governance."

Based on Rhodes and Dunleavy's formulation (1995), we map the development of postcommunist core executives with a focus on eight dimensions: the location of the executive within the political system, with an emphasis on the relations between the government, the president, and parliament, as well as between the government and political parties; an outline of the executive terrain, covering the main departmental structures and key agencies, with a focus on the question of fragmentation; the development of the prime minister's powers; the powers of the finance minister, particularly in the context of the budgetary process discussed in chapter 8; patterns of cabinet decision making, with a focus on procedures governing the preparation of decisions and those establishing the agenda and decision taking in cabinet sessions, different degrees of collegiality and collectivity, and the use of coordinating devices (e.g., cabinet committees, deputy prime ministers, and cabinet presidiums); party-based political coordination devices; the powers and organization of the center of government; and the politics–administration nexus, with a particular focus on the legal status of officials and their position within the core executive.

The Location of Executive in the Political System

Our empirical analysis begins by locating the central executive within the political system. We focus on the relationship between the government, the presidency, and parliament and between the government and political parties. The former relationship has been a key preoccupation of the comparative government literature (Dimitrov and Goetz 2000). Much of the discussion has revolved around the distinction between presidential and parliamentary democracies (for a review, see Lijphart 1992) and, more recently, Duverger's model of semipresidentialism (Bahro, Bayerlein, and Veser 1998). Each of these categories does, of course, cover a range of distinct variants. In fact, as Sartori (1994, 83) has argued with reference to parliamentary systems, they appear to "differ so widely among themselves as to render their common name a misnomer for a deceitful togetherness."

Our main concern is with the centrality of the executive in the political system; in particular, we seek to assess whether it has become the dominant force in policy formation (Goetz and Wollmann 2001). Accordingly, we study efforts to clarify the boundaries between executive tasks and other types of political activity and to concentrate executive powers in the government (Goetz and Margetts 1999), notably, by curtailing the executive powers of the presidency and by restricting parliament's capacity for independent policy initiatives. In the four countries under scrutiny—Hungary, Poland, the

Czech Republic, and Bulgaria—the 1990s witnessed the progressive limitation of the formal and informal powers of the presidency. The unification of executive power in the government was perhaps most pronounced in Poland. While, at the start of the 1990s, the president was often regarded as the dominant political actor (Jasiewiecz 1997), by the early twenty-first century constitutional reform and the emancipation of the government from the shadow of the presidency had succeeded in reducing the latter to a principally representational role (van der Meer Krok-Paszkowska 1999; but see Millard 2000).

As regards executive–legislative relations, the most critical issue we examine is the question of where the main power of legislative initiative lies and to what extent the executive is able to ensure priority for government-sponsored bills in the parliamentary process. During the early phases of postcommunist transition, the newly democratic legislatures often emerged as strongly independent centers of policy formulation (Ágh 1997; Olson 1997; Olson and Norton 1996), and governments found it difficult to prioritize consideration of their own legislative programs and to control the adoption of bills not sponsored by the government. There are clear signs that party discipline among the parliamentary parties supporting the government has increased considerably, at least in Hungary (Ágh 1997) and in the Czech Republic, where observers have noted a shift from a transformative parliament in the early stages of transition to an arena-type legislature (Kopecký 1996, 2001). However, as in other parts of CEE (see, e.g., Evans and Evans 2001), executive control over parliamentary legislation has remained relatively weak in Poland (Zubek 2001) and in Bulgaria (Dimitrov 2001).

In analyzing the government's interaction with political parties, we are principally interested in the party composition of the government, distinguishing between one-party governments, coalition governments in which the partners can expect to stay together after future elections, and coalition governments in which the parties can expect to run against each other in future contests (Hallerberg 2000). Variation in the political composition of the government can lead to very different choices with regard to the executive's institutional structures and the patterns of interaction between politicians and civil servants (more on this later).

The Outlines of the Executive Terrain

Having located the central executive within the political system, we turn to the evolving structure of the central executive, examining the main departmental organizations and the key agencies (Goetz and Wollmann 2001). Our focus here is on institutional fragmentation, given that this was a hallmark of the communist central executive. The central state apparatus, including the central governmental structures, acted under the direction and control of the Communist Party. At all levels, the state structures were subordinated to the parallel structures of the party, which were responsible for political decision taking. This subordination survived largely intact until the late 1980s; even in Hungary, it was only in 1988—when the reformist wing of the Hungarian Socialist Workers' Party ousted Janos Kadar and took over the party leadership and the government—that the government became decoupled from the party apparatus and the substantive preparation of government decisions shifted from the party bureaucracy to the central state administration. The central executive consisted of a high number of ministries (including the sectoral ministries) and other central agencies. Many of the latter were formally attached to the Office of the Council of Ministers but operated largely autonomously. The central state apparatus thus became institutionally fragmented, and specialized units proliferated.

The disappearance of the Communist Party as the main political coordinating mechanism—following the collapse of communist regimes in 1989—exposed the weaknesses of the fragmented executive system and made it virtually unworkable. Accordingly, throughout the 1990s and the early twenty-first century, there were attempts to streamline the structure of the central executive. We examine the success of these reform initiatives by looking at the reduction of the number of ministries and central agencies, the demarcation of their competencies, and the adoption of common principles for the internal organization of ministries (Goetz and Wollmann 2001).

The Powers of the Prime Minister

Under communism, the power of the prime minister, typically known as the chairman of the council of ministers, vis-à-vis other members of the government was rather weak. The center of political decision taking was the party so that the communist council of ministers was not an arena for deliberation and authoritative decision making but rather a machine for the formal adoption of decisions. Implementation was largely the responsibility of individual ministries. In this context, it is not surprising that—in formal terms at least—the council of ministers was collegiate and collective, with the prime minister being a *primus inter pares.*

In our analysis, we assess the degree to which the power position of the prime minister has been transformed, by looking at the introduction of formal-legal mechanisms, such as a constructive vote of no-confidence (which means that parliament cannot pass a vote of no-confidence in the prime minister without electing a new head of government); the ability of the prime minister to represent the council of ministers; his prerogatives in appointing and dismissing ministers; his power to create ministries and to allocate responsibilities among the members of the government; his ability to control the preparation of submissions to the cabinet; his chairmanship of key cabinet committees; his power to determine the agenda of government meetings and to chair their discussion; and his ability to control the implementation of government decisions. In addition to these formal-legal powers, we analyze the degree of the prime minister's political authority over the cabinet, which is critically reliant on his relationship with the main governing party. A strong political authority, as in the case where the prime minister is the leader of the main governing party, can reinforce his legal prerogatives, but a weak political authority, as in cases where the head of government belongs to a minor party or where party leaders choose to remain outside the government, can severely weaken the effectiveness of his formal powers.

The Powers of the Finance Minister

In the Western European literature, finance ministries are seen as paramount policy shapers and coordinators through their control of the budgetary process (Hallerberg 2000; Hallerberg and von Hagen 1999; von Hagen 1998; von Hagen and Harden 1994). By contrast, in communist systems, the role of the finance ministry was typically weak (Goetz and Wollmann 2001). Thus,

> the role of the ministry of finance in the former command societies was chiefly to provide a source of finance both for physical production and social transfer flows, whose direction and volume were decided elsewhere. The state budget proper was, of course, the responsibility of the ministry of finance, but this was not enough to raise the ministry's hierarchical role above that of most of the line ministries. Compiling the state budget itself was a relatively minor job, compared with "monetising" the whole of the overall production plan. (Allen and Tommasi 2001, 27)

Indeed, in Bulgaria, during the last two years of Zhivkov's reign, the Finance Ministry was abolished altogether.

The postcommunist transition created pressures for the transformation of the standing of the finance ministry. This reposition took place in response to the abolition of state planning and the transition to a market economy and in the face of severe fiscal crises, which virtually all CEE countries encountered during the 1990s. The enhancement of the powers and institutional capacities of the finance ministry provide it with far-reaching control over government policy. This strengthening can be achieved through a variety of mechanisms. One such instrument may be the preparation by the finance minister of a medium-term fiscal framework as a basis for the annual budgetary process. The finance minister may also be given the power, either alone or with the prime minister, to set the overall limits of expenditure and to determine the limits for each line ministry. This power gives the minister of finance a dominant position in budget negotiations with line ministries. Finally, during the last stage of the budgetary cycle (the implementation of the budget law adopted by parliament), the finance minister may exercise control through ensuring that all payments are transacted via a treasury system, or a single government account.

Next to such coordinating powers and control of the budgetary process, the minister of finance's standing vis-à-vis his cabinet colleagues is also affected by exogenous enabling constraints, such as the existence of an independent central bank with an explicit remit to control inflation; agreements with international bodies such as the International Monetary Fund that incorporate fiscal policy targets; or use of instruments such as currency boards, which tie the amount of money a government can issue to the amount of its foreign currency reserves.

Patterns of Cabinet Decision Making

The cabinet has the potential of being the prime coordinating mechanism in the executive. In most Western European systems, it acts, in formal terms, as the political forum for taking major policy decisions and as the apex of the government as an administrative authority. While both dimensions— the political and the administrative—coexist, cabinets differ in the relative weight they attach to each. In Western Europe, Britain is at the political end of the spectrum, in that the cabinet is perceived mainly as a governing institution rather than as an administration. The function of administration is placed squarely with the civil service, while the cabinet concentrates on shaping the main outlines of public policy. At the other extreme, in countries such as Austria, the administrative role of the cabinet is much stronger, and it gets involved in a great deal of legal-administrative detail (Blondel and Müller-Rommel 1997).

Political and administrative coordinating mechanisms cannot always be easily separated. The preparation of items for presentation to the cabinet has to meet conditions that are both formal-legal and political. Such conditions may include a requirement for consultation with all the affected line ministries and the ministry of finance, with disputes either resolved before the cabinet meets or clearly indicated in the cabinet submission. In cases where there are standing cabinet committees, a discussion or even a preliminary decision in the relevant committee may be required. Similarly, in cases where there are deputy prime ministers with responsibilities across a number of ministries in a particular policy area, consultation with or approval by the deputy prime minister may be a condition for the submission of an item to the cabinet. A similar role may be played where a formally recognized presidium of the government exists. Discussions at these different levels are inevitably concerned with both legal and political aspects. Items for decision taking typically need to pass through the center of government. This procedure may be little more than a formal-legal exercise, designed to ensure, for instance, that submissions to the cabinet follow a standard format and meet time requirements and are compatible with existing legislation and the EU *acquis communautaire*. However, the center may also act as a political screening mechanism, aiming to ensure that items submitted to the cabinet are consistent with the general policy program of the government.

Party-Based Political Coordination Devices

Party-based political coordination mechanisms rely principally on positions in party organization rather than on positions in government. For instance, a prime minister may choose to coordinate the work of his cabinet colleagues not primarily through the machinery of government but through the party hierarchy. Similarly, coalition management regularly requires the deployment of a range of coordination devices. Müller and Strom's detailed comparative study (2000) of coalition governments in Western Europe identifies a broad range of such devices, including written coalition agreements that specify the size of the government, the allocation of portfolios, detailed procedural rules for the operation of the coalition, and specific policy commitments. Other conflict-management mechanisms include, for example, informal inner cabinets and party summits. Our empirical analysis has been concerned with tracing the development of coordination devices of this kind.

The Powers and Organization of the Center of Government

In the communist system, the center of government—that is, the Office of the Council of Ministers—acted as the government's registrar, exercising little control over the activities of ministries and other central agencies (Goetz and Wollmann 2001). It did not function as an instrument for exercising prime ministerial control over other members of the government, nor did it operate as a cabinet office, in spite of the fact that, in formal terms, the communist constitutions provided for a cabinet-type government with a high degree of collegiality and collectivity. The fact that coordination was carried out largely by the Communist Party, with direct links between party institutions and individual ministries, made communist governments operate as ministerial rather than cabinet governments.

Formal coordinating powers granted to the prime minister, the finance minister, the cabinet, and even party-based devices are unlikely to be effective unless underpinned by the appropriate remolding of the inherited center of government. Here, three broad types of center of government may be distinguished: the center as the prime minister's vanguard, which serves as a means of exercising prime ministerial authority; the center as the guardian of collective responsibility, designed to ensure the authority and smooth operation of a collegiate and collective government; and the center as government registrar, where the center is essentially reduced to the function of recording and processing decisions taken elsewhere. The center is less engaged in substantive coordination than it is in keeping track of the activities of the ministries and channeling their proposals into the cabinet.

The Politics–Administration Nexus: Professionalization of the Civil Service

In both intention and effect, policies aimed at establishing professional career-type civil services in CEE have gone beyond a concern with core executive capacity building. If efforts to strengthen the core executive have aimed at improving coordination, the thrust of public service reform has been to establish the institutional prerequisites for a professional central administration (Goetz and Wollmann 2001). There has been a remarkable degree of agreement on the need for creating career civil services among national administrative reformers, international agencies, and academic observers. While in Western Europe there are signs of a deprivileging of the civil service and a growing convergence in the rights and responsibilities of civil servants and ordinary public employees (Bekke and van der Meer 2000), in CEE professionalization at the level of the central state administration has been regarded as being equivalent to the creation of a body of civil servants separate from the bulk of public employees. The guiding inspiration has been the classical Weberian official, whereas managerialist conceptions have scarcely featured in the reform debate (Goetz 2001b). The communist inheritance of a politicized personnel system was identified early on as a decisive obstacle to improved governance that only determined efforts at professionalization and depoliticization could overcome.

Viewed from the perspective of core executive development, professionalization and depoliticization are of special significance when it comes to senior officials. They play a key role in coordinating the political apex of the executive (the prime minister, ministers, and other executive politicians) and the ministerial administration; that is, they operate directly at the interface of politics and administration and are critical to the effective linking of political and administrative coordination mechanisms (Goetz and Wollmann 2001). It is because of this special position that there is a close connection between professional policy competence and political skills. In some Western European countries, the interpenetration of party politics and administration at the top levels of the ministerial administration is recognized in law, as in the case of Germany's *politische Beamte*; in others, it is a tacitly accepted feature. The British Whitehall model of a strictly party/politically neutral top civil service is the exception rather than the rule (Bekke and van der Meer 2000; Page and Wright 1999). Professionalization on the one hand and the development of "political craft" (Goetz 1997) by senior officials on the other may thus be seen as part of the process of strengthening the coordinating capacity of the central executive.

CONCEPTUALIZING POSTCOMMUNIST EXECUTIVES

The systematic collection of data on the eight dimensions of executive development helps to unpack the "black box" of postcommunist executives. But, given the longitudinal and cross-country comparative design of the study, how can one best grasp the main developmental trends? To do so, we develop a conceptual framework that allows for generalization without excessive simplification and distinguishes between types of government, types of core executive, and types of center of government (see table 2.1).

Our conceptual framework is based on the development of—and, in important respects, the modification of—Rhodes and Dunleavy's concept of core executive (1995). While formulating the concept of core executive to signify "the complex web of institutions, networks and practices surrounding the prime minister, cabinet, cabinet committees," Rhodes and Dunleavy (1995, 12) fail to differentiate between this concept and the concept of type of government. Ultimately, they conflate the two concepts, thus reducing the analytical content of core executive from a term indicating a separate set of institutions to merely a heuristic device for the empirical determination of the type of government. The conflation of the two concepts is based on the implicit assumption that the type of government and type of core executive necessarily co-vary. This assumption may be justified in some cases but not in others.

Our conceptual framework provides a clear analytical distinction between types of government, types of core executive, and types of center of government. This analytical distinction opens up the possibility to investigate

Table 2.1. Types of Government, Core Executives, and Centers of Government

Type of Government	Type of Core Executive	Type of Center of Government
Prime ministerial government	Centralized prime ministerial	Prime minister's vanguard (Prime Minister's Office)
Cabinet government	Centralized cabinet	Guardian of collective responsibility (Cabinet Office)
Ministerial government	Decentralized ministerial	Government registrar (Office of the Council of Ministers)

the relationships—reinforcing or not—that may exist between the three types. We define the type of government as the formal-legal constitution of the government. The key question here is, what is the source of legal authority for the formation of the government? We use the well-known distinction between prime ministerial, cabinet, and ministerial governments. Prime ministerial government is based on the legal authority of the prime minister, who, once elected by parliament, can appoint and dismiss ministers at his discretion, without parliamentary approval. By contrast, cabinet government exists when the cabinet as a whole, rather than the prime minister, is elected by parliament and bears collective responsibility to parliament for its actions. Finally, ministerial government is based on the legal-constitutional preeminence of ministers who make decisions within their own departments (Rhodes and Dunleavy, 20). The minister is responsible for all the actions taken by his department, and neither the prime minister nor the cabinet may intervene legitimately. The distinction between prime ministerial, cabinet, and ministerial governments is continuous rather than dichotomous, and most governments for most of the time operate on the basis of a combination of the three principles (Blondel and Müller-Rommel 1997; Rhodes and Dunleavy 1995).

The same observations apply when we move from considering types of governments to analyzing the types of core executives with which they are typically associated. In centralized prime ministerial core executives, a small number of key institutions and actors dominate the business of pulling together and integrating government policy and "act as final arbiters of conflict between different parts of the government machine" (Rhodes and Dunleavy 1995, 12). These institutions derive their authority—formal or informal—from the dominant position of the prime minister within the government, and coordination is chiefly concerned with maintaining and securing the effective exercise of that authority. The prime minister's dominance in decision making expresses itself in different ways: by the capacity to decide policy questions in any policy area in which he takes an interest; by deciding key issues that set the parameters for the remaining areas of government policy; or by defining a governing "ethos" that leads to predictable and consistent solutions to most policy problems (Rhodes and Dunleavy 1995, 15). In centralized cabinet core executives, too, the number of specialized coordinating institutions is small, and they may resort to hierarchy in their relationships with other parts of the executive; but coordination is driven by considerations of effectiveness and efficiency in cabinet decision making and of ensuring that both the prime minister and the ministers adhere to the collective will of the government. The authority of the core executive is, accordingly, principally derived from the cabinet. A centralized cabinet core executive, on the two dimensions identified by Blondel and Müller-Rommel (1997) for a cabinet government, is distinguished by a high degree of collegiality among ministers, with the prime minister being merely "an equal among equals," and by a high level of collectivity, with an emphasis of the collective responsibility of the cabinet. Finally, in a decentralized ministerial core executive, we can expect to find only very limited government-wide coordinating mechanisms. Most ministers are almost entirely absorbed by the affairs of their departments and pay only intermittent attention to the policy problems confronted by their colleagues. Coordination at the level of government itself is weak; coordination largely takes place within individual ministries rather than among them.

Core executives, as noted earlier, go well beyond the center of government, but the position of the latter is regularly among the key defining features of the former. Thus, a centralized prime ministerial core executive suggests a center of government in the form of a Prime Minister's Office that acts as the prime minister's vanguard. Its prime function is the projection of prime ministerial power. Typical mechanisms include the creation of ministry desks to monitor and, where necessary, steer the activities of ministerial departments; a center that, with the authority of the prime minister, acts as gatekeeper to the cabinet; interministerial committees that are attended by center-of-government staff and often chaired by them; or the creation of units for strategic analysis to enhance long-term planning capacity. Thus, the Prime Minister's Office is configured in a way that allows the head of the government to exercise his power over the government in the most effective manner.

Under conditions of a centralized cabinet core executive, the center of government will tend to take the form of a Cabinet Office, controlled by a powerful cabinet secretary or a minister of cabinet rank who is responsible to the cabinet as a whole. The center exists to ensure the smooth operation of a collegiate and collective government and to ensure its authority. Finally, in a ministerial government, the center is essentially reduced to the function of government registrar, recording and processing decisions taken elsewhere. The center is less engaged in substantive coordination than it is in keeping track of the activities of the ministries and channeling their proposals into the cabinet. The Office of the Council of Ministers under communism closely approximated this model.

Table 2.1 summarizes the types of government, core executives, and centers of government that act as reference points for our empirical analysis. Of course, the reality of postcommunist government has been a great deal messier than such neat typologies suggest. Governments, core executives, and centers of government rarely come in the form of pure types but are usually, at best, approximations of one or the other. Comparative analysis cannot proceed without such typologies; but in trying to compare the outcomes of institutional development, it also relies on reservations and caveats. Equally, it is important to stress that there is no straightforward causal chain between type of government, core executive, and center of government. As set out here, the three are certainly logically linked; but, in practice, they may well diverge. For example, prime ministerial government tends to give rise to a center that acts as the prime minister's vanguard, but other factors may intervene. An instance of such a disjuncture could be observed in the Czech Republic during the first Klaus government of 1992–1996. Klaus's hold over both his ministers and his party meant that the government approximated a prime ministerial type even though, formally, it retained the character of a cabinet government. But Klaus took few steps to transform the center of government into an effective tool for the exercise of prime ministerial authority and preferred to rely, instead, on personalist power resources and party-based coordination mechanisms that bypassed the center of government.

THE CORE EXECUTIVE AND THE BUDGET

As noted in chapter 1, the West European literature has been reluctant to link particular executive arrangements to specific policy outcomes (Dimitrov and Goetz 2000). There is certainly no lack of detailed case studies that examine failures of the executive, as the growing literature on policy disasters attests (e.g., Gray and t'Hart 1998). But while one may derive "negative lessons" from studies of this type, systematic inquiries into the policy consequences of different executive configurations are rare.

To seek to link institutions and policy makes sense for a number of reasons. Implicit in the concept of "core executive" is the need to go beyond formal structural description and analyze coordination in action. Indeed, the coordinating practices of the core executive can scarcely be understood outside their role in the policymaking process. Thus, the analysis of Western European core executives has largely been conducted through case studies of particular policy areas and issues (Rhodes and Dunleavy 1995; Wright and Hayward 2000). The area chosen here for the study of the impact of core executive institutional configurations is the budgetary process. The preparation of the annual state budget is the most demanding coordination task that the executive is likely to face on a regular basis. It engages all parts of the executive, as virtually no branch of government is unaffected by budgetary decisions; it absorbs both political and administrative players; it is a long, drawn-out process rather than a short event; and it is typically regulated at least in part through statutory if not, in fact, constitutional legislation. Moreover, as it needs to be carried out by all governments and is recurrent, it especially lends itself to longitudinal comparative analysis.

Chapter 8 examines the impact of the configuration of core executives on budgetary performance. Using a framework of analysis that builds on the work of von Hagen, Harden, and Hallerberg (Hallerberg 2000; Hallerberg and von Hagen 1999; von Hagen 1998; von Hagen and Harden 1994), we explore the hypothesis that centralized core executives lead to better budget performance, defined in terms of the level of the general government fiscal deficit, than do decentralized core executives.

EXPLAINING VARIATION IN CORE EXECUTIVE TRAJECTORIES

Our attempt to account for core executive trajectories privileges domestic variables and includes, as noted in chapter 1, structural conditions, critical junctures, and actor constellations and choices. The most important structural condition has undoubtedly been the institutional legacy of communism. Although, as argued at the outset, the organization and functions of executives under communism across Central and Eastern Europe followed a common model, important differences existed. Hungary in particular was marked by a growth in coordinating capacity within state institutions during the 1970s and 1980s. In Poland, Czechoslovakia, and Bulgaria, by contrast, the classic characteristics of the communist executive system—most notably, its institutional fragmentation and the weakness of integrative mechanisms other than the leading party—survived without major modifications. Equally, there were differences in the state personnel system, with the process of professionalization advancing furthest in Hungary, spurred by the adoption of far-reaching economic reforms in the 1960s (György 1999). A key institutional development was the setting up of a National School of Public Administration in 1977, designed to improve the professional skills of the state administration. The school became an advocate of the professionalization of administrative personnel by means of introducing a career system based on merit and separated from politics. While the criterion of political reliability was never fully discarded, Balázs argues that at the end of the 1980s the Hungarian personnel system increasingly exhibited features of a career system comparable to Western European public administrations (1993, quoted in Meyer-Sahling 2003). Poland also made some limited progress in the direction of professionalization, indicated by the adoption of a special civil service law in 1982. Czechoslovakia and Bulgaria, on the other hand, while accepting greater professionalization in practice, maintained the rhetorical emphasis on political loyalty. The differing institutional legacies made it easier for Hungary and, to a lesser extent, Poland to move to depoliticized and professional civil service systems after 1989 than for the Czech Republic and Bulgaria.

The emphasis we place on critical junctures has developed in response to what empirical observation suggested. Two main critical junctures can be identified: the fall of communism and the crisis of governance in the mid-1990s. All four of the countries experienced these crises, but they did so in different ways. The end of the communist dictatorship took the form of a negotiated transition in Hungary and Poland; regime collapse in Czechoslovakia; and a delayed, communist-led democratic transition in Bulgaria. The pattern of regime change had a significant impact on the development of types of government and core executives. In Hungary, the Communist Party and the opposition agreed on the need for a strong head of government, once the communists' preferred option of a powerful president was disposed of through a referendum. In Poland, by contrast, the communists succeeded in pushing through the establishment of a directly elected president with wide-ranging powers, thus setting the scene for future conflict between the president and the government. In Czechoslovakia, the collapse of the regime and the seemingly unchallenged legitimacy enjoyed by the Czech Civil Forum and the Slovak Public against Violence made it possible for the two umbrella movements to rule without concerning themselves too much with the reform of executive structures. The dissolution of the Czechoslovak federation at the end of 1992 and the adoption of a Czech constitution did not entail an unambiguous decision on the type of government to emerge; for much of Prime Minister Klaus's tenure, the core executive resembled a centralized prime ministerial model, but Klaus's position owed more to fluctuating political constellations than to constitutional powers. Finally, in Bulgaria, the continuing dominance of the former Communist Party and the intense struggle between party leaders and the head of the government made it impossible to undertake any formal measures that would have strengthened the prime minister's authority.

The mid-1990s crisis of governance took the form of a fiscal crisis. As chapter 8 documents in detail, the precise timing and severity of this crisis differed from country to country. It was severely destabilizing in the case of Bulgaria, serious in Hungary and Poland, and comparatively modest in the Czech Republic. The most immediate effect of this critical juncture was on the budgetary core executive. In Bulgaria, it spurred the creation of a currency board, whereas in Hungary and Poland, a short-term centralization of budgetary powers set the path for a subsequent strengthening of the budgetary core executives. In the Czech Republic, because the crisis was more modest, it did not have the capacity to break the resistance against the strengthening of the minister of finance, with the result being that the Czech Republic has suffered a chronic budgetary crisis for much of the time since. More generally, this second critical juncture had a major influence on the type of core executive that took shape: it reinforced the trend toward prime ministerialization in Hungary; spurred the concentration of policymaking powers within the Polish executive; contributed to election of the Kostov government in Bulgaria in 1997, which after years of rapid turnover, signaled a period of stabilization and consolidation; and left the Czech executive in a state of limbo.

In terms of actor constellations and choices, we concentrate on political parties. This focus merits some elaboration. Political parties—as party-in-government—are key actors within the executive; the executive influences their identities and choices as party-in-parliament and extraparliamentary party; conversely, the parties make choices about the executive in general and the core executive in particular. We are not particularly well served by the academic literature on the impact of political parties on executive structures. Much writing has been concerned with the role of parties in government formation, especially coalition formation and cessation, and the allocation of ministerial portfolios (Laver and Budge 1992; Laver and Schofield 1990; Riker 1962; Strom, Budge, and Laver 1994; Taylor and Laver 1973). By contrast, their impact on patterns of government once a cabinet has been formed has received far less attention. The major contribution to this field, Laver and Shepsle's *Making and Breaking Governments* (1996), makes the argument that in multiparty systems, coalition government inevitably tends toward ministerial government in which all ministers are equal and collective responsibility is weak. In this view, coalition policy is ultimately implemented through ministerial departments, for which individual ministers are responsible. There is little room for effective coordination of individual ministers.

Laver and Shepsle's view (1996) has been challenged, most notably by Müller and Strom (2000), who point out that there are a number of mechanisms that can be used to coordinate policy across ministerial departments in coalition governments. Some of these mechanisms operate within the formal government structures, such as cabinet committees. Others may operate outside these structures and may include, inter alia, coalition agreements, coalition committees, informal inner cabinets, and meetings of the leaders of the coalition parties ("coalition summits").

Both Laver and Shepsle (1996) and Müller and Strom (2000) focus on multiparty systems, which tend to produce coalition governments, rather than two-party systems, which favor the emergence of single-party governments or coalitions dominated by one party. Blondel and Cotta, in their work on party government (1996, 2000), consider the case of a two-party system, but their analysis focuses on the relative influence of·the party vis-à-vis the government—that is, the relative importance of party-based versus government-based institutions, rather than on the internal configuration of either set of institutions.

The most comprehensive model of the effect of political parties on the configuration of government institutions has been developed by Hallerberg and von Hagen (Hallerberg 2000; Hallerberg and von Hagen 1999; von Hagen 1998).[1] Their model has been developed with specific reference to the configuration of institutions operating in the field of budgetary policy, and, as noted, our analysis of budgetary policy in chapter 8 builds on this framework. But the model can also be applied, with appropriate modification, to account for institutional choices about the executive as a whole.

In a series of works, von Hagen, Harden, and Hallerberg have developed a typology of budgeting institutions, based on their degree of centralization (Hallerberg 2000; Hallerberg and von Hagen 1999; von Hagen 1998; von Hagen and Harden 1994). They identify two methods of centralization: delegation and fiscal contracts. Delegation involves the granting of special powers to individual participants in the budgetary process, such as the finance minister and the prime minister, who can be assumed to have a more comprehensive view of the budget than that of other actors. Fiscal contracts are binding agreements negotiated among all the participants in the budgetary process, without lending special authorities to any one of them. Having developed a typology of budgeting institutions, von Hagen and his co-authors have tested the impact of these institutions on fiscal performance, finding consistently that centralized institutions deliver better fiscal performance, defined in terms of the level of the fiscal deficit, than do decentralized institutions. In terms of both the number of cases and the length of the time series, the most extensive study was carried out by Hallerberg and von Hagen (1999), and it examined the effect of budgeting institutions on fiscal deficit in the fifteen EU member states for the period 1981–1994.

In contrast to most studies of institutional configuration, which employ an analytical narrative approach (for a classic example, see Wildavsky 1964, 1986; for a recent notable study, see Schick 1993), von Hagen's work uses quantitative estimates of the configuration of budgeting institutions. This approach involves the setting up of indices of centralization, translating qualitative information about budgeting institutions into quantitative measures (von Hagen 1998). Even as a foundation for statistical analysis, these indices have important limitations. As von Hagen himself notes, "such indices have only an ordinal interpretation, they provide rankings of countries within a sample. A second implication is that indices are sample-specific, index values for countries in different samples are extremely difficult to compare" (von Hagen 1998, 17). A more fundamental weakness of this approach, as pointed out by Schick, is that "it reduces all institutions to a simple classification, and in so doing, it ignores substantial differences among governing systems" (1993, 194). Another important weakness, as Hallerberg (2000) recognizes, is that this approach finds it difficult to analyze the development of institutions over time. In a work attempting to explain why and how Belgium and Italy managed to achieve a remarkable turnaround in their fiscal performance in 1993–1998 and meet the Maastricht fiscal deficit criterion, Hallerberg carries out a qualitative analysis of the changes in the budgeting institutions in these countries, of the reasons behind these changes, and of the impact of these changes on the fiscal deficit (Hallerberg 2000). The analytical framework developed by Hallerberg in the aforementioned work is particularly appropriate for the study of executive institutions in CEE, given the fact that these institutions have undergone substantial transformation since the fall of communism in 1989.

Hallerberg and von Hagen have also been involved in the development of explanations for the choice of different budgeting institutions. In their 1999 study, they link the choice of delegation or fiscal contracts to the number of parties within the government, positing that one-party governments are likely to accept delegation to a powerful finance minister and coalition governments can be expected to choose fiscal contracts. Both types of government can also opt for decentralized institutions. Hallerberg and von Hagen (1999) find considerable supporting evidence for their hypotheses. Of the twelve states with coalition governments, eight used fiscal contracts and three had decentralized institutions. Of the three states expected to use delegation, two did and one used decentralized institutions. In his 2000 study, Hallerberg refines the analysis of the party composition of government, distinguishing between coalition governments composed of parties that expect to run together in future elections and coalition governments in which the partners anticipate competing against each other. The first type of coalition government would behave in a way similar to that of a one-party government. The second type of coalition government is unlikely to agree to delegation but may still achieve policy coordination through fiscal contracts (Hallerberg 2000).

The link between the number of parties in the government on the one hand and the configuration of budgeting institutions on the other is based on the degree of commonality of political preferences in the government and on the recognition that budgeting has the characteristics of a common pool resource problem. In a one-party government and, to a lesser extent, in a coalition government in which the parties expect to run together in the next election, ministers are likely to have shared political preferences and can therefore accept delegation to a finance minister and/or prime minister. Because budgeting is a collective pool problem, in a decentralized executive configuration, where ministers have the freedom to set their own budgets, they will select amounts that are larger than what is collectively optimal for the government. The reason is that a spending minister receives the full benefit of any additional expenditure allocated to one's department but only needs to take into consideration that part of the extra taxation that is payable by his constituency. Delegation to a finance minister and/or prime minister can overcome the collective pool resource problem, based on the assumption that these two ministers are motivated by the general interest of the government and do not suffer from the imbalance between spending and taxation incentives, which characterizes the spending ministers. In a coalition government in which the partners do not expect to contest the next election together, the low degree of commonality of political preferences

makes delegation problematic. In such a government, the collective pool resource problem can be resolved through the establishment of fiscal contracts
in which all the parties participating in the government commit themselves
to an overall spending target and are therefore guided by the collective interest of the government in considering the spending claims of each ministry
(Hallerberg 2000; Hallerberg and von Hagen 1999; von Hagen 1998).

Hallerberg and von Hagen's institutional choice model (1999) lends itself
to application beyond the area of budgetary policy and provides a key to
explaining degrees of centralization of executive institutions more generally.
In the case of the delegation approach, for instance, as the authors themselves recognize, the enforcement of fiscal discipline is not simply a matter
of granting the finance minister some specific powers in the budgetary process. What makes it possible for the finance minister to employ the powers
delegated to him is the support he receives from the prime minister, and
that in turn depends on the prime minister's position in the cabinet and his
powers vis-à-vis the line ministers (217). In order to apply Hallerberg and
von Hagen's institutional choice model to general executive institutions, we
need to modify their typology and explanatory framework. Delegation to
a prime minister and/or a finance minister can be seen, in terms of the typology we have developed in table 2.1, as a centralized prime ministerial
core executive. Fiscal contracts can be expected to occur in a centralized
cabinet core executive, alongside other mechanisms that promote the collective cabinet responsibility, such as coalition agreements and an influential
cabinet office. Finally, multiparty cabinets without fiscal contracts or other
instruments are likely to lead to the emergence of decentralized ministerial
core executives.

Once reformulated in these terms, Hallerberg and von Hagen's institutional choice model provides a plausible explanation for the emergence of
different types of core executive. A one-party government and, to a lesser
extent, a coalition government consisting of parties that expect to run together in future elections can lead to the creation of a centralized prime
ministerial core executive through delegation of power to the prime minister and/or finance minister. A coalition government in which the partners
do not expect to contest future elections together can establish a centralized
cabinet core executive by the use of fiscal contracts or other instruments promoting collective responsibility. In the absence of such mechanisms, such a
coalition government is likely to have a decentralized ministerial executive.

While the explanatory framework provided by Hallerberg and von Hagen
is undoubtedly useful, it could be developed in two main directions. First,
their framework does not distinguish between executive-based and party-
political coordination mechanisms, assuming implicitly that the two operate
together. This is not always the case, however. It is possible that the effectiveness of one set of mechanisms could compensate for the weakness of

the other but also that the presence of one set of mechanisms could inhibit the development of the other.

Second, it would be useful to link the number of parties taking part in government and their pattern of interaction to the shape of the party system. While we do not seek to develop a systematic theory of party systems, it may nevertheless be useful to indicate some ways in which the party systems may influence the party composition of governments. In a bipolar system, based on two main parties or two blocs of parties, we can expect to see the formation of one-party governments or coalition governments with partners that expect to run together in forthcoming elections. In a multipolar system, we are likely to see the formation of coalition governments composed of parties that do not expect to run on the same ballot in future elections.

We also have to consider developing party systems in which parties may lack clear programmatic identities or sharply defined constituencies and systems that are dominated by one party on the basis of its "revolutionary" credentials. In the former case, parties would find it difficult, given their lack of clear policy preferences, to commit themselves to any policy measures, such as fiscal targets, to be incorporated in coalition agreements. In other words, in developing party systems, a centralized cabinet core executive is unlikely to work and is likely to degenerate into a free-for-all ministerial executive. In the case of a party system dominated by one "revolutionary" party, that party can expect to stay in power for the foreseeable future and would have little incentive to lock in its successors through institutional reforms. It may therefore choose to exercise its dominance not through the centralization of executive structures but through party-based mechanisms, much as the Communist Party did before 1989.

The causal linkage between number and patterns of interaction of parties in government on the one hand and types of core executive on the other is certainly not sufficiently robust to claim any lawlike quality; nor does it explain all of the eight dimensions of core executive development, let alone types of government, equally well. It offers a relatively straightforward explanation as far as the powers of the prime minister and finance minister, patterns of cabinet decision making, and the organization of the center of government are concerned, and one can also see the link between government composition and degrees of fragmentation of the executive terrain.

NOTE

1. The section from this paragraph to the end of the chapter draws partly on Dimitrov (2005). Permission from PrAcademics Press.

II

CORE EXECUTIVE TRAJECTORIES IN FOUR COUNTRIES

3

Hungary: A Core Supreme

Martin Brusis

This chapter analyzes the development of core executive institutions in Hungary from 1989 to 2001. It starts with a brief overview of the development of the Hungarian party system and its impact on government formation and then proceeds to map the executive's relationship with presidency, parliament, and political parties. This discussion demonstrates that executive power has increased with each of the three governments that have been in office since the transition to democracy. Against this background, the chapter proceeds to show how the central executive has evolved into a government capable of strategic prioritization, coordination, and arbitration. The following sections first give an overview of the institutional changes in central governmental administration and then focus on the prime minister's position by studying the evolution of his powers. We argue that there has been a clear and continuous trend toward the development of a centralized prime ministerial core executive. Next, we analyze the development of the cabinet and party-based political coordination mechanisms and examine the evolving powers of the center of government. Finally, we turn to the politics–administration nexus, analyzing and explaining the trend toward regulated politicization of top administrative personnel.

THE DEVELOPMENT OF PARTY SYSTEM AND GOVERNMENT FORMATION, 1989-2001

Hungary was the first CEE country to develop a well-functioning party system, with a major party on the left and one on the right. This has meant that all the governments since the transition to democracy have been dominated by one major party, the leader of which has invariably become the prime minister. Hungary's democratic system emerged from a negotiated transition that was characterized by preceding state socialist reforms of the economic and governmental system, a relative absence of mass mobilization and an early differentiation of groups and parties opposing the state socialist system. Having ousted the old party leadership in May 1998, the reform socialists took radical actions leading to a market economy with its corresponding regulatory framework, accepted a multiparty system, and negotiated the transition to democracy with the emerging opposition parties. The first democratic elections, in April 1990, led to the formation of a coalition government headed by prime minister József Antall and consisting of three conservative and Christian democrat parties: the Hungarian Democratic Forum (MDF), the Christian Democratic People's Party (KDNP), and the Independent Smallholders' Party (FKGP). Antall had the strongest political authority in the government and chaired the MDF as the leading party of the governing coalition. The successor party of the state socialist party, the Hungarian Socialist Party (MSZP), and two liberal parties, the Alliance of Free Democrats (SZDSZ) and the Alliance of Young Democrats (FIDESZ), became opposition parties. Although the coalition government experienced numerous changes in its leading personnel, including the death of Prime Minister Antall in December 1993, and fluctuation in its parliamentary basis of deputies, it remained in power until the end of the electoral period. Its composition is depicted in table 3.1. The Antall government continued the economic reforms that had been started by the last state socialist government and established the framework for a "social market economy" in Hungary.

In the second parliamentary elections, held in May 1994, the MSZP won a clear absolute majority but decided to form a coalition government together with the SZDSZ. This was remarkable insofar as it indicated the weakness of the cleavage between postsocialists and the parties emerging from the former opposition to the state socialist system. The government was led by Gyula Horn, the chairman of the MSZP, and it stayed in power for its full term of office. Table 3.2 shows its composition. It implemented a major economic stabilization program in 1995 known as the "Bokros package." The economic reforms entailed severe conflicts between the modernization-oriented and the trade-unionist wing of the MSZP. Among the opposition parties, changes occurred insofar as a radical populist split-off from the MDF established its own party, the Party of Hungarian Truth and Life (MIÉP); the KDNP became marginalized; and the FIDESZ renamed itself the Alliance of Young Democrats–Hungarian Civic Party (FIDESZ-MPP), moving toward the right pole of the political spectrum.

The third parliamentary elections, in May 1998, enabled the FIDESZ-MPP to create a coalition government with the FKGP and the MDF, headed by Viktor Orbán, FIDESZ-MPP chairman until December 1999. The MSZP got

Table 3.1.   Composition of the Antall/Boross Government

Name	Position	Party
József Antall (since 12/1993, Péter Boross)	Prime minister	MDF
Ferenc Rabár (12/1990–2/1993, Mihály Kupa; since 2/1993, Iván Szabó)	Finance	Nonaffiliated, nonaffiliated, MDF
Géza Jeszensky	Foreign Affairs	MDF
Ferenc József Nagy (1/1991–2/1993, Elemér Gergatz; since 2/1993, János Szabó)	Agriculture	All FKGP
Lajos Für	Defense	MDF
Bertalan Andrásfalvy (since 2/1993, Ferenc Mádl)	Education and Culture	MDF, nonaffiliated
Sándor Gyôriványi (since 1/1991, Gyula Kiss)	Labor Affairs	All FKGP
László Surján	Welfare	KDNP
Balázs Horváth (12/1990–12/1993, Péter Boross; since 12/1993, Imre Kónya)	Interior (deputy prime minister)	All MDF
István Balsai	Justice	MDF
Péter Ákos Bod (12/1991–2/1993, Iván Szabó; since 2/1993, János Latorcai)	Industry and Trade	All MDF
Béla Kádár	International Economic Relations	Nonaffiliated
Sándor K. Keresztes (since 2/1993, János Gyúrko)	Environmental Protection and Regional Development	All MDF
Csaba Siklós (since 2/1993, György Schamschula)	Transport, Communication, and Water Management	All MDF
András Gálszécsy (12/1990–2/1992)	Minister without portfolio	MDF
Ferenc Mádl (5/1990–2/1993)		MDF
Tamás Szabó (since 1/1992)		MDF
Ferenc József Nagy (since 1/1991)		FKGP
Balázs Horváth (12/1990–2/1993)		MDF
Tibor Füzessy (since 6/1992)		KDNP
Jenô Gerbovits (5/1990–1/1991)		FKGP
Péter Boross (7/1990–12/1990)		MDF
Gyula Kiss (5/1990–1/1991)		FKGP
Katalin Botos (12/1990–1/1992)		MDF
Ernô Pungor (since 12/1990)		Nonaffiliated
Total appointed ministers: 38	Total ministries: 13	

Note: FKGP: Independent Smallholders' Party; KDNP: Christian Democratic People's Party; MDF: Hungarian Democratic Forum.

Table 3.2.   Composition of the Horn Government

Name	Position	Party
Gyula Horn	Prime minister	MSZP
László Békesi (3/1995–2/1996, Lajos Bokros; since 3/1996, Péter Medgyessy)	Finance (deputy prime minister)	MSZP
László Kovács	Foreign Affairs	MSZP
László Lakos (since 12/1996, Frigyes Nagy)	Agriculture	All MSZP
György Keleti	Defense	MSZP
Gábor Fodor (since 1/1996, Bálint Magyar)	Education and Culture	All SZDSZ
Magda Kovács Kósáné (since 12/1995, Péter Kiss)	Labor Affairs	All MSZP
Pál Kovács (4/1995–11/1996, György Szabó; since 12/1996, Mihály Kökény)	Welfare	All MSZP
Gábor Kuncze	Interior (deputy prime minister)	SZDSZ
Pál Vastagh	Justice	MSZP
László Pál (7/1995–9/1996, Imre Dunai; 9/1996–10/1996, Tamás Suchman; since 10/1996, Fazekas Szabolcs)	Industry, Trade, and Tourism	All MSZP
Ferenc Baja	Environmental Protection and Regional Development	MSZP
Károly Lotz	Transport, Communication, and Water Management	SZDSZ
Béla Katona (7/1994–3/1995) István Nikolits (since 4/1995) Tamás Suchman (3/1995–9/1996)	Minister without portfolio	All MSZP
Total ministers appointed: 26	Total ministries: 12	

Note: MSZP: Hungarian Socialist Party; SZDSZ: Alliance of Free Democrats.

the largest share of votes but failed to attain a parliamentary majority with the SZDSZ. These two parties and the MIÉP formed the parliamentary opposition. In the course of the years, the FIDESZ-MPP leadership managed to co-opt the MDF; integrate political representatives of the KDNP's successor party, KDSZ (Alliance of Christian Democrats), and the moderate right-wing split-offs from the MDF; and contribute to the disintegration of the FKGP—thus, contrary to the Solidarity Electoral Action (AWS) leadership in Poland, it proved able to unite the rightist political camp. All this was achieved under the constraint of a very narrow parliamentary majority of initially 213 out of 385 deputies, which declined to 194 when the FKGP fell apart. Table 3.3 shows the composition of the Orbán government.

Table 3.3. Composition of the Orbán Government

Name	Position	Party
Viktor Orbán	Prime minister	FIDESZ-MPP
László Kövér (7/1998–5/2000)	Deputy prime minister and minister without portfolio	FIDESZ-MPP
István Stumpf	Minister heading the Prime Minister's Office (deputy prime minister since 11/01)	Nonaffiliated
Zsigmond Járai (since 2/2001, Mihály Varga)	Finance	Nonaffiliated, FIDESZ-MPP
János Martonyi	Foreign Affairs	Nonaffiliated
József Torgyán (since 2/2001, Imre Boros)	Agriculture and Rural Development	FKGP
János Szabó	Defense	FKGP
Zoltán Pokorni	Education	FIDESZ-MPP
József Hámori (since 1/2000, Zoltán Rockenbauer)	National Cultural Heritage	Nonaffiliated, FIDESZ-MPP
Tamás Deutsch	Youth and Sports	FIDESZ-MPP
Árpád Gógl (since 1/2001, István Mikola)	Health Affairs	All nonaffiliated
Péter Harrach	Social and Family Affairs	KDSZ
Sándor Pintér	Interior	Nonaffiliated
Ibolya Dávid	Justice	MDF
Attila Chikán (since 1/2000, György Matolcsy)	Economic Affairs	All nonaffiliated
Pál Pepó (6/2000–11/2000, Ferenc Ligetvári; since 12/2000, Béla Turi-Kovács)	Environmental Protection	All FKGP
Kálmán Katona (6/2000–11/2000 László Nógrádi; since 12/2000, János Fónagy)	Transport, Communication, and Water Management	All FIDESZ-MPP
Imre Boros Ervin Demeter (since 5/2000)	Minister without portfolio	FKGP
Total ministers appointed: 28	Total line ministries: 14	

Note: FIDESZ-MPP: Alliance of Young Democrats Hungarian Civic Party; FKGP: Independent Smallholders' Party; KDSZ: Alliance of Christian Democrats; MDF: Hungarian Democratic Forum.

The stability of governing coalitions in Hungary has been facilitated by an electoral system that combines majority and proportional elements and tends to produce clear governing majorities in parliament. The electoral system is a result of the political transition as well as Hungary's parliamentary system of government, where the president has a comparatively weak constitutional position. Árpád Göncz became president of the republic in 1990

Table 3.4. Hungarian Parliaments, Presidents, and Governments, 1990–2002

			Governments	
Parliaments	*Presidents*	*Prime Minister*	*Support in Parliament*	*Party Composition*
May 1990	Árpád Göncz, first term, 1990–1995	József Antall, June 1990–December 1993; Péter Boross, December 1993–May 1994	Majority: 229 of 386 seats	MDF, KDNP, FKGP
May 1994	Árpád Göncz, second term, 1995–2000	Gyula Horn, June 1994–May 1998	Majority: 278 of 386 seats	MSZP, SZDSZ
May 1998	Ferenc Mádl, 2000–2005	Viktor Orbán, June 1998–April 2002	Majority: 213 of 386 seats	FIDESZ-MPP, MDF, FKGP

Note: FIDESZ-MPP: Alliance of Young Democrats Hungarian Civic Party; FKGP: Independent Smallholders' Party; KDNP: Christian Democratic People's Party; MDF: Hungarian Democratic Forum; MSZP: Hungarian Socialist Party; SZDSZ: Alliance of Free Democrats.

and remained in office for a second term until August 2000. The changes of governments and presidents are summarized in table 3.4.

THE LOCATION OF THE EXECUTIVE IN THE POLITICAL SYSTEM

This section argues that the Hungarian executive has consistently increased its powers in relation to the president, parliament, and political parties. The actor constellation of the political transition resulted in the rejection of a parliamentary-presidential model of government, and the political role of the president was reduced to representative functions during the Antall government's term of office. The parliament initially had strong control powers and constituted the focus of the political process but has under the Orbán government lost its centrality and its scope of influencing decision making. The executive has also increased its control over the major governing party, if one compares the compliance of FIDESZ-MPP deputies or party rank and file with the MSZP of 1994–1998 and the MDF of 1990–1994.

In comparison with the Bulgarian, Czech, and Polish cases, the Hungarian transformation can be characterized as being executive driven already in its early stage. Not only is this due to the already mentioned elitist mode of transition and the majority-favoring electoral system, but it originates from the founding constellation of political actors.

First, the executive became the stronghold and instrument of state socialist reformers to push through far-reaching changes against a reluctant party bureaucracy and in the presence of a parliament lacking democratic legitimation. Executive performance in economic crisis management and preemptive systemic reforms were a strategy of regaining a political legitimacy that had been eroded by the party's acceptance of a multiparty system and the political pluralization. Second, the new elites, having won the first democratic elections of April–May 1990, agreed to strengthen the executive in order to ensure and improve governability. The "pact" concluded between the MDF and the SZDSZ in May 1990 reduced the number of laws requiring a two-thirds majority in parliament and introduced a constructive vote of no-confidence that was confined to the prime minister.

The executive was further strengthened by weakening the president and the parliament. The position of the president was relatively quickly downgraded to representation and ceremonial functions. In a first step, the initial attempt of state socialist reformers to move the Hungarian system of government toward a parliamentary-presidential type failed in the political constellation of the transition period. The constitutional reform of 1989 had replaced the previous collective presidential council by the position of a president in order to reestablish continuity with the precommunist system of government and to preserve a part of the socialists' power, since the party could present a very popular candidate (Imre Pozsgay). While the state socialist reformers succeeded in equipping the president with relatively strong constitutional powers, they failed to combine these powers with the direct election of the president.

The liberal opposition parties in the national roundtable negotiations of summer 1989 preferred the indirect election of the president by the new, democratically elected parliament, where they hoped to gain the majority of seats. They initiated a referendum about, inter alia, whether the president should be elected after the parliamentary elections, which turned into a manifestation of widespread disapproval of the state socialist regime, with the side effect of reinforcing the indirect election (and delegated legitimacy) of the president. As a result, the constitutional position of the president is characterized by a certain tension between a relatively weak, indirect democratic legitimation and the relatively strong, formal powers that overlap with the powers of the executive.

According to the constitution in force, the Hungarian president represents the Hungarian state, symbolizes the unity of the nation, and "shall guard the democratic functioning of the state organization." The president may initiate legislation and referenda. He may declare a state of war or a state of emergency whenever the parliament is unable to take such a decision. The president may also dissolve the parliament if it, on four occasions within twelve months, expresses its no-confidence in a government or if parliament does not, within forty days, elect the prime minister–designate of the president after a lost vote of confidence. The president may return a bill with his comments to parliament for reconsideration ("political veto")

or may ask the constitutional court to review a bill he considers unconstitutional ("constitutional veto"). A presidential refusal to sign a bill can
be overruled by a simple majority in parliament. The president appoints
and dismisses state secretaries and deputy state secretaries upon the proposal of the prime minister. To perform some of his functions, the president requires the countersignature of the prime minister or another relevant
minister.

In a second step, the executive prevailed in power struggles with the president during the Antall government's term of office. President Árpád Göncz,
who was proposed by and affiliated with the SZDSZ, initially interpreted
his role and powers as counterbalancing the centralization attempts of the
executive. For example, the president in 1990 refused to sign the bill on
property compensation and asked the constitutional court for a review of
the bill that led to the annulment of parts of the legislation. In 1992, the president refused to accept the prime minister's nomination of vice presidents
for public radio and television. However, the constitutional court in several
decisions rejected the notion of a division of executive power between the
executive and the president and established a restrictive interpretation of the
powers of the president (Körösényi 1999, 423).[1] The Horn and the Orbán
government did not enter into major conflicts with the president, which was
partly due to the political affinity of Göncz and Mádl with the respective
governing parties.

With respect to the parliament, encouraging parliamentary plurality, debate, and institutional autonomy had been a strategy of state socialist reformers in their struggle with party hardliners in the second half of the eighties.
The national roundtable talks led to constitutional amendments and laws
that enhanced the control functions of the parliament and declared the parliament the "supreme organ of state power and popular representation,"
suggesting a superiority not existing in other transition country constitutions
(Elster, Offe, and Preuss 1998, 95). The political role of the first democratic
Hungarian parliament has been salient insofar as it had to adopt numerous
basic laws in order to implement the change of system.

The MDF-SZDSZ pact and the ensuing constitutional amendments, however, increased the constitutional autonomy of the executive in relation to
parliament. According to the constitution, parliamentary discretion in ap-
proving and dismissing governments is limited. Approval of the government
program is linked to the election of the prime minister. The composition of
the cabinet is determined by this election and is not subject to a vote of
parliament. While ministries have to be established or abolished by law,
ministers can be changed irrespective of parliament. Parliamentary deputies
have to elect another prime minister if they want to dismiss a government.
Parliament may not submit a motion of no-confidence against single members of government, although individual ministers are accountable not only

to government but also to parliament. Members of parliament can pose questions or submit interpellations, but even if the minister's reply is not accepted by parliament, this does not lead to his or her removal or resignation.

Since the time of the Antall government, the factual influence of the parliament on the executive has declined, which is, inter alia, indicated by the fact that the number of parliamentary session days fell from 318 (first three years of the Antall government) to 293 (Horn government) and further to 218 (Orbán government). Whereas Prime Minister Antall attended 68 percent of these sessions, Horn and Orbán attended 33 percent and 35 percent of the sessions.[2] The Orbán government reduced the parliamentary session times from the original thirty-seven to forty-two weeks per year to approximately seventeen weeks per year by convening the parliament only every third week during the session periods.

THE OUTLINES OF THE EXECUTIVE TERRAIN

This section describes how the Hungarian executive has been subject to progressive functional integration, organizational differentiation, and legal institutionalization. Economic government has been subject to the most far-reaching changes. State socialist reforms had already replaced the sectorally differentiated branch ministries by a smaller number of ministries (industry, internal trade, external trade) and numerous semi-independent central agencies in the eighties. The first democratic government was thus faced with a comparatively modernized central governmental administration that facilitated, through its organizational fragmentation, interorganizational bargaining and professional-organizational autonomy. This posed a policy conflict between safeguarding vital service functions for the economic transformation on the one hand and reestablishing political control on the other.

The Antall government introduced the term *government* instead of *council of ministers* in order to emphasize the shift from sectoral to functional integration and from fragmentation to political control. The government maintained the former Ministry of Foreign Trade under the new name of Ministry of International Economic Relations and integrated the formerly separate Ministry of Industry and Ministry of Internal Trade into a Ministry of Industry and Trade. The National Planning Office and the Price Office were dissolved, and their remaining functions and personnel were transferred to the Ministry of Finance. The Labor Affairs Office was transformed into the Ministry of Labor Affairs.

Whereas the standing order of the last state socialist governments had mentioned sixteen central agencies and institutions supervised by the council of ministers, the Antall government initially reduced, and in 1991 skipped, all references to these institutions. They were either dissolved or subordinated to ministries (and, if the latter, possibly institutionalized by laws specifying the regulatory role of the government). The Antall government took control of the privatization agency established by the previous government and endowed a minister without portfolio with the supervision of privatization. In addition, it created a minister without portfolio responsible for the already established system of commercial banks. Both institutional arrangements reflected the compromise between reestablishing political control and maintaining professional rationality criteria. As a leading official in the Antall government noted, Antall tried to strictly separate the political sphere from the administration. The prime minister "thought that the prime minister's office had to have a certain political role, but that the political responsibility should rest with himself and his office should remain politically neutral" (interview, February 2001).

The Horn government committed itself to organizational continuity and comparatively incremental changes. It dissolved the Ministry of International Economic Relations and integrated its departments into the Ministry of Industry and Trade and the Ministry of Foreign Affairs. The Ministry of Industry and Trade was transformed into a Ministry of Industry, Trade, and Tourism. The leading role in economic policy formulation was assigned to the Ministry of Finance. This leadership remained contested during the Horn government and even more during the Antall/Boross period (more on this later). The Horn government also reduced the number of ministers without portfolio.

The Orbán government undertook a far-reaching restructuring. It split up the two "human" ministries (welfare; education and culture) into five (social and family affairs; health; education; national cultural heritage; youth and sport) and dissolved the Ministry of Labor Affairs, which it perceived as a stronghold of trade unions. It transformed the Ministry of Industry, Trade, and Tourism into a Ministry of Economics and thus established a lead ministry responsible for, and representing interests of, the entire economy. The tasks inherited from its predecessor ministry referred to industrial, energy, and trade policy; support of tourism; foreign investment; small- and medium-size enterprises; and consumer protection. In addition, the Ministry of Economics received responsibilities in the areas of wage and labor market policy, interest reconciliation with trade unions and business associations, and, from May 2000 onward, labor affairs from the former Ministry of Labor Affairs. Further tasks of the ministry were housing, competition, innovation, and technology policy. In December 1999 some tasks were transferred from the Ministry of Economics to the Ministry of Foreign Affairs and the Ministry of Education. Figure 3.1 shows organizational changes of ministries and major economic policy agencies since 1989.

Németh Government 1989–1990	Antall/Boross Government 1990–1994	Horn Government 1994–1998	Orbán Government 1998–2002
Office of the Council of Ministers	Office of the Prime Minister	Office of the Prime Minister	Office of the Prime Minister
Ministry of Foreign Affairs	Ministry of Foreign Affairs	Ministry of Foreign Affairs	Ministry of Foreign Affairs
Ministry of Defense	Ministry of Defense	Ministry of Defense	Ministry of Defense
Ministry of Justice	Ministry of Justice	Ministry of Justice	Ministry of Justice
Ministry of Finance	Ministry of Finance	Ministry of Finance	Ministry of Finance

National Planning Office

Price Office

State Asset Agency

State Development Institute

State Asset Agency / State Asset Holding Company

State Treasury

State Asset Agency / State Privatization and Asset Management Company

Hungarian Investment and Development

Banking Supervisory Authority

Economic Competition Office

State Audit System

State Privatization and Asset Management Company

Hungarian Development Bank

Hungarian Banking and Capital Market Supervisory Authority

Economic Competition Office

Hungarian Development Bank

Hungarian Banking and Capital Market Supervisory Authority

Economic Competition Office

Figure 3.1.   Structural Changes in Central Governmental Administration. *Source:* Personal Compilation.

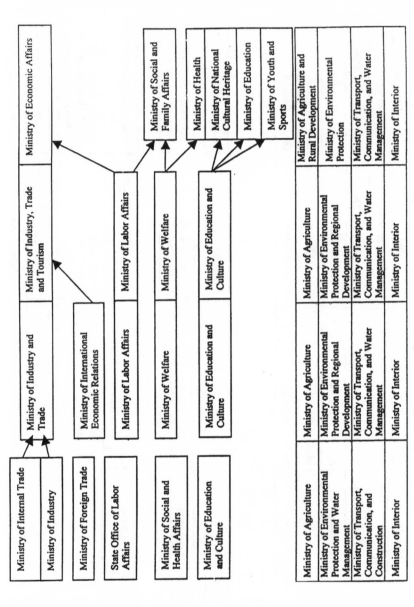

Figure 3.1. *(Contd.)*

Since the political transition, successive Hungarian governments have adjusted the standing order to their own priorities and concepts of governance. The state socialist government of Károly Grósz was the first to publish its standing order in July 1988. The Antall government and the Horn government each adopted new standing orders, and the Orbán government (as well as the state socialist government of Miklós Németh) substantially changed the extant standing order when they entered office. Apart from the government resolutions on the standing orders, other resolutions and decrees regulate, inter alia, the status of cabinet committees and the prime minister's office.

The number of ministries in the three governments between 1990 and 2001 varied between twelve and fourteen. The number and names of ministries are stipulated by law, as required by the Hungarian constitution. The tasks and powers of each ministry are determined by decree. There is no common standing order of the ministries that would stipulate common organizational elements. Although already the Horn government planned to introduce common criteria for the internal organization of ministries, each ministry still has its own standing order. The number of staff in a ministry is fixed and may be changed only by the cabinet. Ministers have bodies of personal advisors with differing sizes and role perceptions. All governments since 1990 have also comprised ministers without portfolio who have been charged with different tasks and whose number has varied between two and five.

Comparing the institutional changes implemented by successive governments, one does not find a clear pattern of "decreasing invasiveness," that is, fundamental changes in the wake of the political transition and ensuing minor adjustments reflecting the ongoing consolidation of the executive. The emergence of a Ministry of Economic Affairs and the increasingly detailed procedures set out in successive standing orders of the government and of individual ministries certainly reflect the general and linear processes of functional integration, differentiation, and institutionalization. However, the organizational restructuring carried out by the Orbán government was at least as far-reaching as the changes realized by the Antall government. It can be argued that this is not a deconsolidation but has been facilitated by the consolidation that made executive performance less dependent on continuity in administrative structures.

THE POWERS OF THE PRIME MINISTER

This section analyzes the establishment of a prime ministerial type of government in Hungary, and the progressive trend toward a centralized prime ministerial core executive. The moderately strong role of the prime minister envisaged by the constitution has been shifted to a chancellor-type model by the Antall, Horn, and Orbán governments. All three governments have increased the formal and real powers of the prime minister and have strengthened his administrative support basis.

The modifications of the constitution agreed during the political transition in 1990 clearly established the prime minister as the source of formal-legal authority of the government, thus laying the foundations for prime ministerial government. According to the constitution, the prime minister may determine and change the cabinet members irrespective of parliament. A 1997 law stipulates that the prime minister exercises the rights of an employer with respect to his ministers. The prime minister also proposes political and administrative state secretaries for appointment. According to the law, the prime minister has to take into account the opinion of the respective minister (appointment of a political state secretary) or base his proposal on the minister's proposal (administrative state secretary). The constitutional right of the president to appoint state secretaries has had a merely formal significance.

The position of the prime minister has been strengthened further by introducing the requirement of a constructive vote of no-confidence, directed at the prime minister rather than the cabinet as whole. The resignation procedure of a prime minister or cabinet member is regulated in detail by a law that has further enhanced the powers of the prime minister.[3] If a minister wants to resign, he has to involve the prime minister and submit a declaration to the president. If the prime minister resigns, the mandate of the government terminates as well.

During the Horn government, the MSZP tried to entrust the prime minister with the right to appoint deputy state secretaries but failed to convince its coalition partner, who insisted on the appointment right of the ministers.[4] It succeeded, however, in shifting the right of appointing the heads of the regional bodies of state administration from the minister of interior to the prime minister. The coalition agreement of the Orbán government gave the prime minister the right to raise a veto against the administrative state secretaries appointed by his ministers. This agreement strengthened the prime minister's political authority in using his legally codified nomination right. In May 2001, the prime minister's power over key administrative personnel was substantially enhanced in connection with the creation of the senior executive service. He was enabled to appoint the three hundred members of the newly established *grand corps*.

The prime minister's formal-legal authority has served as the foundation of the development of a centralized prime ministerial core executive. It has to be noted that there is an ambiguity in the Hungarian constitution with respect to the prime minister's powers to direct and coordinate the work of his fellow ministers. On the one hand, according to the constitution, it is the cabinet that shall "direct the work of the ministries . . . and coordinate their activities" (art. 35.1c). The prime minister may not give instructions to the ministers. Both the prime minister and the ministers may issue decrees, which, however, may not conflict with any law or any decree or resolution of the government. Both the prime minister and the ministers may attend and address the sessions of the parliament. Ministers may "direct the branches of public administration falling within the scope of their responsibilities and control the organs subordinated to them" (art. 37.2), and they are accountable for their decisions.

On the other hand, the constitution stipulates that the prime minister "shall preside over the meetings of the cabinet" (art. 37.1). He must sign the decrees and resolutions of the government and should provide for their implementation (art. 37.1). The procedural rights of the prime minister increase his powers.[5] He formulates and signs the decisions of the cabinet and sends the submissions for parliamentary debate to the chairman of the parliament. The prime minister may—in exceptional and justified cases—issue a resolution of the government during the time between two cabinet meetings in order to define tasks of the government, conduct international negotiations, sign and approve international agreements, organize visits, carry out appointments and dismissals, and confer honors and may do so in other cases on the basis of an explicit authorization of the government. If a minister wants to postpone tasks envisaged in the work plan of the government for more than a month or to terminate these tasks, he has to ask the prime minister for permission. The prime minister may ask a minister to account for the implementation of resolutions of the government.

While cabinet decisions are adopted with a majority of the votes and all members of the government have an equal right to vote, the prime minister's vote decides in case of a tie. In practice, the prime minister's position in cabinet meetings has been additionally strengthened by the fact that he usually applies the principle of negative voting (Verebélyi 1996, 200). According to a leading civil servant under the Horn government, "the prime minister did not specifically ask the individual cabinet members for their approval or refusal on each item. The prime minister asked only for dissenting opinions, and most dissenting opinions were only mentioned in the notes of the meeting" (interview, February 2001). Whereas the rule of positive voting stipulates that every minister may articulate his opinion on a submission, the rule of negative voting states that only those ministers may speak who have objections. Negative voting thus forces dissenting ministers to take a potentially isolated position against the prime minister in front of the cabinet instead of allowing them to influence the formation of a cabinet opinion in the course of an open discussion.

The prime minister's formal powers have been enhanced by his position as leader of the main governing party. The first prime minister after the democratic transition, Antall, a charismatic politician, was able to choose close, personal associates to lead the three key ministries of his government (foreign affairs, interior, and finance; Lengyel 1993, 20).[6] In a similar fashion, the Horn government relied on the legal, political, and social resources of prime ministerial power, but it also tried to further refine and codify the operating procedures of the executive. While the ostensible intention was to facilitate collegiate government by a system of cabinet committees (see the following section), observers classified the actual operation of the executive as resembling a chancellor-type model—that is, a model where cabinet decisions are de facto taken by the prime minister himself and ministers are less participants than advisors in the decision-making process (Sárközy 1995).

The Orbán government established a more distinct subordination of ministers to the prime minister and enhanced the prime minister's position further by placing a minister instead of an administrative state secretary at the top of the prime minister's office.[7] Contrary to the previous cabinet, eight of the eighteen ministers in Orbán's initial cabinet were experts who were not members of the governing parties or of parliament (Szente 1999). As these ministers lacked a political backing in a governing party, their political authority depended on the prime minister. According to a close observer of Hungary's executive, "the prime minister managed to survive the intra-PMO [Prime Minister's Office] rivalries and the conflicts with the coalition partners due to the existence of the personal advisors' *cabinet*, but the price was that 'they shifted the prime minister up to the heaven' so that 'we cannot see him'" (interview, June 2000).

PATTERNS OF CABINET DECISION MAKING

Interministerial coordination in the Hungarian executive has been increasingly institutionalized and differentiated since the political transition. The initial workload of cabinet meetings was reduced by several processes: the conference of administrative state secretaries introduced in 1990 has developed into an effective filtering and structuring institution; the introduction of an Economic Cabinet Committee in 1990 and further cabinet committees from 1994 onward have improved political coordination and dispute resolution among ministers; the PMO has attained agenda-preparing and de facto gatekeeping functions for cabinet meetings; these developments have been facilitated by increasingly "normal" politics, with major systemic reforms having been accomplished.

During the Grósz and Németh governments, the council of ministers met regularly, usually twice per week; its members had equal voting rights and adopted decisions with the simple majority of the votes; and the vote of the chairman of the council of ministers decided in case of a tie. The standing order specified and structured the issue areas that could be discussed in the meetings of the council of ministers. The large number of permanent invitees to meetings of the Grósz cabinet (thirteen), who represented societal organizations and agencies but lacked a voting right, indicated the fragmentation of the late state socialist executive and its preoccupation with sectoral issues. The Németh government reduced the group of invitees and introduced a Cabinet of the Council of Ministers, which functioned as an inner cabinet in order to preclarify "conceptual questions that formed the political profile of the Council of Ministers."[8] Apart from key ministers, the head of the Office of the Council of Ministers participated in this cabinet, and other members of the council of ministers were invited depending upon the issues debated.

The Antall government established a weekly conference of administrative state secretaries, which consisted of the leading civil servants from each ministry and was chaired by the administrative state secretary heading the PMO. The conference had its greatest political influence under the Antall government, compared to both the state socialist and the later governments.[9] Since the new political leaders lacked experience and were faced with an extremely crowded political agenda, many genuinely political issues were shifted to and settled by the conference. Administrative and deputy state secretaries figured as the official representatives of their ministries, who signed and commented on submissions to the cabinet (Verebélyi 1996, 199). In 1991–1992 the PMO attained a stronger role in the preparation of cabinet meetings. Its administrative state secretary coordinated the work schedule of the government, had to be informed of any draft envisaged for the cabinet, and monitored whether a draft corresponded to the government's standing order. In 1993, the government introduced a regular meeting of political state secretaries to coordinate between the three governing parties and its relations with the parliament. In addition to this format, coordination within the governing coalition was performed by assigning political state secretaries of one coalition party to a ministry headed by another coalition party. Of the thirteen ministries in the Antall government, eleven were organized in this way. Following initial conflicts between the minister of finance and other government actors involved in economic policymaking, the Antall government established an Economic Cabinet Committee chaired by the finance minister.

The Horn government preserved the conference of administrative state secretaries and established three new cabinet committees in addition to the economic committee. The Governmental Cabinet Committee decided on principal and urgent political questions and consisted of the prime minister (chair), the minister of interior (leading minister of the junior coalition partner SZDSZ), the minister of foreign affairs, and the minister of finance. Both the head of the prime minister's advisory body and the administrative state secretary of the PMO were permanent invitees to the committee.

The other two new cabinet committees were dealing with national security and EU integration. The Economic Cabinet Committee continued to
be chaired by the minister of finance and was authorized to coordinate the
reform of the public finances and to take positions on budgetary and fiscal
policy issues (Bánsági 1996, 150–51). Its position was strengthened insofar as the cabinet had to base its resolution on the draft of the economic
committee. Initially, the economic committee decided by voting; the second
finance minister of the Horn government, however, reserved for himself the
right to decide whether the committee should decide by voting or leave the
decision to him.

The cabinet committee system originated from a proposal of a Hungarian
expert on public administration who suggested strengthening the collegiate
character of government instead of creating a chancellor-type concentration
of powers in the hands of the prime minister (Kormány 1996; Verebélyi
1996). "The prime minister should be stronger than a 'primus inter pares,'
and the cabinet should be more than a 'simple federation of ministers'" (interview, June 2000). It was argued that most small European states successfully
applied collegiate forms of governance and that Hungary lacked institutions
counterbalancing the chancellor's powers in the German model—the *Länder*
governments and the Bundesrat. The cabinet committees and the Council for
Coalition Coordination replaced the regular meetings of political state secretaries. Among the twelve ministries, five were organized as mixed ministries
with political state secretary and minister differing in their party affiliation
(Szente 1999). The Horn government also reduced the number of ministers without portfolio from four to two and appointed two deputy prime
ministers: the minister of interior (and leading representative of the SZDSZ)
and the minister of finance. The regular conference of administrative state
secretaries attained a stronger coordinating role, and a wider circle of actors
was informed of drafts of cabinet decisions.

The Orbán government retained the governmental, national security, and
economic cabinet committees; dissolved the committee on European integration; and introduced a committee on home affairs. Since the political
leaders of the coalition parties participated in the cabinet, the governmental
committee was initially envisaged for coalition coordination but was soon
replaced by bilateral talks. The Economic Cabinet Committee was chaired
by the minister of economic affairs instead of the finance minister, reflecting the lead role assigned to the Ministry of Economic Affairs. In order to
facilitate an open exchange of opinions and information and to strengthen
the team spirit of the cabinet, the government held informal cabinet meetings in addition to the formal meetings. (For a review of each government's
cabinet committees, see table 3.5.) The practice of mixed ministries was
retained only between FIDESZ-MPP and MDF, not for the FKGP-led ministries. Furthermore, three positions of political state secretary were given to
a moderate right-wing party that had failed to enter parliament.

Table 3.5. Cabinet Committees in Hungarian Governments

Németh	Antall/Boross	Horn	Orbán
Cabinet of the Council of Ministers		Governmental Committee	Governmental Committee
	Economic Committee	Economic Committee	Economic Committee
		National Security Committee	National Security Committee
		European Union Integration Committee	Committee for Home Affairs

Source: Personal compilation.

Several reforms strengthened the coordination function of the PMO, corresponding to its enhanced role and the concept of chancellor-type government: the conference of administrative state secretaries was enlarged with the deputy state secretaries leading the Office of the Government and the ministry desks in the PMO, as well as with the heads of offices of the ministers without portfolio; the political state secretary responsible for the strategy of the government became a permanent invitee to cabinet meetings; and, apart from the meetings between the minister heading the PMO and the chairmen of the parliamentary groups of the governing parties, the personal advisors of the minister heading the PMO and the PMO staff responsible for relations with the parliament were invited to the meetings of the presidency of the FIDESZ-MPP parliamentary group.

According to the standing order of the government, the cabinet decides with the majority of its members, and all members of the government have equal votes. The administrative state secretary of the PMO prepares a draft agenda that is sent to the participants of the meeting. Following consultation with the Governmental Cabinet Committee, the prime minister decides on the final agenda. The agenda consists of three parts: submissions proposed for adoption without debate, submissions proposed for general debate, and special issues (Borók, Fekete, and Horváth 2000, 16). Seventy percent of the items on the agenda of the cabinet meeting are decided by a single voting procedure.[10]

All the ministers and—on the basis of a resolution of the government—the political state secretary of the PMO, the president of the Central Statistical Office, the heads of central agencies (in accordance with the supervising member of the government), the commissioners of the government, and—with the preceding contribution of the prime minister—other organs and persons may submit documents to the cabinet meeting. Every document envisaged for the cabinet meeting has to be submitted to the minister heading the PMO. Ministers, state secretaries, authorized deputy state secretaries, commissioners of the government, heads of state organs with national purview, or their authorized deputies may exercise the right of opinion on a draft submission. The author of the draft submission must ask those members of the government who are affected by the topic of the draft submission to express their opinions prior to the cabinet meeting. He is expected to engage in a consensus-seeking process with those who have voiced an objecting opinion. For some specific issues, the opinions of other state bodies and extra-governmental institutions have to be requested.

The cabinet may decide without a debate if the draft submission is prepared correctly and if those authorized to give their opinions agree with the submission or if the submission aims at the proclamation of international treaties already approved by the government. Major government decisions (e.g., comprehensive draft acts, important decrees of the government, and programs) are prepared in a two-step procedure consisting of a debate and agreement on principal questions and the preparation and determination of detailed arrangements.

The conference of administrative state secretaries takes place nine days before the cabinet meeting, discusses all the submissions envisaged for the cabinet meeting, and prepares cabinet decisions. The conference may initiate the discussion of a submission in the relevant cabinet committee prior to the cabinet meeting. While the minister heading the PMO is the formal chair of the conference, the conference is usually chaired by the administrative state secretary of the PMO. Although the political decision-making role of the conference has decreased in comparison with that of the Antall period, its decision-shaping influence is still high, since the prime minister and the minister heading the PMO used to accept 90 percent of the agenda items prepared by the conference.[11]

PARTY-BASED POLITICAL COORDINATION DEVICES

The cabinet has tended to be the main mode of political coordination in Hungary; while party-based coordination mechanisms also exist, they have been limited in importance. In the Antall government, the chairmen of the coalition parties co-coordinated their policy in cabinet or in noninstitutionalized meetings. The Horn government institutionalized coordination by creating a Council of Coalition Coordination, consisting of the prime minister; the minister of interior and the minister of finance; and the chairmen of the coalition parties, the leaders of the parliamentary groups, and representatives delegated by both coalition parties. The standing order of the Horn government explicitly listed several issues that required an ex-ante coordination and agreement between the representatives of the governing parties. The council was envisaged to meet only if the prime minister and the minister of interior did not reach agreement on an issue. Once established, the council turned into a regularly meeting body used by the coalition parties to discuss any question requiring agreement (Sárközy 1995, 294). According to a Hungarian expert, the council, instead of providing coordination, facilitated "games of non-confidence," which destroyed the Horn government.[12]

The Orbán government established a cabinet committee and a weekly meeting with the leaders of the parliamentary groups. The cabinet committee was envisaged for political coordination and consisted of the prime minister (chairman of FIDESZ-MPP), the deputy prime minister and the minister heading the PMO, the minister of agriculture and rural development (chairman of FKGP), and the minister of justice (chairwoman of MDF). This structure was soon replaced by bilateral talks between the FKGP chairman and the prime minister.[13] The weekly meetings between the minister heading the PMO and the leaders of the parliamentary groups of FIDESZ-MPP, FKGP, and MDF served to explore the degree of parliamentary support for submissions to cabinet and parliamentary debate. Further participants of these meetings were the parliamentary experts of the parties, the political state secretary of the PMO responsible for the strategy of the government, and the employees of the PMO responsible for the relations with the parliament and the preparation of the meetings of government. Both coordination mechanisms, however, failed to settle the political conflicts between the FIDESZ-MPP and the FKGP. These conflicts and the related power struggles within the FKGP led to the ousting of FKGP leader József Torgyán in February 2001 and to the disintegration of the FKGP, depriving the Orbán government of its parliamentary majority.

THE POWERS AND ORGANIZATION OF THE CENTER OF GOVERNMENT

The trend toward a centralized prime ministerial core executive has been supported by the increasing salience and prime ministerial orientation of the Hungarian center of government. As for other aspects of the Hungarian executive, the roots of this development can be traced back to the last state socialist government of Miklós Németh, which upgraded the secretariat of the council of ministers to an "office." By strengthening the policy-coordinating role of this office, reformers tried to increase their scope of action and detach the government from the more rigid and traditionalist party and sectoral bureaucracies. However, the office did not attain a policy-shaping role but remained a primarily technical-bureaucratic organ (Szilvásy 1994, 457). The office provided services to the chairman of the council of ministers and to all ministers. In addition, Németh and his deputy prime ministers had their own

I. Prime Minister
A. Head of Cabinet Title State Secretary
   1. Administrative Deputy Head of Cabinet
   2. General Deputy Head of Cabinet
   3. Secretariat of the Prime Minister
   4. Government Spokesperson
   5. Press Office
   6. Documentation
   7. Protocol Department
B. Administrative State Secretary
   1. General Deputy State Secretary
     a. Legal and Administrative Secretariat
     b. Office for Complaints
     c. Management Office
   2. Deputy State Secretary
     a. Budget and Control Department
     b. Financial and Economic Department
     c. Information Technology Secretariat
     d. Information Technology Coordination Office
     e. Internal Control Organization
   3. Secretariat of the Administrative State Secretary
   4. Personnel and General Services
   5. International Relations Secretariat
C. Political State Secretary (PSS) Information Policy
D. PSS Youth Policy
E. PSS Information Policy
F. PSS Church Relations
G. PSS Church Relations
H. PSS Information Policy
I. Main Advisor Foreign Affairs
J. Minister without Portfolio (MwP) Science and Technology
K. MwP Privatization
L. MwP Security Services
M. MwP Agricultural Property Reform
N. Secretariat Science Policy

Figure 3.2.   Internal Structure of the Prime Minister's Office, December 1993.

secretariats and groups of external advisors. An advisory body to the council of ministers had been established already by the previous government.

The Antall government transformed the office of the council of ministers into the PMO. The structure of the PMO is illustrated by figure 3.2 (Kodela and Szilvásy 1997). From 1990 until 1994, its staff amounted to approximately 510 employees. The PMO provided direct assistance to the prime minister by, inter alia, commenting on bills submitted to the cabinet; organizing the prime minister's relations with the parliament, parties, and civil society organizations; and preparing prime ministerial documents for other state organs. The PMO was equipped with planning and analytical capacities, provided administrative support for the ministers without portfolio, and was charged with various tasks not related to a line ministry.

To provide the prime minister with economic policy expertise and to create an independent unit of strategic economic thinking and decision making, a secretariat on economic policy was created within the PMO in July 1990. In September 1991, the PMO units directly supporting the prime minister's work were integrated into a Prime Minister's Cabinet Office (Miniszterelnöki Kabinetiroda). Advisors existed for the following issue areas: foreign policy; public administration, legal and judicial affairs, environmental protection; defense and national security; home affairs, churches, parliamentary coalition, and opposition parties; economic policy; social policy and interest representation; education and minorities; and information policy. In addition, Antall consulted a body of personal advisors consisting of ethnic Hungarian émigrés in influential positions abroad.

The new organization of the PMO was criticized because it established a residual government, collecting all institutions not fitting into line ministries, and it concentrated far-reaching powers in the hands of the administrative state secretary heading the PMO without making him accountable to parliament (Szilvásy 1994, 465).

The Horn government streamlined the PMO organization by reducing the number of ministers without portfolio and the number of tasks not related to line ministries. An economic policy unit, a unit for youth issues, a secretariat dealing with organized crime and shadow economy, and committees for information technology and telecommunication and for drug abuse prevention were established. The Horn government had a mirror structure insofar as there were deputy state secretaries in the PMO responsible for sectoral issues and, for example, the PMO deputy state secretary for economic issues was invited to the Economic Cabinet Committee. The PMO had three organizational units dealing with budget issues: a unit responsible for the budget chapter of the prime minister, the economic policy department concerned with substantive economic issues (eight staff members in 1997), and a group of legal experts dealing with legality aspects of the budget. The prime minister created his own body of personal advisors who, in contrast to the advisors of Prime Minister Antall, did not have work contracts and positions in the PMO and did not participate in the operative management of the government.

The Orbán government has developed the PMO into a state "chancellery" that is to serve as a "flagship" for the government (see figure 3.3).[14] The plan of the government was to increase the PMO staff to 470 employees. The government placed a minister at the helm of the PMO and made the PMO responsible to supervise the privatization, to exercise the state's property rights in state treasury assets, and to perform strategic guidance over the government's audit office and the regional units of public administration supervising local self-governments and coordinating regional and spatial policy. With the law on the senior executive service, the PMO was charged with the task of qualifying the top-level civil servants belonging to the service. The Office of National and Ethnic Minorities, the Office of Ethnic Hungarians

I. Prime Minister
  A. Political State Secretary, Head of the Prime Minister's Cabinet
  B. Minister, PHARE Program
  C. Minister, Civilian Secret Services
    1. Superintendent of National Security
  D. Head of the Prime Minister's Office
    1. Minister's Cabinet
      a. Department of Privatization
    2. State Secretary, Public Administration and Regional Policy
    3. State Secretary, Security and Defense Policy
    4. Government Commissioner, Danube Issues
    5. Government Commissioner, Y2K Problem
    6. Political State Secretary, Overall Government Strategy
      a. Governmental Strategy Analyses Department
      b. Economical and Social Analyses Department
      c. Political Analyses Department
      d. European Integration Department
      e. Working Group of Integration Strategy
      f. Department of Civic Relations
    7. Administrative State Secretary
      a. Head of the Ministry Desks, Deputy State Secretary
        i. Economic and Financial Policy Desk
        ii. Public Policy Desk
        iii. Agriculture, Environment, and Infrastructure Policy Desk
        iv. Public Law and Home Affairs Desk
        v. Political State Secretary, Foreign Affairs and Defense Desk
        vi. Main Division of Management of Treasury Property
      b. Deputy State Secretary Government Office
        i. Secretariat of Law and Public Administration
        ii. Parliamentary Secretariat
        iii. Department of Citizens Contacts
        iv. Office of Administration
      c. Deputy State Secretary, Budget and Management
        i. Budget Department
        ii. Department of Finance and Accounting
      d. Deputy State Secretary, Information Technology
        i. Information Strategy and Coordination Department
        ii. Department for Outstanding Governmental IT Projects
        iii. Government Network and IT Department
      e. Head of Personnel
        i. Secretariat of Foreign Affairs
        ii. Personnel and Public Services Department
        iii. Secretariat of the Ex-Prime Minister
      f. Government Control Office
      g. Secretariat of Coordination of Public Procurement
    8. Government Spokesman, Political State Secretary
      a. Press Department
      b. Communications Center
      c. Department of Information

Figure 3.3.   Internal Structure of the Prime Minister's Office, June 2001.

in Neighboring States, and the Secretariat of Church Relations, which had been attached to the PMO in the previous government, were transferred from the PMO to line ministries.

The main structural change was to establish three new organizational units within the PMO: a Communication Office, a Center for Strategic Analysis, and ministry desks. The Center for Strategic Analysis was created to provide a strategic planning capacity for the PMO. Communication activities were increased by establishing a Strategic Communication and Media Office led by the spokesperson of the government. The five ministry desks were modeled according to the *Spiegelreferate* in the German chancellor's office, corresponding to the portfolios of line ministries and staffed with forty to forty-five employees. The ministry desk officials participate in the meetings of ministers, state secretaries, and heads of departments within the line ministries and in the ministerial preparation of legislation. They provide a sectoral expertise independent from the line ministries and perform coordination functions between ministries and the PMO and between individual ministries.

Initially, the Orbán government planned to establish the positions of four political state secretaries linked to the newly established cabinet committees for home affairs, economy, national security, and government. These political state secretaries should be supported by secretariats, and they should use the ministry desks to prepare and coordinate the cabinet committee meetings. The objective was to improve the filter function of the cabinet committees, thus increasing the function of the cabinet meeting as a strategic decision-making body. Since the FKGP did not accept a strengthened coordination role of the PMO for the cabinet committees, the government in December 1999 entrusted the political state secretaries with the task of supervising the ministry desks. The relationship between political state secretaries and ministries with related task areas was less clearly defined than in the case of the ministry desks (cf. also Sárközy 1999).

Within the PMO a separate "cabinet" of personal (ad hoc and permanent) advisors supports the prime minister directly. Under the Orbán government, this body consisted of approximately twenty-five persons with FIDESZ-MPP affiliation and constituted an additional expert basis available for the prime minister. The minister heading the PMO had his own advisory body (Stumpf 1999, 327).

The upgrading of the PMO to a chancellery was subject to political and scholarly debate. The opposition parties contended that the enhanced coordination role of the PMO would restrict the democratic accountability of the government. While the ministers would continue to be formally responsible, decisions would be taken behind the scenes, by the ministry desks and state secretaries of the PMO, or by the inner circle of the FIDESZ-MPP.[15] Some legal experts asserted that the centralization of executive power would contradict the collegiate model of government prescribed by the Hungarian constitution.[16] The government argued that the strengthened position of the PMO was to ensure that the government did not fall victim to lobby interests and that it remained capable of realizing its strategic aims. István Stumpf, the minister heading the PMO explained that the aim of the PMO is to "support the prime minister that he can govern the country and will not be preoccupied with balancing different interests and making decisions exposed to daily dilemmas... not being captured by the state apparatus."[17]

The operation of the ministry desks on the one hand entailed conflicts with the line ministries. An advisor to a minister complained that some ministry desk experts would behave like bosses of the ministers. Ministers intending to submit a draft to the government had to gain the prior support of the ministry desk. With this de facto control powers, the desks would resemble the former party apparatus.[18] In the case of those ministries held by politicians from the FKGP and the MDF, ministerial autonomy is politically protected by the coalition arrangement. The ministries led by FIDESZ-MPP politicians or unaffiliated experts seem to be more susceptible to political control and steering attempts of the ministry desks since most desks are staffed with experts having insider knowledge of the ministry.[19] The most visible conflict occurred between the FKGP-led minister of environment and the respective ministry desk. The expert heading the desk, who was a former state secretary in the Ministry of Environment, criticized the minister for lagging behind in preparing laws necessary to transpose EU environmental legislation.

On the other hand, rivalries occurred between the personal advisors' *cabinet* of the prime minister and the ministry desks in the PMO, which represent different organization principles:[20] while the former body copied the model of the French *cabinet ministeriel*, which embodies the idea of personal expertise attached to political leaders, the ministry desks, like their German template, provided intrabureaucratic and formally institutionalized expertise.

THE POLITICS–ADMINISTRATION NEXUS

This section analyzes the attempts of Hungarian governments to strike a balance between the twin imperatives of depoliticization of the bulk of administrative personnel and the regulated politicization of a top layer of administrative positions, which could help the executive in the discharge of its coordinating functions. A clear trend could be observed toward a strengthening role of the prime minister in the appointment of top-level personnel, reinforcing the centralized prime ministerial nature of the Hungarian core executive.

Attempts to create a civil service operating according to professional rationality criteria reach back to the 1970s and were closely linked to the reform socialist strategy of shielding and decoupling the executive from party influence. As a result, administrative personnel who were recruited according to professional performance criteria prevailed at the time of the political transition, enabling the Antall government to pursue a personnel policy of continuity. The MDF leadership decided that former members of the Hungarian Socialist Workers' Party (MSZMP) should not be entrusted with political positions but accepted that the top administrative positions could be staffed with ex-members of the party. However, all compromised persons were excluded from holding such posts. Therefore, many former medium-level civil servants (deputy heads of departments and below) were promoted to leading positions. The new heads of administration had fairly recent university educations and had not been involved in politics.

The government's approach was to clearly separate political and administrative roles, which was reflected in the early law on the provisional regulation of the state secretaries' legal status (May 1990). The law replaced the previous posts of deputy ministers, state ministers, and state secretaries by the posts of "administrative" and "political" state secretaries. This separation of roles was modeled according to the German example of a division of roles between a civil servant state secretary and a *parlamentarischer Staatssekretär*. By institutionalizing such a model, the government intended to preserve the know-how of the former state administration through keeping the best professionals as administrative state secretaries in order to integrate and balance the governing coalition by co-opting important political figures as political state secretaries, "title" state secretaries (i.e., detached from the ministerial hierarchy), or as ministers without portfolio. Four positions of political state secretaries and four positions of ministers without portfolio were created in the framework of the PMO. In addition, each ministry obtained one political state secretary. In its practical personnel policy, the Antall/Boross government refrained from implementing major reshuffles. Among the 177 persons holding leading state positions in the Antall/Boross government—ministers and political, title, administrative, and deputy state secretaries—sixty-three had a leading position already in the previous government (Szilvásy 1995).

Since the Antall government attached high importance to forming a professional and reliable civil service and could draw on reform socialist preparations, Hungary adopted civil service legislation already in March 1992. According to the law, the personnel of central and local government was classified as civil servants, and other public sector employees, including employees in the health and education system, were defined as public servants. The scope, terms, and conditions of employment and the procedures for personnel management were codified in detail.

The main political controversy concerned whether employment conditions of civil servants should be regulated in a more flexible way in order to facilitate greater managerial autonomy (SZDSZ, FIDESZ) or the exclusion of former communists (conservative wing of the MDF; Meyer-Sahling

2001). These concerns were accommodated insofar as the legislation granted more discretion to ministers with respect to appointing and dismissing civil servants. Although civil servants were appointed for an unlimited period, ministers could, for example, replace civil servants by restructuring their ministry. The civil servant law restricted the political activity of civil servants to participating as candidates in the parliamentary or local elections and excluded them from taking other public roles in the name or interest of a party and from positions in political parties. To perform political functions, the law envisaged the legal role model of a political advisor. However, successive Hungarian governments only rarely resorted to the role model of the political advisor. Rather, they placed more political representatives in leading civil service positions. Most of the heads of ministerial advisory bodies acted as political advisors of the ministers but were employed as civil servants (deputy state secretary, head of division).

Political state secretaries, ministers, and the prime minister were not covered by the civil servant law. Their status continued to be regulated by the 1990 law, until the constitutional court in 1996 declared this provision unconstitutional because the system hitherto in force would still bear the traces of a party state government. Reacting to this ruling, the Horn government, which sought to develop a stronger legal codification and institutionalization of its work, in 1997 adopted the law on the legal status and responsibilities of the state secretaries and members of government.

This law continued to distinguish political from administrative state secretaries and classified the latter as civil servants. In appointing political state secretaries, the prime minister was given greater discretion than that with respect to administrative state secretaries (as discussed earlier), and the appointment of a political state secretary terminates with the end of a government's term of office. The law enabled the ministers to propose the appointment of several political state secretaries, which relieve administrative state secretaries in bigger ministries of political tasks they had to perform hitherto (Verebélyi 1998, 326). Only the political state secretary may represent the minister in plenary sessions of the parliament and in meetings of the cabinet. If the political state secretary is unable to attend a cabinet meeting, he may be represented by the administrative state secretary, but the administrative state secretary is not entitled to vote for his ministry in governmental decisions. For sessions of a parliamentary committee, the minister may send the political state secretary or may appoint, if the political state secretary is prevented from participating, another leading state representative or mandate a civil servant to give a statement.

Administrative state secretaries are appointed for an unlimited period. Similar to the legal regulation of the political state secretary and contrary to the rules for other civil servants, a dismissal of an administrative state secretary does not need to be justified. However, in case of a dismissal, the administrative state secretary has to be offered another leading position in the state administration. If he refuses the alternative position, his dismissal is treated like a dismissal of a public servant; that is, notice periods and financial compensations apply. If an administrative state secretary resigns, he will also be entitled to a compensation.

According to the law, a political state secretary may not instruct an administrative state secretary except if the instruction is given by a political state secretary deputizing for the minister. Deputy state secretaries direct the work of the organizational units of a ministry on the basis of the instructions of the administrative state secretary. The deputy state secretary is appointed (for an unlimited period) and dismissed by the minister upon the proposal of the administrative state secretary. The deputy state secretary may represent the administrative state secretary but not the minister. If no specific legal regulation exists, the administrative state secretary exercises employers' rights with respect to the deputy state secretary. In order to draw clearer boundaries between administrative and political functions, the law abolished the previous position of a title state secretary.

In 1997 the civil servant law was modified to distinguish more clearly between civil servants and political associates of government. The modification allowed the government to employ political advisors on the basis of a contract lasting for a limited time. Their employment relationship is linked to the minister and the government, and their salary may be negotiated freely. The government is obliged to specify in a resolution how many political advisors it wants to employ in each ministry. The number of political advisors is limited to fifteen per ministry.

When the Horn government entered office, it appointed ninety-six ministers and political, administrative, title, and deputy state secretaries, among which forty-six held leading positions also in the Antall/Boross government; three held leading positions in the Antall/Boross and Németh governments; and eight persons reentered government, having been in leading positions under the Németh government only (Szilvásy 1995, 473–74).

In May 2001 the Orbán government amended the civil servant law to establish, inter alia, a senior executive service. The prospect of membership in this corps was envisaged to create additional incentives for senior civil servants to continue their careers in the state administration. The law set up a senior executive service of a maximum of three hundred civil servants, who are appointed by the prime minister and cannot be dismissed against their will. To strengthen financial incentives, the wage compression ratio—that is, the ratio of the highest and lowest civil service salary categories—was raised from 3.4 to 6.0 and, in the case of senior executive servants, to 13.0. The Orbán government fixed the number of deputy state secretaries in each ministry (usually four per ministry), ending the previous practice of ministers individually deciding on the number of deputy state secretaries.

In practice, the legal construction of separate political and administrative roles has not been applied and maintained by the Hungarian governments in their personnel policy (Szente 1999; Vass 1999). Incoming governments since 1990 have tended to replace most of the administrative state secretaries and nearly half of the deputy state secretaries they found in post. The Antall government replaced nine of the fourteen administrative state secretaries that it inherited from its predecessor; the Horn government replaced nine of the thirteen administrative state secretaries and twenty of the forty-eight deputy state secretaries, and the Orbán government replaced thirteen of the fifteen administrative state secretaries and twenty of the fifty-three deputy state secretaries (Szente 1999). Governments have also actively replaced administrative and deputy state secretaries in the course of their terms in office, as documented by table 3.6. Moreover, the table indicates

Table 3.6. Administrative and Deputy State Secretaries Replaced by Governments during their Terms of Office

	Administrative/Deputy State Secretary		
Ministry	Antall[a]	Horn[b]	Orbán[c]
Prime Minister's Office	0/2	0/3	0/1
Finance	1/2	0/5	1/2
Agriculture and Rural Development	0/5	1/2	0/4
Economy	—	—	1/6
Trade, Industry, and Tourism	2/1	2/4	—
International Economic Relations	0/2	—	—
Interior	0/1	0/4	0/1
Defense	0/4	0/1	1/2
Justice	0/1	0/0	0/3
Foreign Affairs	1/2	1/4	1/4
Youth and Sport	—	—	1/2
Health	—	—	2/2
Environment	1/5	1/4	2/6
Transport and Water Management	0/1	0/0	2/4
Labor Affairs	0/3	0/1	—
Education and Culture	0/3	0/7	—
Education	—	—	1/1
National Cultural Heritage	—	—	1/1
Welfare	0/2	1/3	—
Social and Family Affairs	—	—	1/4
Total	39 (5/34)	44 (6/38)	57 (14/43)

Source: *Hungarian Economic Weekly*, 13 January 2001.
Note: Changes of staff during the first 2.5 years of a government's term of office, excluding the initial three-month setup period of each government and changes of work areas.
[a]1 September 1990–15 December 1992.
[b]1 October 1994–15 January 1997.
[c]1 October 1998–15 January 2001.

an increasing degree of personnel changes which can be interpreted as a growing politicization of the top echelons of administration. The degree of politicization is confirmed by research on recruitment patterns. Between 1990 and 1999, only 15 of approximately 180 administrative state secretaries were recruited according to a civil service career pattern, that is, among the deputy state secretaries (Szente 1999, 34). There are also tendencies of a growing affiliation of administrative state secretaries with political parties: between 1998 and 2001 the number of administrative state secretaries who were members of a political party rose from one to four.[21]

This politicization of leading administrative positions can be explained with the important role they play in the political governance in Hungary (Szente 1999). Ministers performed only weak and selective political steering and control functions in the case of highly visible and controversial issues, but most of the everyday decision making was initiated and prepared by the administration. The conference of administrative state secretaries attained a decision-shaping role under the Antall government, and administrative state secretaries fulfilled tasks of political state secretaries, such as representing their ministries in parliamentary committees. As a consequence, top administrative positions became politicized, either compensating for the absence of governance by political leaders or as a means of exercising political governance more effectively. Due to the policy-shaping activism of administrative state secretaries, the role of the political state secretary could not unfold as intended in the legislation. On the one hand, political state secretaries remained decoupled from the ministerial bureaucracy, lacking the accumulated insider knowledge of administrative state secretaries. On the other hand, some political state secretaries strove to be charged with the responsibility for professional units in their ministries (e.g., refugee and migration issues were supervised by the political state secretary in the Ministry of Interior; Szente 1999).

The Hungarian academic and political debate on the politicization of leading civil service posts has fluctuated between concepts of technocratic and political government. One reform proposal of the mid-nineties argued that a professional economic crisis management could only be achieved if not only state secretaries but also ministers were appointed according to their professional expertise instead of their political allegiance (Sárközy 1996). In contrast, another author contended that the informal powers of leading civil servants in the process of decision making and their formal discretion rights in the policy implementation stage rendered the political neutrality of public administration a priori an unrealistic assumption (Körösényi 1996). Policy-oriented recent reform proposals have suggested downgrading the administrative state secretary's role to a core of administrative functions and replacing the political state secretary with just one state secretary fulfilling a clearly political role (Szilvásy 1998; Verebélyi 1996).

Table 3.7. Types of Government, Core Executives, and Centers of Government in Hungary, 1990–2002

Type of Government	Type of Core Executive	Type of Center of Government
1990–2002: Prime ministerial	1990–2002: Centralized prime ministerial	1990–2002: Prime minister's vanguard

CONCLUSION

The analysis of the development of executive structures in Hungary presented in this chapter, shows a clear trend toward prime ministerial government (see table 3.7).

Hungary's "founding" constitution clearly designated the prime minister as the source of formal-legal authority for the government. Following the German chancellor model, the prime minister can only be dismissed by a constructive vote of no-confidence, which, significantly, is directed against him and not the cabinet. The prime minister has the power to appoint and dismiss ministers without seeking parliamentary approval. The prime minister's legal authority has served as the basis for the development of effective coordinating institutions, which have been supported by the prime minister's political authority, derived from his position as the leader of the main governing party. This has created a centralized prime ministerial core executive, which has been reinforced by the transformation of the center of government into a prime minister's vanguard. The prerogatives of the prime minister's office reached their high point under the Orbán government, with the establishment of ministry desks, responsible for overseeing the work of line ministries. The centralized prime ministerial nature of the core executive was also expressed in the prime minister's extensive powers over the political-administrative nexus, including the right to propose political and administrative state secretaries for appointment in all the ministries. The change in the appointment system for top-level administrative personnel in 2001 led to a strengthening of the prime minister's power, with the right to appoint all the members of the newly established grand corps. To summarize, Hungary presents the clearest example in our four case studies of reinforcing linkages between the types of government, core executive, and center of government and of close correspondence between intraexecutive institutional arrangements and party-political mechanisms.

NOTES

1. Note that the constitutional court posed a major obstacle to executive government during the Antall and Horn years, as it declared several of these governments'

major political projects unconstitutional, developing the doctrine of an invisible constitution. Since the change of judges in 1998, the court has tended to a more restrained interpretation of its political role, thus conceding more autonomy to the executive.

2. *Hungarian Economic Weekly* (*HVG*), 8 September 2001.

3. Law 79/1997, on the legal status and responsibility of members of government and state secretaries.

4. *HVG*, 28 June 1997.

5. Government resolution no. 1088 of 20 September 1994, on the standing order of the government.

6. The Antall government first introduced the official term "prime minister" (*miniszterelnök*) instead of "chairman/president of the council of ministers" (*minisztertanács elnöke*).

7. Prime Minister Horn also wanted to give the administrative state secretary heading the PMO the status of a minister, but the SZDSZ refused such a strengthening of prime ministerial power.

8. Council of Ministers' resolution no. 1028 of 26 February 1989 on the modification of the standing order of the Council of Ministers.

9. Interviews with officials of the Antall government, 20 June 2000 and 14 February 2001.

10. Interview with a Hungarian expert, 7 June 2000.

11. Interview with a Hungarian government official, 20 June 2000.

12. Interview with a Hungarian expert, 7 June 2000.

13. Interview with a Hungarian expert, 19 June 2000.

14. Compare with www.kancellaria.gov.hu/hivatal/feladat/main_e.html, accessed December 2001; see also the attached organigram obtainable from the chancellery's website.

15. *HVG*, 29 May 1999.

16. *HVG*, 29 May 1999.

17. *HVG*, 3 October 1998.

18. *HVG*, 29 May 1999.

19. Interview with a Hungarian expert on public administration, 7 June 2000.

20. Interviews with Hungarian experts, 19 and 20 June 2000.

21. *HVG*, 13 January 2001.

4

Poland: A Core Ascendant?

Radoslaw Zubek

This chapter analyzes the development of core executive institutions in Poland over a period of fourteen years, from 1989 to 2003. In particular, our account investigates the position of the executive in the Polish political system, its internal organization, and the linkage between political appointees and public officials. The chapter starts with a brief overview of the development of the Polish party system between 1989 and 2003 and its impact on cabinet formation. The two following sections proceed to map the development of the executive's relationship with presidency, parliament, and political parties and discuss the institutionalization of the central government administration. The main body of the chapter examines in detail the position of the Polish prime minister; the modalities of cabinet coordination and the significance of other political coordination mechanisms; the reform of the center of government; and the professionalization of the civil service.

THE POLISH PARTY SYSTEM AND CABINET FORMATION, 1989–2003

The Polish party system has moved gradually from a system dominated by a single umbrella organization (1989–1991), through a highly pluralist system (1991–1993), to a seeming consolidation on a bipolar basis (1993–2001), and a new phase of turbulence from 2001 onward (see Antoszewski 2002; Szczerbiak 1998). Until 2001, the increasing concentration of the party system led to a progressive decline in the number of parties supporting the executive, producing a relatively high incidence of two-party majority coalitions and single-party minority governments.

Between September 1989 (the collapse of communism) and December 2003 (the cutoff point for the present study), Poland had five parliamentary elections and eleven governments.[1] From 1989 to 1991, the Polish party system was dominated by the Solidarity Trade Union. By late 1988, the Polish United Workers' Party (PZPR) had recognized that the rise of Solidarity was making the country ungovernable and had tried to bring it into the system through the roundtable accords. The elections of 1989 became a political victory for Solidarity, which won all the available seats in the Sejm (the lower chamber) and all but one of the seats in the Senate, in spite of the fact that only 35 percent of the seats in the the Sejm were available for contestation, while the remaining 65 percent were preallocated to the PZPR and its two satellite parties, the United Peasants' Party (ZSL) and the Democratic Party (SD). Solidarity's unprecedented political legitimacy allowed it to dominate the first postcommunist government, where it held half of all positions, including the offices of the prime minister—Tadeusz Mazowiecki—and the finance minister. The remaining ministerial portfolios were split between the two ex-satellite parties, while the communists retained control over the ministries of home affairs, defense, transport, and foreign economic relations.

The split in Solidarity—which started in late 1990, partly along ideological lines and partly as a result of a power struggle between Mazowiecki and Solidarity's founder, Lech Walesa—marked the transition from a dominant party to an unstable party system. Defeated by Walesa in the presidential elections of December 1990, Mazowiecki resigned as prime minister and was replaced by Jan Krzysztof Bielecki, whose government relied more on presidential support than on parliamentary majority. Its ministers were recruited from five offshoots of Solidarity. The process of the fragmentation of the party system culminated in the October 1991 elections, held under an exceptionally proportional electoral system. As many as twenty-nine parties entered the parliament, with no one party commanding more than 14 percent of the seats. A highly heterogeneous lower chamber produced an unstable political environment, a situation that was exacerbated by frequent clashes between the government and President Walesa. The two successive governments formed between 1991 and 1993 were both multiparty minority cabinets and turned out to be short-lived. The Olszewski government, formed in December 1991, lasted only until June 1992 and was supported by four parties.[2] In July 1992, Hanna Suchocka of the Democratic Union (UD) was appointed prime minister and formed a new government supported by seven political parties.[3] The Suchocka government collapsed in May 1993 as a result of a vote of no-confidence called for by the Solidarity Trade Union.

The elections in September 1993, held under a revised electoral law providing for a percentage threshold, marked the onset of consolidation of the party system on a bipolar basis, until the process was partially reversed in 2001. The percentage of seats held by the largest party increased from 13.84 percent in the 1991–1993 parliament to 37.17 percent in the 1993–1997 parliament and 43.69 percent in the 1997–2001 parliament, while the number of effective parties dropped from 9.8 to 3.9 and 2.9, respectively (Antoszewski 2002, 145). The Left was the first to achieve consolidation. The Democratic Left Alliance (SLD), PZPR's successor party, won the 1993 elections, followed closely by the Polish Peasant Party (PSL), representing farmers' interests. The SLD and PSL held together almost two-thirds of all seats in the lower chamber. The next parliamentary elections, of September 1997, brought about the consolidation of the Right, as the elections were won by the Solidarity Electoral Action (AWS), a conglomerate of several right-wing parties clustered around the Solidarity Trade Union, which campaigned on a radical reform platform. The share of seats held by the two largest parties—the AWS and the SLD—increased to almost 80 percent. The parliamentary elections in September 2001 saw a partial reversal of consolidation, with the number of effective parties increasing from 2.9 in the previous parliament to 3.6. The percentage of seats held by the largest party—the SLD, 46.95 percent—reached the highest point in Poland's post-1991 parliamentary history (Antoszewski 2002, 145), but this proved only a temporary gain, as the SLD increasingly fell victim to internal conflicts. Both the AWS and the Freedom Union (UW) splintered in 2000–2001 and failed to win any seats in either of the two chambers (see Szczerbiak 2002, 2003). Their space was filled by two smaller center-right parties—the Civic Platform (PO) and the Law and Justice Party (PiS)—and two populist parties—the Self-Defense and the League of Polish Families (LPR).

The gradual consolidation of the party system up to 2001 led to a decline in the number of parties forming governing coalitions. The majority government formed by Waldemar Pawlak in October 1993 relied on the support of two parties—the SLD and the PSL. In March 1995, Pawlak was replaced by Jozef Oleksy (SLD), who in turn was forced to resign in January 1996 and was replaced by Wlodzimierz Cimoszewicz (SLD). After the September 1997 elections, the AWS formed a two-party majority government with the UW under the premiership of Jerzy Buzek. This coalition, however, collapsed in mid-2000, and Buzek carried on as a single-party minority government until the next elections, in 2001. After these elections, the SLD formed a three-party coalition government under Leszek Miller, which relied on 257 seats in the 460-member lower chamber and was supported by the SLD, the PSL, and the Labor Union (UP). The PSL was, however, ejected from the coalition in March 2003 (see table 4.1).

In sum, the growing bipolarity of the party system up to 2001 created conditions favorable to the emergence of smaller, mainly two-party governing coalitions. There were, however, factors that militated against the cohesiveness of governments. In Poland, the Left–Right divide stems from historical cleavages—ex-communist versus dissident—rather than ideological cleavages. As a result, while coalition parties in all governments since 1989 have tended to share a common lineage, they have often been deeply divided

Table 4.1. Prime Ministers, Cabinets, and their Supporting Parties, 1989–2003

Prime Minister	Months in Office	Status	Coalition Parties (no.)	Coalition Parties
Tadeusz Mazowiecki	16	Nonparty	—	—
Jan Krzysztof Bielecki	11	Presidential	5	KLD, PC, ZChN, SD, ROAD
Jan Olszewski	6	Minority	4	PC, ZChN, PL, PChD
Hanna Suchocka	10	Minority	7	UD, KLD, ZChN, PL, SLCh, PPG, PChD
Waldemar Pawlak	16	Majority	2	SLD, PSL
Jozef Oleksy	11	Majority	2	SLD, PSL
Wlodzimierz Cimoszewicz	20	Majority	2	SLD, PSL
Jerzy Buzek	31	Majority	2	AWS, UW
Jerzy Buzek	16	Minority	1	AWS
Leszek Miller	16	Majority	3	SLD, UP, PSL
Leszek Miller	10[a]	Minority	2	SLD, UP

Source: Personal compilation.
Note: AWS: Solidarity Electoral Action; KLD: Liberal Democratic Congress; PC: Center Alliance; PChD: Christian Democratcs; PL: Peasants' Alliance; PPG: Polish Economic Alliance; PSL: Polish Peasant Party; ROAD: Civic Movement Democratic Action; SD: Democratic Party; SLCh: Christian Peasants' Alliance; SLD: Democratic Left Alliance; UD: Democratic Union; UP: Labor Union; UW: Freedom Union; ZChN: National Christian Union.
[a] Until December 2003.

on economic and social policy (see Rydlewski 2000, 13–21). With reference to the ideas introduced in chapter 2, the coalition parties in the 1991–1993 and 1997–2001 parliaments can be regarded as having been unlikely to run together in the next parliamentary elections. Indeed, the splits of governing coalitions in 2000 and 2003—around the midterm of the parliament— support this argument. Moreover, the catchall nature of the AWS served to further undermine the stability of the AWS-UW coalition between 1997 and 2000. On the other hand, the parties that formed the governing coalition in the 1993–1997 parliament and in the early years of the parliament elected in 2001—the SLD and the PSL—found that they had little choice but to stay together, in spite of the PSL's misgivings. The complications of coalition governance have had a pervasive impact on the configuration of executive leadership in Poland: whereas the challenges of modernization and, more recently, Europeanization favored a centralized prime ministerial or cabinet core executive, party coalition dynamics as well as constitutional traditions have pulled toward a more ministerial executive.

THE LOCATION OF THE EXECUTIVE IN THE POLITICAL SYSTEM

Relations with the Presidency

Between 1989 and 2003, the precise balance of power between the Polish executive and the president was shaped as much by political expediency as by deliberate institution building. In 1989, the decision to have the presidency reinstated and to furnish it with extensive powers was guided primarily by the need to contain a Solidarity-led government. Whereas the opposition nominated the prime minister, the Communist Party retained close control through its president. In a similar fashion, direct popular elections for the presidential office were introduced largely to boost the presidential chances of Prime Minister Mazowiecki in 1990—to no avail, as it later turned out (see Rokita 1998, 147). The drafting of the 1992 interim constitution marked the beginning of a more deliberate process of shaping the relations between government and president, although the tumultuous experience of the first two years of Walesa's presidency loomed large in the debate (Brzezinski 1998). The new constitutional regime reduced some of the president's powers, most notably, his discretion in dissolving parliament and control over cabinet formation. At the same time, it did offer the president new levers, often more implicit than explicit, such as control over ministerial appointments for foreign affairs, defense, and home affairs. As it soon transpired, Lech Walesa was quick to maximize his new powers with regard to both the Solidarity-led government and the postcommunist government and was a master at exploiting legal loopholes (Jasiewicz 1997; Szablowski1997).

In 1997, at the time of the drafting of a new constitution, there was a growing consensus that Walesa's ambition of strong presidency had largely undermined executive leadership, and a decision was made to significantly curb the powers of the presidency. The president lost the right to be consulted on appointments for the previously "presidential" portfolios. His influence in cabinet reshuffles was curbed so that he could not reject the prime minister's candidates. Also, under the 1997 constitution, he no longer has the right to chair the cabinet. Although the president has been granted a new right to convene and chair a Cabinet Council, which comprises the prime minister and all ministers, this new body has no formal decision-making powers and so far has met only sporadically. The president has retained the veto over parliamentary legislation, but, contrary to the 1992 constitution, he may not veto the budget. At the same time, the parliamentary majority necessary for overriding the veto has dropped from two-thirds to three-fifths.

In shaping the government–president nexus, three nonconstitutional factors played an important role. First, the president's influence increased where he faced incohesive multiparty governing coalitions (Krok-Paszkowska 2001). Walesa in 1991–1993 and Kwasniewski in 1997–2001 carried more political sway than might be expected from their legal powers because they were able to exploit fractures within the coalition cabinets. Second, political affinity between the government and president clearly mattered. President Kwasniewski did not veto a single bill during a friendly SLD-PSL government between 1995 and 1997 and vetoed only one in 2001–2003 under the SLD-PSL-UP government; but he did veto 30 laws out of a total of 667 passed by parliament under the AWS-UW government between 1997 and 2001 (see www.prezydent.pl). The president's ability to wield informal influence increased with friendly governments, as was most evident with Kwasniewski's opposition to the SLD-PSL government's attempt in 2001–2002 to browbeat the central bank into lowering interest rates (Paradowska 2002). In a fashion similar to that of Vaclav Havel in the Czech Republic, Kwaúniewski also established informal communication channels, mainly through Friday dinners attended by both postcommunist and opposition leaders (interview, May 2000). Finally, personal styles mattered. Although constitutionally powerful, Wojciech Jaruzelski, communist president between 1989 and 1990, chose to use his powers only sparingly (Jasiewicz 1997, 164). That situation changed when Walesa became president in December 1990, with a clear ambition to play a more active, if not leading, role in its relationship with the government. Indeed, the Bielecki cabinet was the closest that Poland ever came to having a presidential government. Aleksander Kwasniewski, president after 1995, largely pursued an unassertive presidency, under both the more semipresidential and the 1997 constitutional framework (Jasiewicz 1997). He undertook only ten legislative initiatives in the 1993–1997 parliament, sixteen in the 1997–2001 parliament, and seven in the parliament elected in 2001 (data up to November 2003; see www.prezydent.pl).

All in all, between 1989 and 2003, the executive became more autonomous from the presidency, and, where interdependence continued to be present, the executive emerged as the dominant actor. This said, the president continued to wield formal and informal influence on the executive (see Millard 2000).

Relations with Parliament and Political Parties

Under communist rule, parliament was vested with supreme state authority, while the executive was relegated to the position of a "central administrative body." This legacy—further reinforced by a new enthusiasm for parliamentary legitimacy—gave parliament an upper hand in its relationship with the executive, in particular in the early days of transition (see Kreppel 2002; Olson and Norton 1996). However, the discrepancy between the ambition to launch difficult social and economic reforms and the volatility of parliamentary support, most evident in the 1991–1993 period, quickly led to calls for more executive autonomy (Rokita 1998). In effect, under the 1992 constitutional amendment, parliament lost the power to pass resolutions that would bind the government. In budget making, the Sejm ceased to approve a socioeconomic framework for the construction of the state budget. The interim constitution also granted the executive the right to obtain from the Sejm a mandate to issue decrees with the force of parliamentary law. This right, however, remained a dead letter and was not upheld in the 1997 constitutional arrangements. The 1997 constitution made it more difficult to dismiss cabinets by providing for a constructive veto of no-confidence as the only way to bring down a government. Perhaps the most significant change occurred in 1996–1997, when the executive won exclusive competence to determine its internal organization.

Despite moves toward increased autonomy, the executive's position in policymaking has remained heavily constrained by limited agenda control in parliament. Unlike many of its Western counterparts, the Polish executive enjoys few privileges in the legislative process (see Döring 1995). Its submissions are processed according to the same rules as private member or committee bills, though admittedly it can ask the parliament to apply a special accelerated procedure. Parliament may submit drafts in areas where a government draft already exists. Perhaps most significant, it takes only fifteen deputies to submit a draft law. In effect, the government must compete with parliamentary-initiated legislation for scarce time and resources (see table 4.2). In the Second and Third Parliaments, executive-initiated draft

Table 4.2.   Legislative Initiatives Between 1991 and 2001

Origin	Drafts Submitted No.	%	Drafts Adopted No.	%	Success Rate (%)
First Parliament, 1991–1993					
Government	91	27	47	46	52
President	10	3	4	4	40
Senate	9	3	4	4	44
Deputies	199	59	33	32	16
Committees	26	8	14	14	54
Total	335	100	102	100	30
Second Parliament, 1993–1997					
Government	346	42	308	53	89
President	30	4	16	3	53
Senate	19	2	7	1	37
Deputies	363	44	195	33	54
Committees	68	8	58	10	85
Total	826	100	584	100	71
Third Parliament, 1997–2001					
Government	553	48	456	60	82
President	16	1.5	5	0.5	31
Senate	27	2	11	1.5	41
Deputies	469	41	216	29	46
Committees	82	7	63	8	77
Citizens	5	0.5	2	0	40
Total	1,152	100	753	100	65

Source: Personal compilation.

legislation accounted only for between 42 and 48 percent of all legislative drafts submitted for adoption respectively. Although the government enjoyed a higher "success rate" of 89 and 82 percent respectively, parliament was still responsible for initiating between 45 and 40 percent of all bills that eventually became law. This said, there is evidence that this trend was beginning to be reversed toward the end of the period under investigation. In the first year of the Fourth Parliament (2001–2002), executive-initiated legislation accounted for almost 70 percent of all legislation submitted for adoption and approximately 80 percent of all drafts that became law (Lipski 2003). This was no doubt due to the increasing proportion of executive-initiated EU transposition and a more cohesive majority coalition of the SLD-UP-PSL.

Parliamentary dominance has also stemmed from weak executive control over parliamentary parties. The "partyness" of governments (see Blondel and Cotta 1996) has its roots, primarily, in relative incohesiveness of governing coalitions, as coalition parties share a common historical lineage but are often divided on policy issues. In effect, there have been many electoral incentives for coalition deputies to vote against their own government and prime ministers have often faced parliamentary revolts, most frequently under the AWS-UW government in the years 1997–2000 (see, for example, Zasuń 2000). Another factor facilitating party dominance over government has been weak party discipline. In this respect, ex-communist parties—the SLD and the PSL—enjoyed a clear advantage over newly established parties of the Right, whose internal incohesiveness militated against disciplined voting behavior.

THE OUTLINES OF THE EXECUTIVE TERRAIN

Under communism, Polish ministers and their departments were chiefly geared toward implementing policies agreed within the party apparatus rather than toward supporting policy-formulation processes (see Izdebski and Kulesza 1999). As one minister said,

> In the old system there were two administrations: one with decision-making and control powers located in the party central committee and the other with implementation powers located in the government. (interview, December 1990)

The centrally planned economy further pushed Polish ministries toward hands-on management of social and economic policies. This legacy had significant organizational implications. First, overloaded with managerial tasks, the Polish ministerial administration had been broken down into a large number of specialized sectoral ministries. Second, the coordination role of the party apparatus had created disincentives to formal or informal communications between ministries. This lack of administrative coordination had been further exacerbated by frequent interministerial conflicts over state subsidies for "their" state enterprises. Finally, ministerial officials had developed a strong penchant for micromanagement of individual enterprises but showed limited policymaking skills.

The early reformers of 1989–1990 did not attempt a major overhaul of ministerial portfolios and the ministerial administration. An early minister explained this reluctance: "Perhaps it was a mistake not to reform the central administration. But at the time the existing administration seemed sufficient for our purposes" (interview, December 1990). In effect, only quick structural adjustments were made to the administration, most of which took place between December 1989 and July 1991. In December 1989, the Ministry for Transport, Maritime, and Communications was dissolved and replaced by two new ministries: the Communications Ministry and the Transport and Maritime Economy Ministry. The forestry portfolio was transferred from agriculture to the environment ministry, which was renamed the Ministry for Environment, Natural Resources, and Forestry. In July 1990 a new Ministry of Privatization was established to oversee the privatization of state-owned enterprises. In June 1991, the Ministry of Industry (established 1987) and the Ministry of the Internal Market (established 1987) were merged into the Ministry of Trade and Industry.

The reasons for delaying central administrative reforms were numerous. For one thing, the Solidarity decision makers enjoyed enormous popular legitimacy and so had limited motivation to reinforce their positions within the administration. Also, as leaders of a mass labor movement, they shared a strong anti-statist bias and perceived the state as the problem rather than the solution. Reform urgency had also been partly removed by piecemeal administrative reforms undertaken in the mid-1980s that had involved a merging of ministries.

The first attempts to deal with this state of affairs were made by the Suchocka cabinet in 1992–1993, but they fell short of practical implementation, mainly due to a volatile parliamentary support and short-lived character of this government. It was only in 1996–1997 that, after initial unwillingness of the first SLD-PSL government to engage in reform, the second and third SLD-PSL governments under Oleksy and Cimoszewicz succeeded in launching a comprehensive reform of the "economic center of government." Two major factors facilitated the reform. First, the SLD-PSL coalition met with acute problems when implementing its "Strategy for Poland." Although it moved to circumvent ministerial administration by creating a parallel system of working groups empowered to submit proposals directly to the cabinet, this modus operandi faltered at the implementation stage, not least due to the lack of strong central coordination (see Rydlewski 2002, 87–88). A 1995 report concluded,

> The experience with the formulation and implementation of the medium-term program "The Strategy for Poland" confirms that governmental structures have major problems with the formulation of such programs and the center finds it difficult to ensure coordination of the implementation of the adopted plans. (Office of the Council of Ministers [URM] 1995, 8)

Second, since the mid-1990s a consensus started to emerge among the political elites that Poland's economic and legal adaptation to the European Community had proceeded at too leisurely a pace. Legal harmonization had covered only 5–10 percent of the European Community legislation, and it took the Polish administration more than a year to formulate and agree on a timetable for the implementation of the internal market white paper. The forthcoming onset of accession negotiations had placed a high premium on developing stronger central coordination machinery modeled on the experience of the EU member states (Zubek 2005b).

The 1996–1997 center of government reform had four objectives: reconfigure the key economic ministries; establish an EU coordination structure; strengthen the prime minister; reinforce coordination at the cabinet level; and institutionalize a professional civil service. This section discusses the first two objectives; the latter two will be dealt with in the subsequent sections.

The reconfiguration of the economic administration aimed at reorienting ministries from managing to regulating the economy. The industry-based organization of economic ministries was abandoned as a new Economics Ministry took over responsibilities from the Ministry of Industry and Trade, the Ministry for Foreign Economic Relations, and the Central Planning Office. All line ministries, including the Finance Ministry, were deprived of the state assets ownership competences, which were pooled under the roof of a newly established State Treasury. The State Treasury minister was made responsible for general state asset management, including privatization of state-owned enterprises. Supervisory functions concerning the state-owned enterprises were shifted down from ministries to *voivodship* (regional) offices. Finally, economic planning responsibilities were removed from the Central Planning Office and vested in the cabinet and line ministries. A newly established Strategic Studies Center was charged with supporting strategic planning, socioeconomic growth forecasting, and spatial development. As a result of this reorganization, the overall number of ministries fell from seventeen to fifteen, and it remained at about this number in the following years (see figure 4.1).

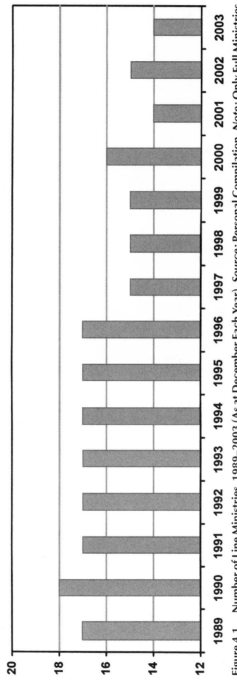

Figure 4.1. Number of Line Ministries, 1989–2003 (As at December Each Year). *Source*: Personal Compilation. *Note*: Only Full Ministries have been Counted.

Perhaps the most significant change introduced in 1996–1997 was the new, flexible system for establishing line ministries. Up to then, ministries had been established under parliamentary legislation, and changes to the ministerial administration had to be agreed by parliament. Now, the powers to establish, abolish, and reorganize ministries were transferred to the cabinet. In a bid to facilitate cross-ministerial flows of information, the reform also provided for a uniform internal structure of Polish ministries. At a political level, political *cabinets* were created in all ministries, staffed by the minister's personal advisors. Two types of junior ministers were assigned to assist the minister: state secretaries and undersecretaries. At the civil service level, ministries were divided into departments (*departamenty*), offices (*biura*), and secretariats (*sekretariaty*). While departments perform policy-related tasks, offices are chiefly responsible for supporting the work of the ministry as a whole. Both departments and offices have been further subdivided into sections (*wydziały*). Secretariats provide support to the minister, committees, councils, and task forces within the ministry. All ministries have units responsible for legal advice, contacts with media, budget and finance, staff training and development, European integration, information technology, public procurement, general administration, defense, complaints processing, and protection of classified information. Ministerial departments and offices have been subordinated to the director-general, who ensures the implementation of tasks specified by the minister, state secretaries, and undersecretaries. Figure 4.2 shows the internal structure of a Polish ministry.

The 1996–1997 reform has also provided for new institutional arrangements for the coordination of EU affairs within central government. The Office of the Cabinet Plenipotentiary for European Integration, located within the URM, was replaced by the Committee for European Integration, a collective supreme authority with competence to coordinate Polish European policy. The committee comprised eight ministers: foreign affairs, internal affairs, economy, finance, environment, labor, agriculture, and justice. It was assisted by a permanent secretariat—the Office of the Committee for European Integration. The new coordination schema was principally modeled on the French SGCI (General Secretariat of the International Committee on European Questions) but also borrowed from the Polish tradition of establishing collective ministerships, such as the Planning Commission and Committee for Scientific Research (Zubek 2005b).

The 1996–1997 reform sparked much controversy, especially with regard to the reconfiguration of the powers of the prime minister, central cabinet coordination, and civil service legislation (see the following sections). The process of reorganizing the economic ministries also became quickly politicized, as coalition parties in the cabinet vied to increase their influence or at least maintain the status quo (Warsaw University Faculty of Journalism and Political Science 1997). More significantly, neither Prime Minister Oleksy

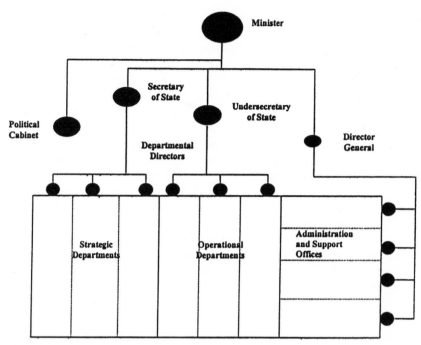

Figure 4.2.   The Internal Structure of a Polish Ministry. *Source*: Adapted from Izdebski and Kulesza (1999, 147).

nor Cimoszewicz demonstrated political determination to support a radical shake-up of the administration, instead calling for caution and minimum disruption to the work of the government (Rydlewski 2002, 86). In effect, the center of government reform stopped short of going beyond organizational changes to revise ministerial prerogatives contained in substantive laws. The communist legacy was broken only partially. As one minister said,

> The 1996–1997 reform has moved in the right direction in combating the sectoralization of the government . . . but this legacy is still there. The "conspiracy" between, for example, the directors of coal mines and departmental directors in the economics ministry is very deeply rooted. The 1996 reform has reorganized the bureaucracy, but the old linkages have reemerged. (interview, December 2000)

THE POWERS OF THE PRIME MINISTER

The fortunes of all Polish premiers since 1989 indicate that strong formal powers provide a necessary but not a sufficient condition for the prime minister to emerge as a forceful head of the government. In fact, despite an upgrading of the prime minister's legal powers, the strength of prime ministerial leadership has been chiefly determined by political and personal factors, such as party standing, the nature of parliamentary support, the presence of important leaders outside the cabinet, personal style, and the popularity of government policies. This weak institutionalization of the Polish premier's position in cabinet owes much to the coalition nature of Polish government; it is also expressed by the limited organizational resources available to the premier at the center of government.

The first Polish noncommunist premier inherited a fairly weak institutional position. Under the communist regime, the prime minister's standing depended less on constitutional powers, which were strictly limited, and more on his stature within the Communist Party (Rybicki 1985). The first postcommunist government, in 1989–1991, was able to operate as a centralized executive but on the basis of the cabinet rather than the prime minister. The fact that the government was dominated by Solidarity gave it an unusual degree of cohesion, laying the basis for a high degree of collective responsibility, but by the same token, the "team" nature of the government made it difficult for the prime minister to claim any special role. Indeed, if any one minister could be seen as taking the lead in the government, it was not Prime Minister Mazowiecki but rather the finance minister and deputy prime minister Leszek Balcerowicz. Balcerowicz entered the government with a compact team of faithful advisors, who, in cooperation with foreign experts, engineered the departure from a centrally planned economy. A close observer characterized their mode of action as follows:

> We entered the government as a group of around ten people. . . . Our work consisted of working out economic policy and seeking support for it within the government. . . . We were quicker and better organized than other parts of the government. We understood better what should be done. . . . To deal with day-to-day problems we set up a few interministerial working groups, which were chaired by our people so that we knew that their actions would be in agreement with the program. (interview, December 2000)

Having provided a strong political impulse for change and established procedural controls over the administration, the Balcerowicz team was content to work with the state structures proficient in executing policies. It was not long, however, before plans for administrative reform had started to be developed (Izdebski 1993; URM 1991, 1992, 1993). The time of "extraordinary politics" that benefited Balcerowicz had passed, and, faced with a more mundane day-to-day policy management, Polish political leaders started to call for a major reconstruction of government structures. The reforms were delayed for a number of years by the weak and unstable coalition governments. The parties participating in these governments could not have a realistic expectation of running together in the next election and therefore had little incentive to agree to the concentration of power in the hands of the prime minister. It was only in the context of the relatively stable SLD-PSL coalition in the 1993–1997 parliament that conditions became favorable for the establishment of more centralized government structures.

A series of reforms in 1996–1997 turned the prime minister into the source of the legal authority for the government, thus creating the basis for a prime ministerial government, although not without important ambiguities. The 1997 constitution provided for a "constructive" vote of confidence as the only way to dismiss the government. The constitution has also introduced a new procedure under which the prime minister can seek to bolster his or her authority by calling for a vote of confidence in the parliament. In June 2003, this procedure helped Prime Minister Miller to regain—albeit briefly—the political initiative after the successful EU referendum.

But it was the 1996–1997 center of government reform that has provided the most significant boost to the formal position of the premier. As part of a legislative package, two crucial laws were introduced: the 1996 act on the council of ministers and the 1997 law on chapters of state administration. Their combined effect has been, first and foremost, to give the prime minister the power to allocate and reshuffle portfolios among ministers by executive regulation. His discretion in this respect is now constrained only by a statutory list of thirty-two "chapters," or areas of state administration. The premier is free to use such chapters as "building blocks" in determining the area of competence of particular ministers.

This move toward a stronger role of the prime minister has not been un-contested and has occurred, at least partly, by subterfuge (Gdulewicz and Mojak 1997; Rydlewski 2002). The original government proposals in 1995–1996 did not envisage a major upgrading of the premier's prerogatives, and further prime ministerialization was opposed by strong forces, including members of the Legislative Council, which advocated collegiality as the cabinet's modus operandi (Rokita 1998, 150; Ulicka 1997). It was only later, during parliamentary committee work and mainly at the behest of the opposition deputies, that specific provisions were inserted to reinforce the position of the prime minister (Gdulewicz and Mojak 1997). Such political controversies were further fueled by the coalition ministers' reluctance to concede powers to the premier. A close observer thus summarized the mood:

> In part [the problems with the reform] had a political background. These took the form of resistance to the idea of strengthening the position of the prime minister, mainly from the PSL ministers and ministers associated with president Walesa (the so-called "presidential ministers"). (Rydlewski 2002, 89)

Disagreements over the extent of the premier's prerogatives have prevented the new 1996–1997 institutional regime from explicitly endorsing a prime ministerial government. Opposition within its own government and parliamentary ranks caused the governing coalition to delay the entry into force of the new portfolio allocation system until 1999. A good example of the inconsistencies between statutory law and the new constitution is the preservation in the constitution of a parliamentary no-confidence vote against individual ministers, even though, under the new statutory regime, they owe their jobs principally to the prime minister.

While there have been important ambiguities in the establishment of a legal basis for prime ministerial government, the emergence of a centralized prime ministerial core executive has proved even more problematic. Strengthening the tendency already evident in the interim 1992 constitution, the 1997 constitution has charged the prime minister with "commanding, coordinating, and controlling" the work of the cabinet. Furthermore, under the 1996–1997 center of government reform, the premier has gained tighter control over the work of individual ministers and the cabinet as a whole. The prime minister may chair any of the cabinet committees. He may also establish and preside over ad hoc committees or advisory councils. The prime minister can request information, documents, and periodic reports on any matter from ministers, directors of central executive agencies, or regional government representatives. He can also ask his chancellery to conduct an audit of the implementation of tasks entrusted to ministers.

Despite the upgrading of the premier's powers, however, the prime ministerialization of the Polish core executive has been less pronounced in practice. Besides limitations resulting from the residual powers of the president and the strength of the legislature, prime ministers have been heavily constrained by political and personal factors. The contrast between Buzek and Miller provides a good illustration. Buzek was generally considered to be a weak prime minister (Hall 1999; Rzeczpospolita 1999; Waszkielewicz 1999). In many instances, he refrained from exercising his formal powers under pressure from coalition party leaders. This was, for example, the case when Buzek tried and failed to use his new appointment powers in a cabinet reshuffle in early 1999 (Subotić 1999). His leadership was undermined, first and foremost, by the incohesiveness of the AWS. Marked programmatic differences and ongoing internal disputes within the AWS pushed Buzek into a constant balancing act between different factions of his own party. His role as prime minister was further weakened by the presence of the AWS leader, Marian Krzaklewski, outside the government. Buzek's authority in cabinet was often challenged by Balcerowicz, deputy prime minister, finance minister, and leader of the AWS's coalition partner, the UW. It is also important to note Buzek's relative parliamentary and political inexperience. An AWS minister said,

The consolidation of the right outside the parliament between 1993–1997 meant that the AWS leaders—Buzek, Krzaklewski, and Plazynski—had not been members of parliament and neither had they served in government. They did not have firsthand experience of parliamentary politics and did not know what made the executive or parliament work. (interview, December 2000)

Personal styles have also mattered. Prime Minister Buzek was said to have been hampered by his excessively conciliatory style. An AWS minister said,

> The position of Jerzy Buzek has been weakened by his conciliatory tactics, which manifested itself in long cabinet meetings, his persuasive attitude toward ministers, a multitude of informal meetings and negotiations. This was in large part a product of his trade unionist mentality and a related inclination for governing by negotiation. (interview, November 2000)

The contrast with Prime Minister Miller could not have been more striking. Leszek Miller was the first prime minister since 1989 to combine his post with leadership of the largest parliamentary party. He was a seasoned political actor with extensive parliamentary and government experience going back to communist times. He had served as labor minister and the minister head of the URM under the 1993–1997 SLD-PSL government. His style in cabinet stood in stark contrast to Buzek's. Drawing on his party and government authority, he was able to enforce effectively cabinet internal rules. For example, if a compromise was agreed in cabinet committees, Miller would not allow ministers to reopen issues in cabinet unless there was an overriding reason for doing so (interview, July 2003). But even Miller was not immune from some loss of authority. As his government became more and more unpopular, Miller's hold on his party and cabinet lessened significantly. This has led one observer to make the following comment:

> When you compare Buzek's and Miller's terms, you have a weak Buzek at the start of his term, but, with time, he was becoming stronger and stronger; Miller was very strong at the beginning of his, but, as time went by, his position has weakened. (interview, July 2003)

PATTERNS OF CABINET DECISION MAKING

Under communism, the cabinet was an unwieldy affair. It consisted of a large number of ministers of varying rank and functioned as a monthly debriefing of ministers, regional governors, and agency chief executives (see, e.g., Stembrowicz 1985). One of the principal challenges of postcommunist government reform has thus been to transform the cabinet into a real center of political decision making. Besides the prime minister's newly won control over the cabinet agenda (see earlier section), the "politicization" of the Polish cabinet has been facilitated by a progressive decline in the number of cabinet-level ministers. The size of the cabinet fell from a maximum of twenty-five under the Suchocka government to a minimum of fourteen under the first Miller government (see figure 4.3). The increasing cohesiveness of coalition parties contributed to this trend, as fewer party factions had to be bought off with cabinet seats. The contrast between the AWS-UW and the SLD-PSL-UP cabinets is a case in point. Another contributing factor has been the flexible portfolio allocation system, which has granted the prime minister extensive powers over cabinet appointments. The cabinet has also shed all its nonessential participants, such as regional government representatives and agency executives. In 2001, the Miller government excluded the central bank governor and the audit office executive from cabinet meetings (Pilczynski 2001). Cabinet sessions have also tended to become shorter with time. The longest sessions were held under Mazowiecki, whose cabinet met at 3:00 pm and lasted until the small hours. The shortest were cabinets under Oleksy, starting at 9:00 am and lasting two to three hours (Subotić 1997).

Smaller size and shorter sessions have undoubtedly made cabinet sessions more focused, but they have been insufficient to deal with the most serious threat to the political nature of cabinet decision making: agenda overload. A high-level official at the Mazowiecki government recollected, "I was surprised to find how detailed cabinet deliberations were; one would think that many of these issues could be dealt with at director level" (interview, December 2000). Dossiers received by ministers before cabinet ran into thousands of pages, and they could hardly be expected to read it all (Subotić 1997).

The pressures of modernization and, later, EU-related policy reforms pushed the number of legislative drafts submitted to cabinet for adoption from three hundred in 1993 to almost six hundred in 2002 (see figure 4.4). As a result, the cabinet had to increasingly rely on precabinet coordination machinery if it was to retain its political-strategic focus.

The first substantial attempts to shift some of the cabinet workload to "precabinet" meetings were made under the Suchocka government. In 1992, the two cabinet committees for economic and social affairs, which dated back to the pre-1989 period, were formalized, and it was decided that all cabinet submissions would first be routed through these committees. The importance of these committees, in particular the Cabinet Economic Committee (KERM), gradually increased over the last decade (see figure 4.5). Under the Buzek government, there were four such standing cabinet committees (economic affairs, social affairs, defense, and regional policy). The members of these committees were appointed from among cabinet ministers by the prime minister. Their membership normally stood at fifteen to sixteen ministers. They were chaired by deputy prime ministers and, after 1997, could also be chaired by the prime minister himself.

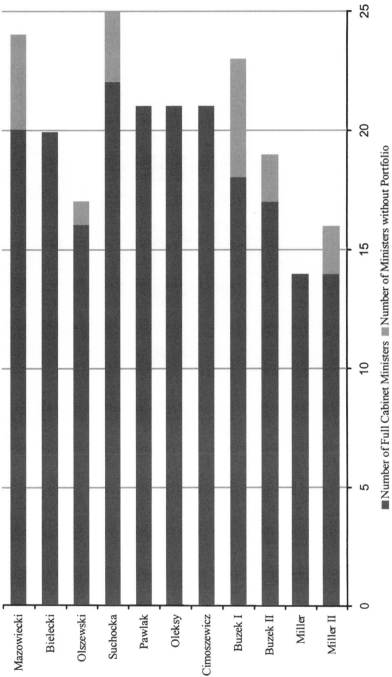

■ Number of Full Cabinet Ministers ■ Number of Ministers without Portfolio

Figure 4.3. The Number of Cabinet-Level Ministers, 1989–2003 (At the Start of Term).

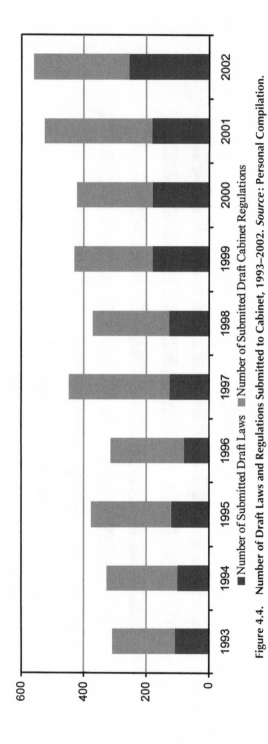

Figure 4.4. Number of Draft Laws and Regulations Submitted to Cabinet, 1993–2002. *Source*: Personal Compilation.

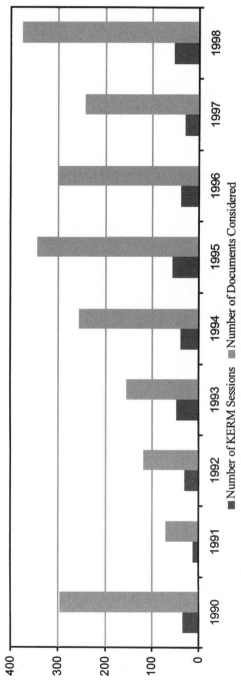

Figure 4.5. Number of Sessions and Agenda Points, Cabinet Economic Committee, 1990–1998.

Legend: ■ Number of KERM Sessions ■ Number of Documents Considered ■ Number of Agenda Points

While the cabinet committees provided an efficient mechanism for administrative coordination, they were less successful in enhancing political coordination. A close observer said,

> Cabinet committees are perceived as a good procedure for administrative coordination; this is not political coordination; although ministers and deputy ministers participate, there is no room for political discussions in these committees. (interview, May 2000)

The sectoral concerns of each of the four cabinet committees under Buzek prevented them from taking an overall government view. As a result, drafts routed through the economic committee often met with opposition in cabinet from social ministers (and vice versa), and political coordination had to be achieved at cabinet level (Rydlewski 2002, 189). The problem of insufficient political coordination below cabinet has been summarized by one official,

> [The existing mechanisms] are dominated by sectoral mentality of bureaucrats who represent narrow sectoral interests of their constituents rather than the overall government policy. Politicians should be involved in the coordination mechanisms much earlier and thus enhance political mediation. (interview May 2000)

Two institutional options for political coordination have been tried in the Polish core executive. As part of the 1996–1997 center of government reform, much hope was placed in ministers' political *cabinets* (see, e.g., Kulesza and Barbasiewicz 1999, 2000). Established by statutory legislation as a permanent element of each ministry's landscape, French-style *cabinets ministeriel* failed, however, to emerge as an important forum for political coordination. Lacking legitimacy, they had to compete for the minister's ear with junior ministers and high-ranking civil servants (interview, December 2000). Their authority was also partly undermined by the fact that they mainly comprised the minister's political and personal friends. A more successful option was that of establishing horizontal coordination at the level of junior ministers (state secretaries or undersecretaries). Indeed, operating at the interface of politics and technical expertise, junior ministers developed, with time, to provide the backbone of political coordination within the executive. The sheer bulk of legislative work, especially in the area of EU transposition, empowered junior ministers, in particular those at the undersecretary level (Zubek 2005a). Indeed, in 2001 the Miller government replaced the four cabinet committees at minister level with a single Cabinet Committee (KRM) at junior minister level. Chaired by the deputy prime minister for finance (and later for economics), it helped to institutionalize the coordination role of junior ministers in their own ministries. In EU affairs, the KRM was mirrored by a junior minister-level preparatory meeting of the Committee for European Integration (Zubek 2005a).

Besides the cabinet committees, other precabinet fora for coordination emerged. At a formal level, all legislative drafts had to be submitted to written interministerial consultations, and, where multiple comments were voiced, conciliation conferences had to be organized. The center of government was also populated with standing or ad hoc task forces, working groups, councils, and committees. A special category of informal coordination were "precooking" meetings of the prime minister with deputy prime ministers, the head of the chancellery, and the cabinet secretary. Such meetings were held under the Oleksy and Cimoszewicz governments on Monday mornings to discuss and prepare the agenda for the Tuesday cabinet meeting (Subotić 1996). In a similar fashion, Prime Minister Miller held regular morning meetings with his closest associates, including the head of the advisors' team, *chef de cabinet*, the head of the chancellery, and the government spokesman (Olczyk and Subotić 2002).

PARTY-BASED POLITICAL COORDINATION DEVICES

In general, coalition governments encourage the downgrading of cabinet-based coordination, as politically salient decisions are decided in extraexecutive coordination mechanisms, linking the government to political parties (see Blondel and Cotta 1996, 2000). In Poland, the development pattern and effectiveness of the party–government linkages has been highly dependent on the cohesiveness of coalition parties (Zubek 2001). Cohesive coalition partners have been more likely to develop centralized institutions for managing intracoalition affairs, which have reinforced party control of the government but have also strengthened the discipline of coalition parties in parliament. The first such meetings were held already by the Mazowiecki government within the so-called Caucus of the Civic Parliamentary Group, the meetings of which were attended by the prime minister. They took a slightly more defined shape under the Suchocka government, when irregular monthly meetings of coalition leaders were devoted to discussing the most controversial issues. The incohesiveness of the parties, however, militated against the establishment of regular centralized mechanisms. A minister in the Suchocka government said, "The meetings were held once a month and dealt mainly with emergency situations. They had no significance for day-to-day political management of the government's work" (interview, May 2000).

It was under the SLD-PSL that a high degree of internal cohesion of the two parties facilitated the development of centralized institutions for managing the party–government nexus. The coalition leaders met on Wednesdays, but the prime minister and deputy prime ministers attended only when important issues were discussed (Subotić 1996). During important parliamentary debates, such as the passage of the budget, coalition meetings were held more often. The AWS-UW coalition found it more difficult to develop a similar extraexecutive system for political management due to the internal incoherence of the AWS. No regular summits of coalition leaders were held, and the onus of political coordination shifted to parliament. The presidiums of the coalition parties' parliamentary clubs met on Monday mornings. This mechanism was, however, largely ineffective. A high-ranking AWS politician said,

> The coalition meets on Mondays at 8:30 before the Tuesday session of the Sejm. These meetings are mostly devoted to the review of upcoming votes in parliament and thus fulfill a reactive, firefighting role. Political decisions are made outside this setting within an informal network of advisors to AWS leader Krzaklewski. (interview, May 2000)

The party leaders met only when a fully blown coalition crisis flared up. However, these ad hoc noninstitutionalized meetings often ended in an impasse (Zubek 2001, 925–28). In contrast, the cohesiveness of the SLD, the UP, and the PSL again facilitated the development of more centralized coordination mechanisms under the Miller government.

THE POWERS AND ORGANIZATION OF THE CENTER OF GOVERNMENT

In designing any center of government, one must confront such issues as who it should support—the cabinet or the prime minister; who should provide support—political advisors or the civil service; and what the nature of that support should be—strategic or administrative (Weller 1991). Institutional choices along these three dimensions are shaped by specific national traditions as well as opportunity structures within which key executive actors—individual and collective—operate. If analyzed in these terms, the Polish center of government has moved—although not in a linear fashion— toward a largely administrative secretariat populated by professional officials and principally geared to support the cabinet process; the part of the center supporting the prime minister has remained rather rudimentary. The key factors that have shaped this development pattern have been the nature of coalition governments and the internal organization of political parties.

The first postcommunist government of Tadeusz Mazowiecki did not opt for a radical shake-up in the organization of the URM, a central institution inherited from the previous regime. The procedural continuity was accentuated by one Solidarity official, who said,

> We had been invited to attend sessions of the communist cabinet chaired by deputy prime minister Ireneusz Sekula even before we formally took power. If the cabinet were about to make a decision that we disagreed with, we could inform the new prime minister–designate who could stop it. This early spell at the URM taught me how the office worked. (interview, December 2000)

This conservative approach petrified the old URM structures in the first few years of transition. Headed by a full cabinet minister, it was nominally responsible for monitoring policy implementation, but its activities were in fact dominated by more mundane tasks, such as the provision of state-subsidized housing, cars, holidays, and other benefits to high-level state officials. Admittedly, some change occurred at staff level. Ten to fifteen percent of over six hundred employees lost their jobs in 1990, but most adapted quickly to the new conditions (interview, December 2000).

By 1992–1993, however, there was already a growing appreciation that the center of government should be substantially reconfigured (see, e.g., Izdebski 1994; Pelczynski 1993; URM 1992, 1993). The need for centralization stemmed from a widespread realization that, for government policies to be more cohesive and responsive, coordination and control capacities should be developed at the center to fill the void after the disappearance of the Communist Party and to counteract operational autonomy of the line ministries. This mood was captured by one of the experts:

> After the party-led power structures were broken in 1989, Poland has lacked a central institution which would shape general government policy and coordinate the actions of line ministries. In other words, the system lacked a stable axis around which line ministries, with their restricted worldviews and particularistic interests, could be mobilized. (Pelczynski 1993)

But while the rationale for change was widely accepted, contending views emerged as to the precise configuration of the reinforced center. The early proposals developed under the Suchocka government envisaged the prime minister as the dominant actor at the center of government and aimed to place most resources in his service. The plans featured a Secretariat of the Government, closely steered by the prime minister's *cabinet* staffed by political advisors. The secretariat was to be subdivided into the prime minister's pillar with policy-development departments and the cabinet's pillar focusing on legal review and secretarial support to cabinet (Izdebski 1993, 28–32).

These early blueprints were never put to a political feasibility test, as the Suchocka cabinet collapsed in 1993 and its successor shelved the reform.

It was only in the context of the 1996–1997 center of government reform that the issue surfaced again. This time a different route was followed, not least because the coalition nature of the SLD-PSL government, as well as the controversies over the extent of prime ministerialization, militated against a radical power shift toward the center (Rydlewski 2000, 2002). Many of the recommendations for a stronger center that were developed in 1992–1993 or within the 1995–1997 OMEGA project failed to find support in government or parliament (The Final Report 1997, 26–29). In effect, the reform focused more on streamlining the cabinet machinery rather than on providing institutional backup to the prime minister.

The new chancellery shed many of the old URM functions, inter alia, supervision of public administration, relations with churches, European integration, cross-border migration. A nonministerial official was put at its helm, and professional and administrative support was provided by civil servants, who were organized into twelve departments. The chancellery started with 486 full-time positions (out of around 750 in the URM); the number of political positions was halved from twenty-eight to fourteen. The premier was supported by a small political *cabinet* attached to his private secretariat. The major departure from the 1992–1993 concepts led one of the ministers involved in the early conceptual work to argue that

> when after three years [since 1993] a law was adopted to establish the [prime minister's] chancellery, it dealt only with the support function for the cabinet as a whole. . . . Besides the misleading name nothing had been incorporated from the old concept of the chancellery. . . . It houses no units developing government strategies, nor professional offices capable of developing programs, the prime minister has no access to timely policy analysis, there are no mechanisms for controlling and enforcing tasks assigned to ministers. (Rokita 1998, 153)

Under the chancellery's first head in the AWS-UW government, Wieslaw Walendziak, important—albeit largely unsuccessful—attempts were made to reconfigure the role of the prime minister's chancellery and of the premier's political *cabinet*. Three factors seem to have brought about these initiatives. First, the Buzek government launched several radical social and economic reforms, and there was a natural expectation that reinforced central coordination would ensure more effective implementation. Second, the AWS and the UW leaders felt a certain kinship with reform blueprints developed in 1992–1993, many of which had been shelved or implemented partially by the SLD-PSL government. They revived some of those early ideas, including that of a stronger prime minister's office. Third, personal political ambitions mattered. Walendziak made no secret of his political ambitions, having been publicly considered as a possible prime ministerial candidate after the 1997 elections. Indeed, his appointment policies led to a widespread belief that he was building a power base within the chancellery, independent of the prime minister (Janicki and Pytlakowski 1998; Subotić 1998).

As the head of the chancellery, Walendziak acted on the premise that the center should be populated by staff who were politically close to the prime minister and were capable of hierarchical coordination vis-à-vis the ministerial bureaucracy (interview, May 2000). When he took office in 1997, he dismissed all high-ranking officials without tenure and moved those with tenure to less-prominent posts. Their places were taken by fourteen new political appointees, including four ministers without portfolio (including Walendziak) and ten secretaries of state and undersecretaries of state (see figure 4.6). Walendziak's associates prepared further plans according to which the chancellery was to be divided into three parts: the prime minister's branch, consisting of the prime minister's political *cabinet*, his secretariat, and all policy departments; the cabinet's branch, consisting of cabinet support departments; and the deputy prime ministers' branch, comprising their secretariats. At the same time, the prime minister's *chef de cabinet*, Wojciech Arkuszewski, moved to strengthen policy support for the premier. He established close linkages with the Coordination and Audit Department and charged it with the monitoring of line ministries. A high-ranking civil servant observed,

> Arkuszewski . . . stressed that the prime minister should actively monitor the work of individual ministers and should not limit himself to being briefed by ministers. This task was to be carried out by the Coordination and Audit Department. . . . The first such task was the monitoring of the implementation of the coalition agreement. The department has broken down the coalition agreement into around three hundred concrete targets and identified ministers responsible for each task. (interview, December 2000)

Arkuszewski also advocated that a small budget office be established within the chancellery to provide the prime minister with budgetary expertise alternative to that of the finance minister (interview, December 2000).

The idea that the prime minister's chancellery should, on the one hand, have a strong political figure as its head and, on the other hand, house the prime minister's *cabinet* providing advice alternative to that of line ministries proved, however, to be unsustainable in political terms. For one thing, Walendziak's attempts at central coordination ran into fierce opposition from line ministers. The contrast between the prime minister, whose position was subject to significant political constraints, and an activist head of the chancellery also gave rise to speculations as to the real locus of power.

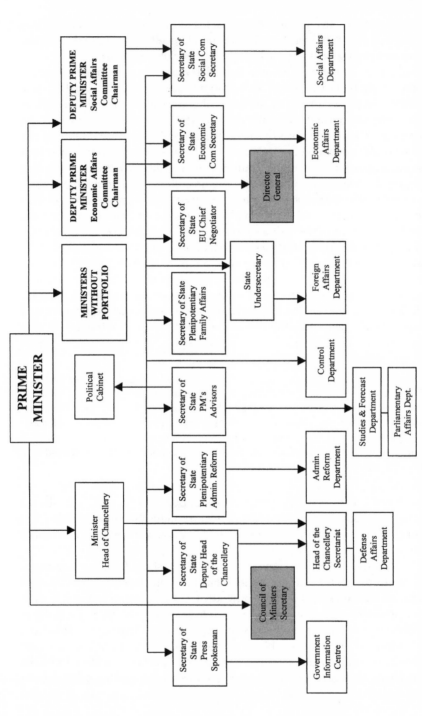

Figure 4.6. Internal Structure of the Prime Minister's Chancellery, February 1998 (Simplified). *Source:* Subotić (1998). *Note:* PM: Prime Minister.

The presence of numerous political appointees within the chancellery was widely criticized as excessive politicization (Kublik and Wielowieyska 1997). Given a weak political position of the prime minister and the coalition nature of the government, the activist center was easily neutralized by ministers, and Walendziak was dismissed in 1999.

Arkuszewski found himself in a similar predicament. He soon realized that detailed information on ministerial actions that his staff collected was not put into effective use given Buzek's weak political position (interview, July 2003). The idea of creating a budgetary desk ran into opposition from the finance minister. As a high-ranking official noted,

> The idea never reached implementation stage. At the time when Balcerowicz was finance minister, this would lead to a fervent power struggle within the government. So, as a start, . . . one or two people were employed to perform this function within the Coordination and Audit Department. No further action was taken, because [it] would lead to conflicts with Balcerowicz. (interview, December 2000)

As the concept of a strong political chancellery as a whole proved unfeasible, Arkuszewski's successor at the helm of the political *cabinet*, Kazimierz Marcinkiewicz, moved to fill the political vacuum. Marcinkiewicz reorganized the *cabinet* by dividing all advisors into chief advisors, advisors, and nonremunerative advisors. Regular meetings of all chief advisors started to be held to discuss policy issues and implementation records. A permanent secretariat of the *cabinet* was established, which in December 2000 consisted of twenty-seven people and continued to acquire new tasks, mainly with regard to foreign affairs, speech writing, and the prime minister's diary (interview, December 2000). This strengthened the organizational capacity of the prime minister's *cabinet*, which in 1998 still relied on a permanent staff of only two secretaries (interview, July 2003).

Marcinkiewicz's attempts at interministerial coordination were, however, less successful. Borrowing from the French government's practices, he started to hold meetings of the heads of ministerial political *cabinets*, but this proved unworkable in practice. A close observer said,

> Marcinkiewicz attempted to organize briefings of heads of political *cabinets* from line ministries under his chairmanship but with little success. The main reason for failure was that heads of *cabinets* did not attend in person and delegated their deputies, advisors, and spokespersons. And so the meetings lost sense. (interview, November 2000)

In mid-2000, after the collapse of the AWS-UW coalition and the formation of the AWS minority government, the prime minister's political *cabinet*, under its new *chef*, Teresa Kaminska, moved more actively to establish close working relations with some of the professional departments within the chancellery. Linkages were intensified with a new department, the Policy Analysis Department, which was established following a merger of the Policy Department, the Reform Monitoring Department, and the Analysis and Forecast Department. The Policy Analysis Department, which employed sixteen people, worked predominantly for the prime minister's political *cabinet*, developing new policy initiatives as well as assessing and reporting on implementation of government policy (interview, December 2000). The prime minister's *cabinet* started requesting reports and assessments from the Economic Department, which until then had worked solely for the deputy prime minister chairing the Cabinet Economic Committee (interview, November 2000). A high-ranking official thus described the *cabinet*'s mode of operation:

> Chief advisors communicate with line departments through the *cabinet*'s secretariat. But Mrs. Kaminska, head of the *cabinet*, may approach line departments directly without our intermediation. In fact, she rarely uses the secretariat in this regard. (interview, November 2000)

The *cabinet* under Kaminska expanded its other responsibilities. It comprised six chief advisors (economic affairs, social affairs, foreign affairs, media relations, European integration, press spokesman). There were also twenty nonremunerated advisors. Three of the prime minister's chief advisors regularly attended cabinet sessions, where they actively participated in discussions. The cabinet also functioned as an important institutional link between the prime minister and both the parliament and other parts of the executive (interview, December 2000).

The emergence of a more forceful political *cabinet* pushed the head of the prime minister's chancellery to concentrate on more administrative tasks. This, in turn, pitted the latter against the director-general, with whom he had to share administrative responsibilities. This is perhaps the reason why the office of the director-general was not formally filled in the last two years of the Buzek government. A high-ranking official summarized this situation:

> The director-general is crowded out from the leadership of the chancellery, especially when the head of the chancellery performs a more administrative role that overlaps with that of director-general. This is at least partly because of incompatibility between the law on civil service, which provides for the office of director-general in all ministries, and the law on the prime minister's chancellery. (interview, December 2000)

Under the SLD-PSL-UP government, which came to power in 2001, the prime minister's chancellery as a whole retained its administrative profile, while the position of the prime minister's political *cabinet* within the chancellery declined. The Policy Analysis Department was closed down, and collaboration with line departments went into abeyance. The Social and Economic Affairs Department again refocused to support only the KRM (interviews, July 2003). In contrast to Buzek's government, the prime minister's *cabinet* was divided into two independent teams (Olczyk and Subotić 2002). Grzegorz Rydlewski, Miller's old-time collaborator and former cabinet secretary, headed a team of six advisors, who met a few times a week. Their role was to "produce ideas and warnings and identify weak chains in the government system." Lech Nikolski, Miller's first *chef de cabinet*, had a staff of five and was responsible for maintaining the premier's diary and contacts with coalition parliamentary caucuses and the SLD regional party administration. Nikolski's successor, Aleksandra Jakubowska, operated a more energetic *cabinet* and expanded its staff to nine full-time advisors, a dynamic that pushed her into rivalry with Rydlewski's group (Rybak 2003). Miller's departure from Buzek's concept of a strong political *cabinet* may—in large part—be explained with the former's close control of his party and a natural reliance on party coordination mechanisms for reining in his ministers. In contract to Buzek's minority cabinet status, the coalition nature of the Miller cabinet provided a further disincentive to building strong intraexecutive coordination capacities under the premier.

Both under Buzek and Miller, the chancellery continued to hone its capacities for administrative support to the cabinet as a whole. In 1998–1999, the Parliamentary Affairs Department's capacity to track draft laws in parliament was substantially reinforced as personnel resources were increased from ten to eighteen. A computerized system was developed for tracking the status of drafts submitted to the parliament, with a relevant report prepared for each cabinet session. In managing the linkage between core executive and parliament, the department started to acquire more sophisticated tasks, such as coordinating the formulation of the government's position on draft laws that originated outside the executive; ensuring appropriate government representation in parliamentary committees and plenaries; and providing voting instructions to coalition ministers and parliamentary leaders (interview, December 2000). The chancellery's involvement in legal management was reinforced by the creation, in 2000, of a Government Legislative Center, which became responsible for ensuring good drafting of bills prepared by ministries. In doing so, the center participated in interministerial consultations to monitor quality at all levels (Proksa 2002). Finally, the Cabinet Agenda Department, which in December 2000 employed twenty-seven people, assisted the cabinet secretary in managing document flows before and after each cabinet session. It was charged with coordinating the programming of annual and semiannual cabinet legislative plans. The department collated requests from ministries and then submitted them for consultation to the prime minister's political *cabinet* (interview, December 2000).

THE POLITICS–ADMINISTRATION NEXUS

The postcommunist Polish governments have found it difficult to establish an effective twin-track system for the civil service, distinguishing clearly between low- and middle-level personnel, where the key imperative is professionalization and depoliticization, and top-level administrative positions, where a limited degree of regulated politicization could prove useful. In formal terms, the extent of discretion enjoyed by parties in government over personnel appointments shrunk considerably between 1989 and the early twenty-first century. This change was driven by domestic calls for professionalization of the civil service and supported by external encouragement provided by the Organization for Economic Co-operation and Development and the European Union. This said, two powerful forces complicated the practical implementation of civil service legislation. For one thing, from 1991 to 1992, successive governments resorted to staff politicization in a search for enhanced steering capacity (see, e.g., Staniszkis 1995, 2000). But paradoxically, frequent staff replacements engendered far-reaching unresponsiveness among Polish civil servants, who preferred to obstruct new programs lest the next government punish them for collaboration with predecessors (Pedersen and Zubek 2004). This, in turn, created stronger incentives for more politicization. Second, the nature of Polish coalition cabinets added a further motivation for supporting parties to politicize the administration.

In 1989–1990, the Mazowiecki government predominantly worked with old communist civil servants, except in areas such as privatization, where new ministries were established. The existing ministerial staff shared much of the government's reform enthusiasm and had a good understanding of the communist system, which proved useful in dismantling the old regime. One minister noted, "Most of [the existing] employees were quick to adapt to . . . changes. They found the new system easier to operate in, as there were fewer conflicting signals" (interview, November 2000). The status of the public officials was regulated by the law on state officials of September 1982. Although the law granted tenure to selected public employees, civil servants could be easily hired and fired. In 1991, the Bielecki government attempted to introduce nonpolitical staffing procedures, but it was defeated in parliament. The opportunity to make large-scale staff replacements on political grounds was first resorted to after the parliamentary elections in autumn 1991. The incoming Olszewski government broke away with the initial politico-administrative consensus around the Balcerowicz reforms and used personnel policy to steer the administration in a new direction. The multiparty conflictual nature of the Olszewski government provided a further incentive for staff politicization. Against this backdrop, a new reform proposal was elaborated under the Suchocka government (Hesse and Goetz 1993a). A draft civil service law, adopted by the cabinet in May 1993, envisaged that all state administration employees, including those with tenure, would become contractual employees (URM 1993, 138–42). A special civil service committee would then grant tenure to selected employees on the basis of a professional examination. The draft law, however, foundered on the collapse of the Suchocka government. The new Pawlak government withdrew the draft from parliament and, despite some half-hearted attempts (see, e.g., Subotić 1994), civil service reform stalled. In effect, the "system limbo" of the early transition persisted for the next few years (Nunberg 1999, 43).

A law on civil service was finally adopted within the framework of the 1996–1997 center of government reform under the Oleksy and Cimoszewicz governments (for detailed discussion, see Torres-Bartyzel and Kacprowicz 1999). It opted for a gradual—over a decade—phasing out of the provisions of the 1982 law on state employees. It divided all existing employees of state administration into two groups: employees engaged under the 1982 law and civil servants granted tenure under the new law. The appointment of the latter was managed by a special recruitment committee, whose members were nominated by the prime minister. In addition, the law distinguished between political and permanent positions within the governmental administration by introducing a principle that state secretaries, undersecretaries, and regional governors submit their resignations together with the cabinet. But, when adopting the civil service law, the SLD-PSL government found it very difficult to make a credible commitment to depoliticized recruitment. As a result of protracted political bargaining in parliament, the law gave the prime minister extensive competencies over the civil service, including the appointment of a selection committee (Nunberg 1999). The law also did not allow people with less than seven years experience in government to run for senior-level appointments. The first decisions made by the selection committee vindicated the critics of the 1996 law. Briefly before the parliamentary elections, and with full knowledge that the government was heading for an electoral defeat, the SLD-PSL selection committee granted tenure to 116 civil servants in a process riddled with controversial decisions (Paradowska 1998).

The new AWS-UW government under Buzek suspended the implementation of the 1996 law and passed a new civil service law in December 1998 (it came into force in mid-1999). The new law formally curbed political discretion in three important respects. First, it extended civil service status to all existing state employees working in ministries, central agencies, and *voivodship* offices. Members of the civil service were divided into two categories: public employees engaged under a contract of employment governed by the general labor law and civil servants awarded tenure under a special appointment procedure provided in the civil service law. Second, under the new law, tenure was granted based on the results of a formal written examination administered by the newly created Office of the Civil Service. Finally, the new regulations provided for competitions to be organized when recruiting for senior civil service posts—that is, secretary of the council of ministers, directors-general, department directors, and section directors. Such competitions were open only to civil servants under tenure, but the law provided for a transitional period until mid-2004, during which civil servants without tenure could also run for these offices.

The partyness of the AWS-UW government militated against the effective implementation of these rules. In a bid to insert party-loyal activists into the administration, ministers resorted to circumventing the regulations they had previously endorsed. Perhaps a most blatant example was provided by the practice of making "temporary" appointments to senior director positions (*pełnienie obowiązków*). As the practice showed, such provisional placements turned out to be surprisingly permanent, with staff frequently staying in office for the entire government term (Paradowska 2001). In December 2001, the SLD-PSL-UP government under Miller moved to legalize this practice through the amendment of the civil service legislation. A new article 144a made it possible for ministries to recruit from outside the civil service for provisional appointments to senior positions. This article was, however, struck down by the constitutional court in December 2002. The Miller government further tried to remove certain governmental agencies from being subject to civil service legislation (Urząd Służby Cywilnej 2002, 9).

As a result, despite a stringent regulatory regime, the Polish civil service continued to be subject to a far-reaching politicization, mainly at senior and middle levels. The process of granting tenure to civil servants proceeded very slowly. Between 1997 and 2002, tenure was awarded to 1,148 of a total of 118,000 public employees, accounting for less than 1 percent of the total government workforce. This slow pace was mainly due to a small number of applications from within the service. Perhaps more important, it was the widespread tampering with the regulatory framework that enabled political parties to insert political appointees to senior civil service posts (see table 4.3).

In January 2003, the number of senior positions occupied by officials tenured under the 1996 or 1998 law accounted for only 4.5 percent of all senior positions in line ministries. In contrast, the proportion of officials engaged under general labor contracts and tenured under the 1982 law

Table 4.3. Senior Civil Service Posts in Line Ministries

	All	Labor Law Contract	Tenure: 1982 Law[a]	Tenure: 1996/1998 Laws	Other	Vacant[b]
July 2000	810	306	252	37	55	160 (n/a)
July 2001	781	239	212	45	42	243 (n/a)
July 2002	715	124	164	32	40	355 (323)
January 2003	769	112	164	36	44	413 (379)

Source: Urząd Służby Cywilnej (1999, 2000, 2001, 2002).
[a]These tenures will be automatically transformed into labor law contracts from 2004, but proposals are pending to extend them further.
[b]The number of position filled with temporary placements.

stood at 14.5 percent and 21 percent respectively. The largest proportion—54 percent—was held by people recruited outside the legally required competition through the infamous provisional arrangement (*pełnienie obowiązków*). The number of formal vacancies in senior positions increased from 160 to 413 between 2000 and 2003, with the largest jump after the 2001 parliamentary elections. All in all, these figures demonstrate that civil service reform in Poland has had only a hesitant start.

CONCLUSION

The evolution of the type of government, core executive, and center of government in Poland since the start of transition to democracy exhibits not only a number of reinforcing linkages but also a wide range of incongruities (see table 4.4).

Starting from a relatively weak point in 1989, the executive has been able to strengthen its position with respect to the presidency and parliament. But

Table 4.4. Types of Government, Core Executives, and Centers of Government in Poland, 1989–2003

Type of Government	Type of Core Executive	Type of Center of Government
1989–1997: Cabinet	1989–1991: Centralized cabinet	1989–1997: Government registrar
1997–2003: Prime ministerial	1991–2001: Decentralized ministerial	1997–2001: Prime minister's vanguard—government registrar
	2001–2003: Centralized prime ministerial	2001–2003: Government registrar

while the executive's relationship with the president has been defined in a relative stable form by the 1997 constitution, the executive's relationship with parliament continues to evolve in both its formal and its party-political dimension. While there is some early evidence that parliamentary activism is on the wane, the government's ability to control parliamentary parties has varied widely from cabinet to cabinet. The evolution of the executive's internal organization offers a similarly complex picture. While there has been some progress in reducing the number of line ministries and in establishing common horizontal structures of ministerial administration, recent reforms aimed at reducing the number of central agencies indicate contestation with regard to vertical structures. In examining the evolution of the executive's coordinating capacity, there is clear evidence of a dramatic institutional shift in 1996–1997. The cabinet type of government, inherited from the communist era, was transformed into a prime ministerial government by the 1997 constitution and the 1996–1997 acts on the council of ministers and on chapters of state administration. The prime minister became the source of formal-legal authority for the government, with the power not only to appoint and dismiss ministers at his discretion but also to determine their areas of competence. The prime minister's formal-legal authority has not always been translated, however, into effective centralizing institutions within the core executive, leading to a possible disjuncture between the type of government and the type of core executive. Prime minister Buzek, played the role of a "conciliator" with respect to the line ministers (largely due to his weak position within the governing coalition), through a multitude of informal meetings and negotiations. By contrast, Prime Minister Miller, the first since 1989 to combine his post with the leadership of the largest governing party, was able—at least in the first two years of his premiership, before he was incapacitated by corruption scandals—to enforce a centralized system of decision making within the executive. The prime ministerialization of the core executive has also been kept in check by the ambiguity in the position of the center of government, the capacity of which to serve as the prime minister's vanguard was strictly limited. Finally, the development of a prime ministerial executive has been hampered by the slow adoption and only partial implementation of civil service legislation, making it difficult to achieve a system combining professionalized nonpolitical administrators at the low and middle levels of the civil service, with structured and functional politicization at the top. The Polish case demonstrates the importance of party-political coordinating mechanisms, which could either reinforce the linkages between the formal-legal constitution of the government, the configuration of executive institutions, and the structure and functions of the center of government or produce significant discrepancies between them.

ANNEX

Table 4.5.   The Composition of Polish Cabinets, 1989–2001
Table 4.5a   Tadeusz Mazowiecki Cabinet, 12/9/1989–12/1/1991

Prime minister	Tadeusz Mazowiecki (12/9/1989–4/1/1991)
Deputy prime minister	Leszek Balcerowicz (12/9/1989–12/1/1991)
Deputy prime minister	Czesław Janicki (12/9/1989–6/7/1990)
Deputy prime minister	Jan Janowski (12/9/1989–12/1/1991)
Deputy prime minister	Czesław Kiszczak (12/9/1989–6/7/1990)
Education	Henryk Samsonowicz (12/9/1989–12/1/1991)
Finance	Leszek Balcerowicz (12/9/1989–12/1/1991)
Spatial Development and Construction Industry	Aleksander Paszyński (12/9/1989–12/1/1991)
Culture and Arts	Izabella Cywińska (12/9/1989–12/1/1991)
Defense	Florian Siwicki (12/9/1989–6/7/1990)
	Piotr Kołodziejczyk (6/7/1990–12/1/1991)
Agriculture, Forestry, and Food Industry	Czesław Janicki (12/9/1989–31/12/1989)
Agriculture and Food Industry	Czesław Janicki (01/1/1990– 6/7/1990)
	Temporary head: Mieczysław Stelmach (11/7/1990–14/9/1990)
	Janusz Byliński (14/9/1990–12/1/1991)
Environment and Natural Resources	Bronisław Kamiński (12/9/1989–31/12/1989)
Environment, Natural Resources, and Forestry	Bronisław Kamiński (01/1/1990–12/1/1991)
Labor and Social Policy	Jacek Kuroń (12/9/1989–12/1/1991)
Industry	Tadeusz Syryjczyk (12/9/1989–12/1/1991)
Internal Market	Aleksander Mackiewicz (12/9/1989–12/1/1990)
Home	Czesław Kiszczak (12/9/1989–6/7/1990)
	Krzysztof Kozłowski (6/7/1990–12/1/1991)
Foreign Affairs	Krzysztof Skubiszewski (12/9/1989–12/1/1991)
Justice	Aleksander Bentkowski (12/9/1989–12/1/1991)
Transport, Maritime Industry, and Communications	Franciszek Wielądek (12/9/1989–16/12/1989)
Transport and Maritime Industry	Franciszek Wielądek (16/12/1989–6/7/1990)
	Ewaryst Waligórski (6/7/1990–12/1/1991)
Minister—member of cabinet for the establishment of Communications Ministry	Marek Kucharski (12/9/1989–20/12/1989)
Communications	Marek Kucharski (20/12/1989–14/9/1990)
	Jerzy Slezak (14/9/1990–12/1/1991)
Foreign Economic Relations	Marcin Święcicki (12/9/1989–12/1/1991)
Health and Social Care	Andrzej Kosiniak-Kamysz (12/9/1989–12/1/1991)

(Continued)

Table 4.5a *Continued*

Minister—head of the Office of the Council of Ministers	Jacek Ambroziak (12/9/1989–12/1/1991)
Minister—head of the Central Planning Office	Jerzy Osiatyński (12/9/1989–12/1/1991)
Minister—member of the cabinet for rural development	Artur Balazs (12/9/1989–12/1/1991)
Minister—member of the cabinet for cooperation with political parties and associations	Aleksander Hàll (12/9/1989–12/10/1990)
Privatization minister (ministry established 13/07/1990)	Waldemar Kuczyński (14/9/1990–12/1/1991)
Minister—member of the cabinet, chairman of the Economic Council	Witold Trzciałkowski (12/9/1989–12/1/1991)
Minister—head of the Technical Development and Innovation Office	Jan Janowski (12/9/1989–12/1/1991)

Table 4.5b **Jan Krzysztof Bielecki Cabinet, 12/1/1991–23/12/1991**

Prime minister	Jan Krzysztof Bielecki (12/1/1991–6/12/1991)
Deputy prime minister	Leszek Balcerowicz (12/1/1991–23/12/1991)
Education	Robert Głębocki (12/1/1991–23/12/1991)
Finance	Leszek Balcerowicz (12/1/1991–23/12/1991)
Spatial Development and Construction Industry	Adam Glapiński (12/1/1991–23/12/1991)
Culture and Arts	Marek Rostworowski (12/1/1991–23/12/1991)
Defense	Piotr Kołodziejczyk (12/1/1991–23/12/1991)
Agriculture and Food Industry	Adam Tański (12/1/1991–23/12/1991)
Environment, Natural Resources, and Forestry	Maciej Nowicki (12/1/1991–23/12/1991)
Labor and Social Policy	Michał Boni (12/1/1991–23/12/1991)
Industry	Andrzej Zawiślak (12/1/1991–29/7/1991)
Industry and Trade	Andrzej Zawiślak (29/7/1991–31/8/1991)
	Henryka Bochniarz (31/8/1991–23/12/1991)
Home	Henryk Majewski (12/1/1991–23/12/1991)
Foreign Affairs	Krzysztof Skubiszewski (12/1/1991–23/12/1991)
Justice	Wiesław Chrzanowski (12/1/1991–23/12/1991)
Transport and Maritime Industry	Ewaryst Waligórski (12/1/1991–23/12/1991)
Communications	Jerzy Slezak (12/1/1991–23/12/1991)
Foreign Economic Relations	Dariusz Ledworowski (12/1/1991–23/12/1991)
Health and Social Care	Władysław Sidorowicz (12/1/1991–23/12/1991)
Minister—head of the Office of the Council of Ministers	Krzysztof Żabiński (12/1/1991–23/12/1991)
Minister—head of the Central Planning Office	Jerzy Eysymont (12/1/1991–23/12/1991)
Temporary head of Internal Market	Czesław Skowronek (16/1/1991–23/12/1991)
Head of the Technical Development and Innovation Office	Stefan Amsterdamski (16/1/1991–23/12/1991)
Privatization	Janusz Lewandowski (12/1/1991–23/12/1991)

Table 4.5c   Jan Olszewski Cabinet, 23/12/1991–10/7/1992

Prime minister	Jan Olszewski (6/12/1991–5/6/1992)
Education	Andrzej Stelmachowski (23/12/1991–10/7/1992)
Finance	Karol Lutkowski (23/12/1991–28/2/1992)
	Andrzej Olechowski (28/2/1992–4/6/1992)
Culture and Arts	Andrzej Ściński (23/12/1991–10/7/1992)
Defense	Jan Parys (23/12/1991–23/5/1992)
Agriculture and Food Industry	Gabriel Janowski (23/12/1991–10/7/1992)
Environment, Natural Resources, and Forestry	Stefan Kozłowski (23/12/1991–10/7/1992)
Labor and Social Policy	Jerzy Kropiwnicki (23/12/1991–10/7/1992)
Home	Antoni Maciarewicz (23/12/1991–20/6/1992)
Foreign Affairs	Krzysztof Skubiszewski (23/12/1991–10/7/1992)
Justice	Zbigniew Dyka (23/12/1991–10/7/1992)
Transport and Maritime Industry	Ewaryst Waligórski (23/12/1991–10/7/1992)
Foreign Economic Relations	Adam Glapiński (23/12/1991–10/7/1992)
Health and Social Care	Marian Miśkiewicz (23/12/1991–10/7/1992)
Minister—head of the Office of the Council of Ministers	Wojciech Włodarczyk (23/12/1991–20/6/1992)
Minister—head of the Central Planning Office	Jerzy Eysymont (23/12/1991–10/7/1992)
Minister—member of the cabinet	Artur Balazs (23/12/1991–9/5/1992)
Temporary head of the Privatization Ministry	Tomasz Gruszecki (23/12/1991–10/7/1992)
Temporary head of the Spatial Development and Construction Ministry	Andrzej Diakonow (23/12/1991–10/7/1992)
Temporary head of the Industry and Trade Ministry	Andrzej Lipko (23/12/1991–10/7/1992)
Temporary head of the Communications Ministry	Marek Rusin (23/12/1991–10/7/1992)

Table 4.5d   Hanna Suchocka Cabinet, 11/7/1992–26/10/1993

Prime minister	Hanna Suchocka (10/7/1992–25/10/1993)
Deputy prime minister	Henryk Goryszewski (11/7/1992–26/10/1993)
Deputy prime minister	Paweł Łączkowski (11/7/1992–26/10/1993)
Education	Zdobysław Flisowski (11/7/1992–26/10/1993)
Finance	Jerzy Osiatyński (11/7/1992–26/10/1993)
Spatial Development and Construction Industry	Andrzej Bratkowski (11/7/1992–26/10/1993)
Culture and Arts	Vacant (11/7/1992–11/2/1993)
	Jerzy Góral (11/2/1993–26/10/1993)
Defense	Janusz Onyszkiewicz (11/7/1992–26/10/1993)
Agriculture and Food Industry	Gabriel Janowski (11/7/1992–8/4/1993)
Environment, Natural Resources, and Forestry	Zygmunt Hortmanowicz (11/7/1992–26/10/1993)

(Continued)

Table 4.5d   Continued

Labor and Social Policy	Jacek Kuroń (11/7/1992–26/10/1993)
Industry and Trade	Wacław Niewiarowski (11/7/1992–26/10/1993)
Home	Andrzej Milczanowski (11/7/1992–26/10/1993)
Foreign Affairs	Krzysztof Skubiszewski (11/7/1992–26/10/1993)
Justice	Zbigniew Dyka (11/7/1992–17/3/1993)
	Jan Piątkowski (17/3/1993–26/10/1993)
Transport and Maritime Industry	Zbigniew Jaworski (11/7/1992–26/10/1993)
Communications	Krzysztof Kiljan (11/7/1992–26/10/1993)
Foreign Economic Relations	Andrzej Arendarski (11/7/1992–26/10/1993)
Health and Social Care	Andrzej Wojtyła (11/7/1992–26/10/1993)
Minister—head of the Office of the Council of Ministers	Jan Maria Rokita (11/7/1992–26/10/1993)
Minister—head of the Central Planning Office	Jerzy Kropiwnicki (11/7/1992–26/10/1993)
Privatization	Janusz Lewandowski (11/7/1992–26/10/1993)
Minister—member of cabinet, chairman of the Economic Council	Henryk Goryszewski (11/7/1992–26/10/1993)
Minister for European Union integration	Jan Krzysztof Bielecki (11/7/1992–26/10/1993)
Minister—member of cabinet	Zbigniew Eysmont (11/7/1992–26/10/1993)
Minister—member of cabinet	Jerzy Kamiński (11/7/1992–26/10/1993)
Minister—member of cabinet, chairman of the Social and Political Committee	Paweł Łączkowski (11/7/1992–26/10/1993)
Chairman of the Scientific Research Committee	Witold Karczewski (11/7/1992–26/10/1993)

Table 4.5e   Waldemar Pawlak Cabinet, 26/10/1993–6/03/1995

Prime minister	Waldemar Pawlak (26/10/1993–1/3/1995)
Deputy prime minister	Marek Borowski (26/10/1993–8/2/1994)
	Grzegorz Kołodko (28/4/1994–6/3/1995)
Deputy prime minister	Włodzimierz Cimoszewicz (26/10/1993–6/3/1995)
Education	Aleksander Łuczak (26/10/1993–6/3/1995)
Finance	Marek Borowski (26/10/1993–8/2/1994)
	Grzegorz Kołodko (28/4/1994–6/3/1995)
Spatial Development and Construction Industry	Barbara Blida (26/10/1993–6/3/1995)
Culture and Arts	Kazimierz Dejmek (26/10/1993–6/3/1995)
Defense	Piotr Kołodziejczyk (26/10/1993–10/11/1994)
	Vacant (10/11/1994–6/3/1995)
Environment, Natural Resources, and Forestry	Stanisław Żelichowski (26/10/1993–6/3/1995)
Agriculture and Food Industry	Andrzej Śmietanko (26/10/1993–6/3/1995)
Labor and Social Policy	Leszek Miller (26/10/1993–6/3/1995)
Industry and Trade	Marek Pol (26/10/1993–6/3/1995)
Home	Andrzej Milczanowski (26/10/1993–6/3/1995)

Table 4.5e   Waldemar Pawlak Cabinet, 26/10/1993–6/03/1995

Foreign Affairs	Andrzej Olechowski (26/10/1993–6/3/1995)
Justice	Włodzimierz Cimoszewicz (26/10/1993–6/3/1995)
Transport and Maritime Industry	Bogusław Liberadzki (26/10/1993–6/3/1995)
Communications	Andrzej Zieliński (26/10/1993–6/3/1995)
Foreign Economic Relations	Lesław Podkański (26/10/1993–6/3/1995)
Health and Social care	Jacek Żochowski (26/10/1993–6/3/1995)
Minister—head of the Office of the Council of Ministers	Michał Strąk (26/10/1993–1/3/1995)
Minister—head of the Central Planning Office	Mirosław Pietrewicz (26/10/1993–6/3/1995)
Privatization	Wiesław Kaczmarek (26/10/1993–6/3/1995)
Chairman of the Scientific Research Committee	Witold Karczewski (26/10/1993–6/3/1995)

Table 4.5f   Józef Oleksy Cabinet, 7/3/1995–7/2/1996

Prime minister	Józef Oleksy (4/3/1995–7/2/1996)
Deputy prime minister	Roman Jagieliński (7/3/1995–7/2/1996)
Deputy prime minister	Grzegorz Kołodko (7/3/1995–7/2/1996)
Deputy prime minister	Aleksander Łuczak (7/3/1995–7/2/1996)
Education	Ryszard Czarny (7/3/1995–7/2/1996)
Finance	Grzegorz Kołodko (7/3/1995–7/2/1996)
Spatial Development and Construction Industry	Barbara Blida (7/3/1995–7/2/1996)
Culture and Arts	Kazimierz Dejmek (7/3/1995–7/2/1996)
Defense	Zbigniew Okoński (7/3/1995–22/12/1995)
	Stanisław Dobrzański (5/1/1996–7/2/1996)
Environment, Natural Resources, and Forestry	Stanisław Żelichowski (7/3/1995–7/2/1996)
Agriculture and Food Industry	Roman Jagieliński (7/3/1995–7/2/1996)
Labor and Social Policy	Leszek Miller (7/3/1995–7/2/1996)
Industry and Trade	Klemens Ścierski (7/3/1995–7/2/1996)
Home	Andrzej Milczanowski (7/3/1995–22/12/1995)
	Jerzy Konieczny (29/12/1995–7/2/1996)
Foreign Affairs	Władysław Bartoszewski (7/3/1995–22/12/1995)
	Dariusz Rosati (29/12/1995–7/2/1996)
Justice	Jerzy Jaskiernia (7/3/1995–7/2/1996)
Transport and Maritime Industry	Bogusław Liberadzki (7/3/1995–7/2/1996)
Communications	Andrzej Zieliński (7/3/1995–7/2/1996)
Foreign Economic Relations	Jacek Buchacz (7/3/1995–7/2/1996)
Health and Social Care	Jacek Żochowski (7/3/1995–7/2/1996)
Minister—head of the Office of the Council of Ministers	Marek Borowski (7/3/1995–7/2/1996)
Minister—head of the Central Planning Office	Mirosław Pietrewicz (7/3/1995–7/2/1996)
Privatization	Wiesław Kaczmarek (7/3/1995–7/2/1996)
Chairman of the Scientific Research Committee	Aleksander Łuczak (7/3/1995–7/2/1996)

Table 4.5g   Włodzimierz Cimoszewicz Cabinet, 7/2/1996–31/10/1997

Before the 1996–1997 Center of Government Reform

Prime minister	Włodzimierz Cimoszewicz (7/2/1996–17/10/1997)
Deputy prime minister	Roman Jagieliński (7/2/1996–10/4/1997)
Deputy prime minister	Grzegorz Kołodko (7/2/1996–4/2/1997)
Deputy prime minister	Mirosław Pietrewicz (7/2/1996–31/10/1997)
Education	Jerzy Wiatr (7/2/1996–31/10/1997)
Finance	Grzegorz Kołodko (7/2/1996–31/10/1997)
Spatial Development and Construction Industry	Barbara Blida (7/2/1996–31/12/1996)
Culture and Arts	Zdzisław Podkański (7/2/1996–31/10/1997)
Defense	Stanisław Dobrzański (7/2/1996–31/10/1997)
Environment, Natural Resources, and Forestry	Stanisław Żelichowski (7/2/1996–31/10/1997)
Agriculture and Food Industry	Roman Jagieliński (7/2/1996–10/4/1997)
Labor and Social Policy	Andrzej Bączkowski (7/2/1996–7/11/1996)
Industry and Trade	Klemens Ścierski (7/2/1996–31/12/1996)
Home	Zbigniew Siemiątkowski (7/2/1996–31/12/1996)
Foreign Affairs	Dariusz Rosati (7/2/1996–31/10/1997)
Justice	Leszek Kubicki (7/2/1996–31/10/1997)
Transport and Maritime Industry	Bogusław Liberadzki (7/2/1996–31/10/1997)
Communications	Andrzej Zieliński (7/2/1996–31/10/1997)
Foreign Economic Relations	Jacek Buchacz (7/2/1996–4/9/1996)
Health and Social care	Jacek Żochowski (7/2/1996–31/10/1997)
Minister—head of the Office of the Council of Ministers	Leszek Miller (7/2/1996–31/12/1996)
Minister—head of the Central Planning Office	Mirosław Pietrewicz (7/2/1996–30/9/1996)
Privatization	Wiesław Kaczmarek (7/2/1996–30/9/1996)
Chairman of the Scientific Research Committee	Aleksander Łuczak (7/2/1996–31/10/1997)

After the 1996–1997 Center of Government Reform

Prime minister	Włodzimierz Cimoszewicz
Head of the prime minister's chancellery	Grzegorz Rydlewski (1/1/1997–31/10/1997)
Deputy prime minister	Mirosław Pietrewicz (7/2/1996–31/10/1997)
Deputy prime minister	Roman Jagieliński (7/2/1996–10/4/1997)
	Jarosław Kalinowski (25/4/1997–31/10/1997)
Deputy prime minister	Grzegorz Kołodko (7/2/1996–4/2/1997)
	Marek Belka (4/2/1997–31/10/1997)
Home and Administration	Leszek Miller (1/1/1997–31/10/1997)
Economy	Wiesław Kaczmarek (1/1/1997–31/10/1997)
Culture and Arts	Zdzisław Podkański (7/2/1996–31/10/1997)
Finance	Grzegorz Kołodko (7/2/1996–4/2/1997)
	Marek Belka (4/2/1997–31/10/1997)
State Treasury	Mirosław Pietrewicz (1/10/1996–31/10/1997)

Table 4.5g   Włodzimierz Cimoszewicz Cabinet, 7/2/1996–31/10/1997

Environment, Natural Resources, and Forestry	Stanisław Żelichowski (7/2/1996–31/10/1997)
Agriculture and Food Industry	Roman Jagieliński (7/2/1996–10/4/1997)
	Jarosław Kalinowski (25/4/1997–31/10/1997)
Labor and Social Policy	Tadeusz Zieliński (4/1/1997–31/10/1997)
Head of the Government Center for Strategic Studies	Zbigniew Kuźmiuk (1/1/1997–31/10/1997)
Foreign Affairs	Dariusz Rosati (7/2/1996–31/10/1997)
Justice	Leszek Kubicki (7/2/1996–31/10/1997)
Transport and Maritime Industry	Bogusław Liberadzki (7/2/1996–31/10/1997)
Communications	Andrzej Zieliński (7/2/1997–31/10/1997)
Defense	Stanisław Dobrzański (7/2/1996–31/10/1997)
Education	Jerzy Wiatr (7/2/1996–31/10/1997)
Health and Social Care	Jacek Żochowski (7/2/1996–17/9/1997)
Minister—member of cabinet	Zbigniew Siemiątkowski (1/1/1997–31/10/1997
Head of the Central Spatial Development and Housing Office	Barbara Blida (1/1/1997–27/10/1997)
Chairman of the Committee for European Integration	Włodzimerz Cimoszewicz (15/10/1996–31/10/1997)

Table 4.5h   Jerzy Buzek Cabinet, 31/10/1997–19/10/2001

Prime minister	Jerzy Buzek (31/10/1997–19/10/2001)
Deputy prime minister	Longin Komołowski (19/10/1999–19/10/2001)
Deputy prime minister	Janusz Steinhoff (12/6/2000–19/10/2001)
Deputy prime minister	Leszek Balcerowicz (31/10/1997–8/6/2000)
Deputy prime minister	Janusz Tomaszewski (31/10/1997–3/9/1999)
Labor and Social Policy	Longin Komołowski (31/10/1997–19/10/1999)
Labor and Social Policy	Longin Komołowski (19/10/1999–19/10/2001)
Economy	Janusz Steinhoff (31/10/1997–19/10/2001)
Agriculture and Rural Development	Artur Balazs (19/10/1999–19/10/2001)
Agriculture and Food Industry	Artur Balazs (26/3/1999–19/10/1999)
	Jacek Janiszewski (31/10/1997–26/3/1999)
Foreign Affairs	Władysław Bartoszewski (30/6/2000–19/10/2001)
	Bronisław Geremek (31/10/1997–30/6/2000)
Finance	Halina Wasilewska-Trenkner (28/8/2001–19/10/2001)
	Jarosław Bauc (12/6/2000–28/8/2001)
	Leszek Balcerowicz (31/10/1997–8/6/2000)
Home and Administration	Marek Biernacki (7/10/1999–19/10/2001)
	Janusz Tomaszewski (31/10/1997–3/9/1999)
Health	Grzegorz Opala (7/11/2000–19/10/2001)
	Franciszka Cegielska (19/10/1999–23/10/2000)
Health and Social Care	Franciszka Cegielska (26/3/1999–19/10/1999)
	Wojciech Maksymowicz (31/10/1997–26/3/1999)

(Continued)

126   *Chapter 4*

Table 4.5h *Continued*

Treasury	Aldona Kamela-Sowińska (28/2/2001–19/10/2001)
	Andrzej Chronowski (16/8/2000–28/2/2001)
	Emil Wąsacz (31/10/1997–16/8/2000)
Justice	Stanisław Iwanicki (5/7/2001–19/10/2001)
	Lech Kaczyński (12/6/2000–5/7/2001)
	Hanna Suchocka (31/10/1997–8/6/2000)
Defense	Bronisław Komorowski (16/6/2000–19/10/2001)
	Janusz Onyszkiewicz (31/10/1997–16/6/2000)
Communications	Tomasz Szyszko (16/3/2000–18/7/2001)
	Maciej Srebro (26/3/1999–16/3/2000)
	Marek Zdrojewski (31/10/1997–26/3/1999)
	Temporary Minister Janusz Steinhoff (19/7/2001–24/7/2001)
Regional Development and Construction Industry	Jerzy Kropiwnicki (16/6/2000–19/10/2001)
Environment	Antoni Tokarczuk (19/10/1999–19/10/2001)
Environment, Natural Resources, and Forestry	Jan Szyszko (31/10/1997–19/10/1999)
Culture and National Heritage	Andrzej Zieliński (12/7/2001–19/10/2001)
	Kazimierz Michał Ujazdowski (16/3/2000–12/7/2001)
	Andrzej Zakrzewski (19/10/1999–10/2/2000)
Culture and Arts	Andrzej Zakrzewski (26/3/1997–19/10/1999)
	Joanna Wnuk-Nazarowa (31/10/1997–26/3/1997)
Transport and Maritime Industry	Jerzy Widzyk (12/6/2000–19/10/2001)
	Tadeusz Syryjczyk (8/12/1998–8/6/2000)
	Eugeniusz Morawski (31/10/1997–8/12/1998)
Education	Edmund Wittbrodt (20/7/2000–19/10/2001)
	Mirosław Handke (31/10/1997–20/7/2000)
Science	Andrzej Wiszniewski (19/10/1999–19/10/2001)
Minister—member of cabinet, special services coordinator	Janusz Pałubicki (31/10/1997–19/10/2001)
Minister—member of cabinet	Jerzy Kropiwnicki (31/10/1997–16/6/2000)
Minister—member of cabinet	Teresa Kamińska (31/10/1997–26/3/1999)
Minister—member of cabinet	Wiesław Walendziak (31/10/1997–26/3/1999)
Minister—member of cabinet	Jerzy Widzyk (31/10/1997–26/3/1999)
Minister—member of cabinet	Ryszard Czarnecki (31/10/1997–26/3/1999)
Chairman of the Committee for European Integration	Jerzy Buzek (27/7/1998–19/10/2001)
	Ryszard Czarnecki (31/10/1997–27/7/1999)
Chairman of the Committee for Scientific Research	Andrzej Wiszniewski (31/10/1997–19/10/2001)

Source: www.kprm.gov.pl.

NOTES

1. See annex for composition of successive governments.
2. Centre Alliance (PC), Peasants' Alliance (PL), National Christian Union (ZChN), and Christian Democrats (PChD).
3. Democratic Union (UD), Liberal Democratic Congress (KLD), National Christian Union (ZChN), Christian Democrats (PChD), Peasants' Alliance (PL), Polish Economic Alliance (PPG) and Christian Peasants' Alliance (SLCh).

5

Czech Republic: A Core Neglected

Vesselin Dimitrov and Radoslaw Zubek

This chapter maps the development of core executive institutions in the Czech Republic over a period of twelve years, from 1989 to 2001. It locates the executive within the political system by analyzing the changing party system and its impact on government formation and the executive's relationship with the president, parliament, and political parties. The following sections give an overview of the institutional changes in the central governmental administration and focus on the prime minister's position by studying the evolution of his powers and argue that there has been a lack of progress in establishing effective coordinating mechanisms. Next, the chapter documents the development of the cabinet and the role of party-based political coordination mechanisms before examining the evolving powers of the center of government. Finally, we turn to the politics–administration nexus, explaining the delay in the adoption of civil service legislation.

THE DEVELOPMENT OF PARTY SYSTEM AND GOVERNMENT FORMATION, 1989–2001

During the period under investigation the Czech Republic has moved from a centrally planned communist regime to a market democracy based on the rule of law. The student protests in November 1989 led to a collapse of the communist government. The June 1990 elections produced a new, noncommunist federal Czechoslovak government, which was led by prime minister Marian Calfa and dominated by the Civic Forum and Public against Violence. At the state level, a new Czech government was formed

129

under the premiership of Petr Pithart (Civic Forum). The key role in the management of the economic transition was played by Vaclav Klaus, federal finance minister, who in mid-1991 became leader of the newly established Civic Democratic Party (ODS). After economic reforms were successfully launched in January 1991, the political debate soon centered on the future of the Czechoslovak federation. The June 1992 elections were held amid mounting pressure for the dissolution of the Czechoslovak federation. They produced a new, albeit scaled-down federal government headed by Jan Strasky. The new Czech government was led by Vaclav Klaus. After the elections, Klaus and his Slovak counterpart, Vladimir Meciar, entered into negotiations on the dissolution of the federation, and on 1 January 1993 the Czech Republic became an independent state. The Klaus government, which was formed after the 1992 elections, continued in power until June 1996. It was a coalition consisting of the ODS and three smaller parties: Christian Democratic Party (KDS), which merged with the ODS in 1995; Christian Democratic Union–Czechoslovak People's Party (KDU-CSL); and the Civic Democratic Alliance (ODA). Table 5.1 shows its composition.

The main event of the June 1996 elections was the emergence of a new political power, the social democrats, as the second largest parliamentary party. A coalition government was formed by the ODS, KDU-CSL, and ODA under premiership of Vaclav Klaus. The new cabinet could rely on ninety-nine votes in the two hundred-seat lower chamber and would, thus, closely miss a majority. Table 5.2 shows its composition.

The government's weak parliamentary position was subsequently undermined by the economic crisis of mid-1997 and a financial scandal regarding the ODS's party finances, both of which contributed to the government's collapse in November 1997. In December 1997 Josef Tošovsky (previously the chairman of the Czech National Bank) was appointed a caretaker prime minister. Tošovsky's main aim was to arrange for new parliamentary elections. These were held in June 1998 and were won by the Czech Social Democratic Party (CSSD), who, however, failed to achieve a majority in the lower chamber. Vaclav Klaus (ODS) and Milos Zeman (CSSD) negotiated the creation of a minority social democratic government under the latter's premiership but one supported by the ODS on the basis of a so-called opposition agreement. Table 5.3 shows its composition.

Despite a relatively small total number of governments during the last decade, nearly all possible cabinet configurations have been exhausted. There were two majority governments (both single party and coalition), an interim caretaker government, and two minority governments (both coalition and single party). At the same time, there was one constant factor: the presidency was—with one brief pause—occupied by Vaclav Havel. Table 5.4 summarizes this information.

Table 5.1. Composition of the First Klaus Government

Name	Position	Party
Vaclav Klaus	Prime minister	ODS
Ivan Kocarnik	Deputy prime minister; minister of finance	ODS
Jan Kalvoda	Deputy prime minister; in charge of the civil service and legislation	ODA
Josef Lux	Deputy prime minister; minister of agriculture	KDU-CSL
Karel Dyba	Economic Development	ODS
Jiri Skalicky	National Property Administration and Privatization	ODA
Josef Zieleniec	International Relations	ODS
Petr Pitha (since 5/1994, Ivan Pilip)	Education, Youth, and Sport	KDS
Jindrich Kabat (since 1/1994, Pavel Tigrid)[a]	Culture	KDU-CSL
Jindrich Vodicka	Labor and Social Affairs	ODS
Petr Lom (since 6/1993, Ludek Rubas; since 10/1995, Jan Strasky)	Health	ODS
Jiri Novak	Justice	ODS
Jan Ruml	Interior	ODS
Vladimir Dlouhy	Industry, Trade, and Travel	ODA
Igor Nemec	State Control	ODS
Frantisek Benda	Environment	KDS
Stanislav Belehradek	Economic Competition	KDU-CSL
New ministry since 1/1993, Jan Strasky (since 10/1995, V. Budinsky)	Transport	ODS
New ministry since 1/1993, Antonin Baudys (since 9/1994, Vilem Holan)	Defense	KDU-CSL
Total appointed ministers: 25	Total ministries: 17	

Source: Personal compilation.
Note: KDS: Christian Democratic Party; KDU-CSL: Christian Democratic Union–Czechoslovak People's Party; ODA: Civic Democratic Alliance; ODS: Civic Democratic Party.
[a] P. Tigrid was proposed by KDU-CSL to replace J. Kabat but was without political affiliation.

THE LOCATION OF THE EXECUTIVE IN THE POLITICAL SYSTEM

In analyzing the executive's position within a wider political system, this section focuses on its relationship with the president, parliament, and political parties. With regard to the executive's relationship with the presidency, it is argued that the two executive actors are only narrowly interdependent, and—where such interdependence is present, as is the case, for example, in foreign policy—the core executive has managed to tip the balance in its

Table 5.2.   Composition of the Second Klaus Government

Name	Position	Party
Vaclav Klaus	Prime minister	ODS
Jan Kalvoda (since 1/1997, Vlasta Parkanova)[a]	Deputy prime minister; minister of justice (and the head of Legislative Council)[b]	ODA
Josef Lux	Deputy prime minister; minister of agriculture	KDU-CSL
Ivan Kocarnik (since 6/1997, Ivan Pilip)	Finance	ODS
Miloslav Vyborny	Defense	KDU-CSL
Josef Zieleniec (since 10/1997, Jaroslav Sedivy)	Foreign Affairs	ODS
Ivan Pilip (since 6/1997, Jiri Grusa)	Education, Youth, and Sport	ODS
Jaromir Talir	Culture	KDU-CSL
Jindrich Vodicka (since 10/1997, Stanislav Volak)	Labor and Social Affairs	ODS
Jan Strasky	Health	ODS
Jan Ruml (since 10/1997, Jindrich Vodicka)	Interior	ODS
Vladimir Dlouhy (since 6/1997, Karel Kuhnl)	Industry and Trade	ODA
Jiri Skalicky	Environment	ODA
Martin Riman	Transport	ODS
J. Schneider (since 5/1997, Tomas Kvapil)	Regional Development	KDU-CSL
Pavel Bratinka	Without portfolio	ODA
Total appointed ministers: 24	Total ministries: 14	

Source: Personal compilation.
Note: KDU-CSL: Christian Democratic Union–Czechoslovak People's Party; ODA: Civic Democratic Alliance; ODS: Civic Democratic Party.
[a]Vlasta Parkanova became the minister of justice but was not a deputy prime minister. Jiri Skalicky, minister of environment, became deputy prime minister.
[b]When Kalvoda resigned and Parkanova took over as minister of justice, Cyril Svoboda, until then the deputy head of the Legislative Council, became the head of the Legislative Council.

favor. As for relations with the parliament, it is argued here that the basic features of the Czech parliamentary system foster a closely interdependent relationship between the executive and parliament. But despite the parliament's substantial formal powers, its role in policymaking has been largely tamed by effective coordination between the executive and its supporting parties and, more recently, even opposition parties.

Relations with the presidency have been characterized by a relatively small degree of interdependence. The formal powers of the president have always been limited, but the 1993 Czech constitution has constrained them

Table 5.3.   Composition of the Zeman Government

Name	Position	Party
Milos Zeman	Prime minister	CSSD
Egon T. Lansky (until 11/1999)	Deputy prime minister, foreign and security policy	CSSD
Pavel Mertlik (since 6/2000, also the minister of finance)	Deputy prime minister, economic policy	CSSD
Vladimir Spidla	Deputy prime minister, social policy; minister of labor and social affairs	CSSD
Pavel Rychetsky	Deputy prime minister; head of the Legislative Council	CSSD
Ivo Svoboda (until 7/1999)	Finance	CSSD
Jan Kavan (since, 12/1999 also the deputy prime minister for foreign and security policy)	Foreign Affairs	CSSD
Jan Fencl	Agriculture	CSSD
Vladimir Vetchy	Defense	CSSD
Otakar Motejl	Justice	Nonaffiliated
Eduard Zeman	Education, Youth, and Sport	CSSD
Pavel Dostal	Culture	CSSD
Ivan David (since 2/2000, Bohumil Fiser)	Health	CSSD
Vaclav Grulich (since 4/2000, Stanislav Gross)	Interior	CSSD
Miroslav Gregr	Industry and Trade	CSSD
Milos Kuzvart	Environment	CSSD
Antonin Peltram (since 4/2000, Jaromir Schling)	Transport and Communications	CSSD
Jaromir Cisar (since 4/2000, Petr Lachnit)	Regional Development	CSSD
Jaroslav Basta (since 3/2000, Karel Brezina)	Head of the Office of the Government	CSSD
Total appointed ministers: 24	Total ministries: 14	

Source: Personal compilation.
Note: CSSD: Czech Social Democratic Party.

even further (Wolchik 1997, 170). Most important, under the new constitutional regime, the president is no longer entitled to legislative initiative. He is elected by the legislature and has largely ceremonial functions. He formally appoints and accepts the resignation of the prime minister and his ministers, as well as convenes the parliament and can dissolve it under certain circumstances. The president also appoints judges of the constitutional court, the head of the Supreme Audit Office, and members of the managing committee of the Czech central bank. Admittedly, the president does have some scope for affecting policymaking through, in particular, discretion in

Table 5.4.   Czech Parliaments, Presidents, and Governments, 1990–2003

| | | | Governments | |
| | | | Support in Lower Chamber | Party Composition |
Parliaments	Presidents	Prime Minister		
June 1990	Vaclav Havel, Czechoslovak president	Petr Pithart, June 1990–June 1992	Majority: 127 seats	Single party: Civic Forum (OF)
May/June 1992	Vaclav Havel, Czech president, first term,	Vaclav Klaus, June 1992–July 1996	Majority: 105 votes	Coalition (four parties): ODS, KDS, KDU-CSL, ODA
June 1996	1993–1998	Vaclav Klaus, July 1996–November 1997	Minority: 99 votes	Coalition (three parties): ODS, KDU-CSL, ODA
		Josef Tošovsky, December 1997–July 1998	Caretaker government	—
June 1998	Vaclav Havel, second term, 1998–2003	Milos Zeman, July 1998–2002	Minority: 74 votes	Single party: CSSD

Source: Personal compilation.
Note: CSSD: Czech Social Democratic Party; KDS: Christian Democratic Party; KDU-CSL: Christian Demo-cratic Union–Czechoslovak People's Party; ODA: Civic Democratic Alliance; ODS: Civic Democratic Party.

appointing prime ministers, veto power, and an ability to shape the political debate. This said, however, it must be recognized that such opportunities have seriously shrunk over the last decade. While the president seemingly enjoys a free hand in nominating prime ministers, his room for maneuver has come to be constrained, as governments have had to secure the confidence of the lower chamber of parliament. Thus, whereas in the early period of 1990–1992 President Havel was directly involved in the formation of cabinets, already in the mid-1990s, although reluctantly, he had to nominate the candidates of the largest parliamentary party (ODS in 1996 and CSSD in 1998). His powers in this regard may, however, receive a temporary boost in times of crisis, as is demonstrated by Havel's active role in the formation of a caretaker government led by Josef Tošovský (Kopecký 2001, 146). Similarly, the power of presidential veto has proved to be of limited significance. The main reason is that the veto is fairly easy to override, with only absolute majority of deputies required to do so (Cepl and Gillis 1994, 65). Between

1992 and 1996, four out of seven presidential vetoes have been rejected by the parliament (Kopecký 2001, 156–57). Perhaps the most significant lever available to the Czech president has been his ability to shape the political debate by appealing directly to the general public, political parties, and organized interests. President Havel demonstrated a great skill in having his views heard in his regular Sunday radio addresses, weekly meetings with the prime minister, and Friday meetings with parliamentarians. On many occasions this brought him into conflict with the government, in particular over foreign policy, the role of the Senate, and the regional governments (Wolchik 1997, 184–87). But, although significant, his agenda-shaping powers shrunk considerably. For one thing, the government moved to rein in Havel's activism in this regard by, for example, flatly rejecting his idea of an annual "state of the republic" address. Moreover, as other political actors came of age, Havel's voice, which in the early 1990s had no competition, had to compete for attention with government, parliament, political parties, and organized interests (Wolchik 1997, 188–89).

In contrast to relative autonomy of the two executive actors, the government's relations with the parliament have remained fairly interdependent. The Czech governments are accountable to the first chamber of parliament, the House of Deputies. The constitution provides for a parliamentary investiture of governments when it passes a vote of confidence in the government's program. Members of the government do not have to be, but may be, members of parliament. However, members of government are excluded from the chairmanship (vice chairmanship) of a chamber of parliament and from participating in parliamentary committees or commissions. Members of the government have the right to attend sessions of both chambers of parliament, as well as their committees and commissions. The parliament holds far-reaching control powers over the government. First of all, it determines the organization of the government. Ministries and central agencies are established only by parliamentary acts that specify the contents of ministerial portfolios. The parliament holds wide appointment powers with regard to many central administrative bodies and self-governing municipal authorities (Reschova and Syllova 1996, 85). The lower chamber may also adopt resolutions requesting the government to take legislative action in a particular area (Reschova and Syllova 1996, 95–96). It may bring down the government by a no-confidence vote. While the number of deputies that can propose such a vote is fairly high and stands at fifty (one quarter of all deputies), the parliament does not have to simultaneously indicate a new prime minister. Finally, it is important to note the parliament's role in the budgetary process. A three-reading arrangement offers the lower chamber an opportunity to accept or reject the general parameters of the draft budget—that is, its size, deficit/surplus, and allocations to regions and municipalities.

Yet, despite its wide constitutional powers, the parliament's role in policymaking has over the decade been tamed by effective coordination between the executive and its supporting parties. From the start of transition, party discipline has been relatively high, and governments have generally been able to count on the support of their members of parliament. The use of political coordination mechanisms such as written coalition agreements and coalition councils has eased the interaction between the government ministers and the leaders of the parliamentary parties. The relative effectiveness of channels for feeding in party priorities at an early stage has ensured a high parliamentary cohesion and the necessary legitimacy for government drafts in parliament. As a result, Czech parliamentarians have exhibited a fairly low degree of legislative activism. In 1993, for example, deputies submitted twenty-four draft bills, out of which only sixteen eventually became law. The government, by contrast, submitted sixty-three bills, all of which became law (Reschova and Syllova 1996, 96).

THE OUTLINES OF THE EXECUTIVE TERRAIN

At the structural level, the Czech executive has been subject to horizontal integration at the level of ministerial administration and progressive fragmentation at the level of central agencies. At the same time, the internal organization of ministerial administration has continued to be characterized by a far-reaching differentiation.

The early adjustments in the structure of the central administration were mainly driven by two factors: new economic conditions and progressive defederalization. With regard to the first of these factors, the constitutional amendment of July 1990 reorganized the economic administration at a federal level by abolishing a number of ministries and agencies, including the Ministry of Metallurgy, Engineering, and Electrical Engineering; the Ministry of Agriculture and Food; the Ministry of Fuel and Energy; the Price Control Office; the State Planning Commission; the State Commission for Scientific, Technological, and Capital Construction Development; and the Public Control Committee. At the same time, it established three new ministries (Ministry for Strategic Planning, Ministry of Economy, Ministry of Control) and two new central agencies (Office for Economic Competition and the Committee for Environment). The reorganization of economic management capacities was pursued with similar vigor at the Czech republican level. In 1990 alone five ministries were abolished (Commission for Planning and Scientific and Technological Development,[1] Commission for People's Control, Ministry of Agriculture and Food, Ministry of Forestry and Wood, and the Ministry of

Construction and Building Industry); one was created and soon abolished (Ministry of Engineering Industry and Electronics); four new ministries were established (Ministry of Economic Policy and Development; Ministry of Agriculture; Ministry of Control; Ministry of National Property Administration and Privatization); and one new central agency was created (Work Safety Office).

As a result of the progressive dismantling of the Czechoslovak federation, the existing Czech republican ministries were transformed into ministries of a Czech independent state. Consequently, the number of federal ministries shrank from twelve in mid-1990 to six in October 1992. At the same time, there was a sharp increase in the number of Czech ministries, which at the end of 1993 totaled seventeen, the highest number in the last decade.

Following the breakup of Czechoslovakia, the process of reconfiguring the central administration has begun with a view to streamlining the functioning of the governmental administration. After the 1996 parliamentary elections, the new Klaus government took action to restructure the ministerial bureaucracy, abolishing three ministries and setting one new ministry and an independent central agency. The Ministry of National Property Administration was abolished, and its competencies were transferred to the Finance Ministry. The responsibilities of the Economics Ministry were divided up among four ministries: the Ministry of Finance; the Ministry of Industry and Trade; the Ministry of Transport and Telecommunications; and the newly established Ministry for Regional Development. A new Office for State Information System was also established as new central agency. While the 1996 reorganization seemed to have provided a stable configuration of ministerial bureaucracy for the next four years (no changes between 1996 and 2000), it is interesting to note that precisely in that same period the number of central agencies rose from eight to twelve. In late 2001, the Czech central administration comprised fourteen ministries and twelve central agencies.

With regard to the internal organization of the ministerial bureaucracy, it must be stressed that it has continued to exhibit a far-reaching heterogeneity. Each ministry is responsible for determining its own organizational rules. Thus, ministries are organized into sections (*sekce*; Foreign Affairs, Regional Development, Environment, Defense), divisions (*divize*; Industry and Trade), groups (*skupiny*; Education), or sectors (*useky*; Transport; PHARE 1998, 34). Likewise, wide variations are present in the configuration of the units supporting the work of the minister himself. These vary from Ministry Office (Urad ministerstva), through the Office of the Minister (Kancelar ministra) and Cabinet of the Minister (Kabinet ministra) to the Secretariat of the Minister (Sekretariat ministra). Far from designating mere differences in name, such organizations have different status and position within each ministry.

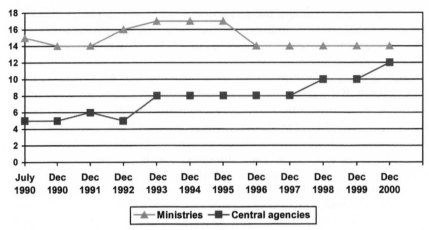

Figure 5.1.   Number of Ministries and Central Agencies, 1990–2000 *Source*: Personal Compilation.

To summarize, figure 5.1 shows the integration and fragmentation tendencies in the Czech executive.[2]

THE POWERS OF THE PRIME MINISTER

The experiences of the last decade offer a fairly mixed picture when it comes to assessing the position of the prime minister. While in formal-legal terms, the government has remained in cabinet mode throughout the 1990s, this has occasionally been overcome by a prime minister who could exercise personal and political ascendancy over his ministerial colleagues.

The Czech constitution establishes a clear legal basis for cabinet government. Having been nominated by the president, the prime minister selects a cabinet and submits it to the president, who must approve it. The parliament does not approve the prime minister but only votes on the program of the entire government. Although the prime minister chooses ministerial candidates, he has little freedom in shaping the structure of his cabinet, as the content of individual ministerial portfolios is determined by parliamentary acts.

The constitution provides little basis for the emergence of a core executive, centralized around the prime minister. While defining the prime minister's role as that of "organizing the work of the cabinet and presiding over its meetings," it does not give him powers to direct or control the work of ministers or give them policy instructions. The work of ministries is directed, controlled, and coordinated by the government (law 122/97, art. 28). The prime minister's low profile is also conspicuous in the government's internal rules and procedures. His formal powers in cabinet sessions are limited and include the granting of the right to speak and the calling for a vote. Although the premier is responsible for preparing the cabinet agenda, ministers accept it at the beginning of each cabinet session. The premier has no direct control over the work of government committees, councils, and other advisory bodies. During interministerial coordination, his office does not enjoy a privileged status.

It is further important to note the relatively minor role envisaged for the prime minister in the budgetary process. While the preparation of the budget is principally guided by the finance ministry, final decisions tend to be made in cabinet, where both the prime minister and finance minister could be easily outvoted by line ministers. Moreover, the prime minister has only limited access to economic expertise autonomous from the Finance Ministry. An attempt to establish a center for medium-term economic planning in the Government Office has largely failed when these competencies were transferred from the Social and Economic Strategy Council to the Charles University (more on this later). Professional support for the prime minister is also restricted in other policy areas. The prime minister may draw on the assistance of specialist advisors housed in the Prime Minister's Office. Yet, such advice is principally of political character. The prime minister lacks recourse to strategic policy advice from a permanent policy analysis and development department. The main reason is that the Government Office, which houses the Prime Minister's Office, provides almost purely secretarial and administrative support to the chief executive, deputy prime ministers, and the cabinet as a whole.

The underinstitutionalization of the prime minister's position could, however, be overcome by party-political factors. Vaclav Klaus, prime minister between 1992 and 1997, was able to run a centralized core executive, especially in his first government (1992–1996). By virtue of his role as the creator and the unchallenged leader of the ODS, which in turn dominated the government, as well as his forceful personality and political-organizational capabilities, he had little difficulty in imposing his policy preferences on his cabinet colleagues (Orenstein 1998, 49). This was most evident in economic policy, where Klaus clearly had an upper hand on issues such as privatization, regulatory reform, and fiscal prudence. As his finance minister of 1992–1997 noted, "Klaus had enormous authority in cabinet. I regularly informed him about fiscal policy developments and his support was very important" (interview, March 2001). A close observer noted,

> Under the Klaus governments, the position of the prime minister, although weak on paper, was extremely strong due to Klaus's forthright personality. He issued direct instructions to ministers, who were not willing to come into conflict with him. This was most evident with regard to the finance minister. (interview, June 2000)

From a political point of view, Klaus benefited from the popularity of his policies among the general electorate. A high place in the opinion polls was, however, due mainly to the prime minister's programmatic decision to make important concessions including the continuation of the social guarantees and welfare programs (Orenstein 1998, 50). In organizational terms, he proved very skillful in building his own party and a strong parliamentary majority. However, Klaus's antibureaucratic bias and a general wariness of bureaucratic power prevented him from institutionalizing a strong prime ministerial government. Milos Zeman, the social democratic prime minister, has not been able to rely on alternative resources to bolster his limited formal powers. As a result, the core executive under him operated in a decentralized manner, with little control over the activities of individual ministers. Apart from his more accommodating personality, he, unlike Klaus, faced competition from within his party and cabinet, in particular from deputy prime ministers. Zeman's low profile has been further accentuated by a new practice of taking votes on each single issue, ranging from cabinet agenda to policy choices. As the head of the Agenda Department in the Government Office observed, "Under the Zeman government votes are taken almost all the time. This was very rare under Klaus" (interview, March 2001).

PATTERNS OF CABINET COORDINATION

The legal framework governing the work of the Czech government provides an important role for the cabinet in determining the legislative and technical quality of the acts submitted to it but gives individual ministers a potentially greater role by giving them responsibility for the substantive content of the acts (law 2/1969, quoted in Kabele and Linek 2004). These legal provisions create a tendency toward a decentralized ministerial executive, with the exception of the arrangements for ensuring good quality legal drafting.

In the Czech Republic, the majority of policy decisions are taken in cabinet. As a result, cabinet meetings tend to be extremely long, often lasting more than several hours. As the head of the Agenda Department of the Government Office noted,

> The cabinet discusses between twenty-five and fifty items every week. The items on the agenda are not divided into A and B points [i.e., in order of priority]. The sessions last from 10:00 am until 5:00 pm and are often prolonged into late evening. (interview, March 2001)

Before 1993 the cabinet was aided in its decision making by a presidium of the government (*predsednictvo vlady*), which was, however, abolished by

Vaclav Klaus, as a communist remnant. A limited coordination of decision making was achieved in the social democratic government of Prime Minister Zeman (1998–2002), through the introduction of three deputy prime ministers, overseeing the work of line ministers in the area of economic policy, social and cultural affairs, and security and defense. The hierarchical powers of the deputy prime ministers vis-à-vis "their" ministers, are not, however, defined clearly. As a close observer noted,

> Technically, deputy prime ministers have power to instruct ministers, to comment on their proposals. No sanctions are envisaged for noncompliance, but a minister who finds himself in disagreement with his deputy prime minister may find it difficult to present proposals to the cabinet. (interview, June 2000)

It has become customary for deputy prime ministers to hold weekly meetings with ministers in their ambit to review the agenda of the forthcoming cabinet session. The Zeman government also revived the pre-1993 concept of a presidium as the pinnacle of the new coordination structure. Accordingly, the cabinet meeting on Wednesday is preceded, first, by the Tuesday meeting of deputy prime ministers with their line ministers and a presidium meeting on Wednesday morning. Unlike in the past, these meetings are not formalized and are not supported by permanent secretariats. As the head of the Agenda Department of the Government Office noted,

> The Zeman government reinstated the presidium but only by a government resolution. The presidium has no official output and so does not generate any work for the Government Agenda Department. The present constitution says that the government acts as a collegial body, so there can be no formal decision-making role for the presidium. (interview, March 2001)

The policy coordination process has been characterized by an increasing degree of fragmentation. Its main tenets are outlined in the legislative rules and the cabinet procedural code. The new legislative rules were adopted in March 1998 (resolution 188/1998), replacing the previous ones dating back to March 1987. Unlike the legislative rules, the cabinet procedural code has been amended by almost each successive government (five times since 1991, most recently in September 2000). Rather than with a draft law, the Czech legislative process starts with the preparation of a factual objective of law (*vecny zamer zakona*), which identifies the main objectives to be achieved and the means to be used. It is drafted by a ministry or any of the other central administrative bodies and forwarded for comments to other ministries, central agencies, the central bank, and the department of EU compatibility at the Government Office, within a so-called cross-sectoral review (*pripominkove rizeni*). At this stage, it also gets distributed to relevant advisory bodies of the government (detailed later). After comments have been provided, they are either incorporated into the draft or negotiated with interested parties. If an agreement has not been reached, a list of differences is drawn up to accompany the draft on its way to the cabinet. Once the cabinet decides to approve a factual objective, the leading ministry can proceed with the preparation of a draft law, which undergoes the same consultation procedure as the factual objective, with only minute procedural differences. The onus of policy coordination has thus shifted to a complex array of advisory and other committees. Between 1990 and 1998 there were fourteen such bodies (supported by the Government Office), of which nine were newly created. The Zeman government increased their number substantially, by creating ten new committees within the first two years in office (see table 5.5). All such bodies may be divided into three principal types: advisory, participatory, and coordinating. The advisory bodies are characterized by a mixed composition that includes—next to government officials—a broad representation of the professions, academia, business, and media. For example, the Council for Social and Economic Strategy, headed by the deputy prime minister for economic affairs, consists of twenty-one members, including ministers (industry and trade; education; environment; interior; finance; transport and communications), representatives of regional government (mayors of Prague and Ostrava); trade unions; business associations; and academics and journalists. Participatory committees bring together representatives of the government and those of societal actors. These bodies provide a platform for relations with, in particular, trade unions, nongovernmental organizations, national minorities, and the Roma population. A good example is that of the Council of Economic and Social Agreement (Tripartite Council), which was set up in 1990 and brings together the trade unions, business associations, and the government. Finally, coordination committees are composed almost exclusively of government ministers. Under the Klaus government, there were two such committees: the Economic Council and the European Integration Council. The Economic Council coordinates the preparation of cabinet decisions on economic policy by reviewing draft documents and submitting its recommendations to the cabinet. The council consists of twenty-one members, of which thirteen have decision rights, while the remaining members enjoy only consultative status. The former comprise two deputy prime ministers (economic policy [chairman]; foreign and security policy), six ministers (finance; labor and social affairs; industry and trade; agriculture; transport and communications; regional development), four academic experts, and the secretary of the council. The latter include one minister (environment), the central bank governor, three office heads (Competition Office; Czech Statistics Office; National Property Fund), and three deputy ministers (interior; defense; and foreign affairs).

Table 5.5.   Advisory Bodies at the Czech Center of Government

1990–1998	*1998–2001*
Supported by the Government Office	
Committee for European Integration	Committee for European Integration
Interministerial Drug Commission	Interministerial Drug Commission
Disabled Board	Disabled Board
Economic Council	Economic Council
Research and Development Council	Research and Development Council
Legislative Council	Legislative Council
Council for Relations with NGOs	Council for Relations with NGOs
Commission for Relocating Bodies of Central Administration	Commission for Relocating Bodies of Central Administration
Council for National Minorities	Council for National Minorities
Interministerial Commission for Roma Community Affairs	Interministerial Commission for Roma Community Affairs
Tripartite Council	Tripartite Council
	National Security Council
	Committee for Protection of Economic Interests
	Council for Social and Economic Strategy
	Commission for Holocaust-Related Property Injuries
	Committee for Children, Youth, and Family
	Council for Human Rights
Supported by Other Ministries	
Czech Commission for UNESCO	Czech Commission for UNESCO
Security of Road Transport	Security of Road Transport
Privatization Commission	Privatization Commission
	Commission for State Information Policy
	Council for Health and Environment
	Commission for Southeast Europe
	Commission for Relations with Churches

Note: NGO: nongovernmental organization; UNESCO: United Nations Educational, Scientific, and Cultural Organization.

While in principle the Economic Council's opinions do not bind the government, some observers note that in practice they often translate into cabinet decisions (Mikule 1998, 5).

When viewed against this background, the arrangements for legal review are characterized by a high degree of horizontal integration. Before a draft objective of law is submitted to the government, it must first be scrutinized by the Legislative Council. The council was established under a 1969 government resolution, but its history goes back to the late 1950s. Most recently, its mode of operation has been amended by government resolution 534/1998. The council provides the cabinet with nonbinding opinions on all draft laws, with respect to their drafting quality, constitutionality, and compliance with international law. It comprises twenty-six members appointed by the government, including civil servants, senior judges, law professors, the ombudsman, and it is currently chaired by the deputy prime minister for legislation. It meets twice a week and discusses, on average, four drafts per session. From April 2000 to March 2001 there were twenty-four sessions, during which ninety-eight drafts were discussed. The council reviews only the more important laws, while the less-significant drafts are screened in its subcommittees, of which there are seven. The work of the council and its subcommittees is supported by a twenty-two-person-strong secretariat at the Government Office.

PARTY-BASED POLITICAL COORDINATION DEVICES

Coalition governments in the Czech Republic have resorted extensively to the use of formal written agreements. The agreement concluded by the ODS, KDS, KDU-CSL, and ODA government in 1992 consisted of two pages and two annexes, running a total of approximately two thousand words. It focused mainly on the allocation of posts within the government but also contained some references to the way in which the coalition partners should cooperate—for example, by holding a joint meeting once a month. The ODS, KDU-CSL, and ODA government in 1996 also concluded an agreement on more or less the same format as the previous one. However, the rules governing intercoalition cooperation were this time elaborated in greater detail. The agreement provided for regular consultations of coalition partners at the level of party leaders, leaders of party groups in parliament (Chamber of Deputies, Senate), ministers, or other specified persons. These consultations were to take place regularly before every meeting of the Chamber of Deputies and before every meeting of the Senate at three levels: party leaders, highest representatives of the parties in parliament, and leaders of party groups in parliament.

The coalition consultation arrangements have not remained on paper. The two Klaus governments have benefited from a highly sophisticated system of consultation and coordination with its supporting parties in parliament (Kopecký 2001, 110–11). Chief among such mechanisms was the so-called Coalition Thirteen, which comprised leaders of coalition parties, the speaker and deputy speaker of the parliament, and the leaders of the coalition parliamentary parties. The Coalition Thirteen met regularly to discuss legislative

Table 5.6.   Frequency of Meetings between Ministers and Coalition Parties (%)

	ODS	KDS	ODA	KDU-CSL
More than once a week	11.8	—	18.2	16.7
Once a week	80.4	28.6	72.7	75.0
Once a month	7.8	57.1	9.1	8.3
A few times a year	—	14.3	—	—
Hardly ever/never	—	—	—	—

Source: Kopecký (2001, 111).
Note: KDS: Christian Democratic Party; KDU-CSL: Christian Democratic Union–Czechoslovak People's Party; ODA: Civic Democratic Alliance; ODS: Civic Democratic Party.

proposals before plenaries and committees in order to screen them for possible disagreements and, where possible, to reconcile differences. These mechanisms were complemented by the so-called Parliamentary Nine (the Coalition Thirteen without party leaders), which met twice a week. Where necessary, coalition party leaders also held separate meetings (the so-called Four). Besides such formalized consultation fora, there were also endless informal meetings between ministers and deputies from their parties in corridors, committee hearings, and even smokers' rooms. Table 5.6 shows the frequency of such informal meetings.

Under the Zeman government, coordination mechanisms were also extended to opposition parties on the basis of the so-called Opposition Agreement with the ODS. The parties agreed to consult each other on matters of foreign and domestic politics before parliamentary debates. This has pushed the CSSD government into constant negotiations with opposition parties about each single draft or new policy. The effectiveness of these negotiations is undermined by the fact, however, that they only take place after a draft law has been presented to parliament and not at the time when the draft is considered by the government. As the head of the Agenda Department of the Government Office noted,

> The Social Democratic government does not negotiate with the ODS in the course of a discussion of a draft in government. It only does so after it submits a draft to the parliament. The result is that a lot of drafts are defeated in parliament. (interview, March 2001)

THE POWERS AND ORGANIZATION OF THE CENTER OF GOVERNMENT

In any analysis of the center of government, one needs to confront such issues as who it should support (cabinet or prime minister), who should provide support (political advisors or civil service), and the nature of that support (strategic or administrative). When viewed through such lenses, the Czech center of government is principally keyed to provide administrative and technical assistance to the government as a whole; in other words, it acts as a government registrar.

The head of the Government Office is appointed and dismissed by the cabinet. Although he attends cabinet meetings, his rank is normally nonministerial, but the current incumbent, Karel Brezina, has combined this position with that of a minister without portfolio since March 2000. In 2001, the office employed about 490 staff and managed a budget of CZK 361,224,000.[3]

Under the Klaus government, there was a deliberate downgrading of the role of the Government Office. As the head of the Agenda Department noted,

> Until the end of 1992 the Government Office was a real center of power. It stood above the ministries. All submissions from ministries had to go through different sections established within the Government Office.
> With the establishment of the Czech Republic [in 1993], this was changed. Klaus weakened the Government Office. This is a paradox because under a strong prime minister, the center was weakened. The reason for this was that Klaus believed that decisions should be made by political appointees and not by civil service. (interview, March 2001)

In spite of his belief in the importance of political appointees at the center of government, Klaus took no steps to establish an effective Prime Minister's Office. His political dominance over ministers was such that he could usually ensure that they would do his bidding, without needing institutional support. As the head of the Agenda Department observed,

> The tendency was to transfer decision-making powers to ministers and leave a small office supporting the prime minister. He did not establish a big Prime Minister's Office, because he thought he could do it all himself. (interview, March 2001)

As a result, under Klaus, the Government Office's internal structure was divided into two main pillars: a government office providing technical and administrative support to the cabinet and an almost skeletal prime minister's office. The former consisted of the head of the Government Office's secretariat, the Personnel Department, the Government Agenda Department, and the Press Department. The latter comprised the Protocol Department, the prime minister's advisors, and the Security and Defense Department. Figure 5.2 presents the internal structure of the Government Office under the first Klaus government (1995). Under Milos Zeman, the Government Office has expanded. Personnel levels almost doubled, from 286 in 1997 to 490 in 2000. The growth reflects a new coordination schema, characterized by the

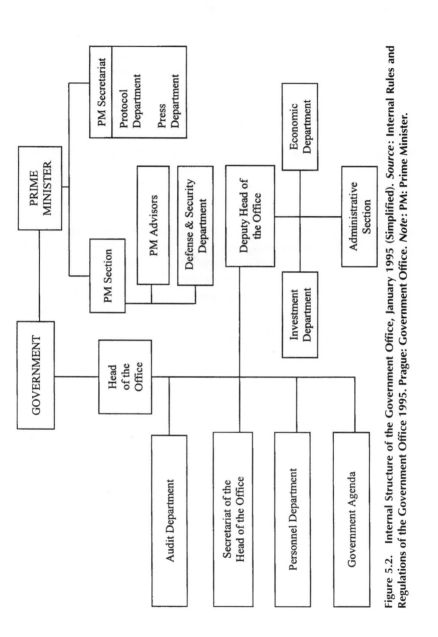

Figure 5.2. Internal Structure of the Government Office, January 1995 (Simplified). *Source*: Internal Rules and Regulations of the Government Office 1995. Prague: Government Office. *Note*: PM: Prime Minister.

presence of four deputy prime ministers: finance, legislation, social affairs, and home affairs. As part of the reorganization, permanent secretariats were established for the deputy prime ministers, who were also given a share of coordination and a team of advisory bodies to chair and supervise. Figure 5.3 shows the organigram of the Government Office in May 2000.

Despite increased structural capacities, the role of the Government Office has remained largely unchanged and has continued to be limited to technical and administrative support. This is best reflected in the profile of its line departments and secretariats, whose support for the chief executive and the cabinet is only sporadically concerned with the substance of policies. In the main, they carry out a technical and legal review of submissions from line ministries. For example, the Agenda Department holds responsibility for preparation of cabinet meetings, checking submission to the cabinet for their compliance with requirements of interministerial consultation and distribution of documents to ministries and the parliament. As the head of the department noted, however, it did not undertake "substantive checks" on submissions from the ministries. The department does take part in the preparation of a government program, on a biannual basis. The program consists of two parts: the legislative program (draft laws), prepared by the Legislative Department at the Legislative Council (detailed later); and the nonlegislative program (concepts, strategies, white papers, etc.), prepared by the Agenda Department. The Agenda Department prepares a monthly report on the implementation of the biannual government program, but this is primarily a technical exercise that is undertaken in a manner that does not threaten the collegiate nature of the cabinet:

> The Government Agenda Department prepares a "control report" on a monthly basis. It discusses the reasons for delay with ministries and presents a report to the cabinet. Any changes in the program must be approved by the cabinet.
>
> All new tasks are keyed into a computer software, and the computer keeps track of the implementation record. (interview, March 2001)

The Legislative Council, whose permanent secretariat employs twenty-two lawyers, checks all draft laws for their drafting quality, constitutionality, and compliance with international law (discussed earlier). A technical profile is also typical of the secretariats of the government advisory and coordination committees. For example, the Tripartite Council employs only three people and provides almost purely technical support. This is also true for the deputy prime ministers' secretariats. For example, the secretariat of the deputy prime minister for economic affairs employs four people (its head, secretary, two part-time advisors), and its role is very limited. The Prime Minister's Office remained relatively weak, with ten permanent advisors and five external advisors, together with a small secretariat (interview, March 2001).

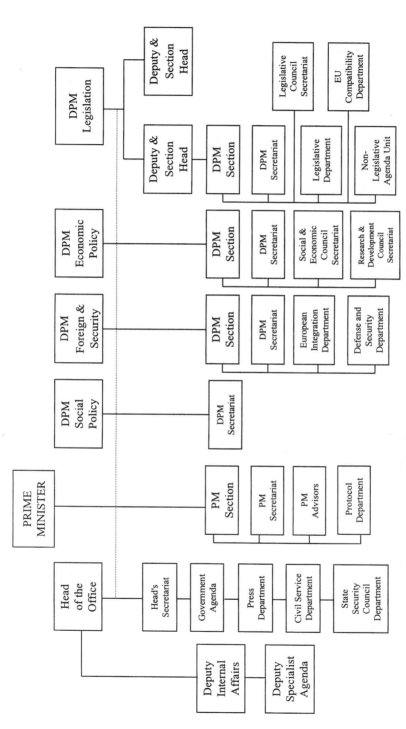

Figure 5.3. Internal Structure of the Government Office, May 2000 (Simplified). *Source:* **www.vlada.cz.**

Where attempts were made to establish more policy-oriented units, these have largely failed, as is demonstrated by the example of the secretariat of the Social and Economic Strategy Council, which found itself in an organizational limbo after the core of the council's planning competencies were moved outside the government to a new Center for Social and Economic Strategy at the Charles University.

The low profile of the center of government reflects the Czech government's inclination to collegial decision making. Thus, the bulk of policy development work is performed by line ministries, while the burden of ensuring cohesion of government policies falls on a web of coordination and advisory committees and, more recently, on deputy prime ministers. As the head of the Agenda Department of the Government Office noted,

> The Government Office supports the entire cabinet. This is stated in the law. There have been attempts to make it more subordinate to the prime minister, but they have never been reflected in the law. (interview, March 2001)

A deputy minister who has been closely involved with the numerous attempts to reform the structure of the government office in the course of the 1990s takes a rather pessimistic view of developments since the start of the democratic transition:

> The government office functioned very well under the Calfa government [1990–1992]. Today it plays a very administrative role, mainly that of supporting the meetings of the cabinet. Also, it houses bodies and committees that could not fit anywhere else. (interview, March 2001)

The reasons for the failure to establish an effective government office have been primarily political. Klaus's party-political dominance in 1992–1996 was such that he considered formal institutional mechanisms unnecessary. As the deputy minister noted,

> Prime Minister Klaus considered public administration reform as unnecessary. . . . He was in favor of a very strong central authority exercised by the prime minister. . . . The quality of central state administration has never been one of Klaus's priorities. He focused on economic growth, privatization, and so forth.
> This is a bit of paradox. Klaus, who wanted to exercise strong central authority, did not attempt to strengthen the central administration. He probably believed that he could exercise hands-on management himself. (interview, March 2001)

Indeed, Klaus took active steps to stop the public administration reform proposals that had already been prepared:

> One of Klaus's first steps as prime minister was to abolish in 1993 the Institute of Legislation and State Administration (headed by Mr. Kalvoda), which was

part of the Czech government (at the level of a central agency). At the time, the institute had just prepared a program for reforming the public administration. Perhaps this was partly the reason why Klaus decided to abolish it. Many people from this institute have transferred to the Home Affairs Ministry. (interview, March 2001)

The shifting of responsibility for the reforms from a central government agency to a line ministry (Home Affairs), underlined the low political priority attached to the reforms. This was amply demonstrated in 1994:

> In 1994 the then minister of home affairs, Mr. Rumel, in cooperation with the then justice minister, Ms. Parkanova, submitted to the government a comprehensive program for reform of the state administration. This program was submitted to the Government Office but never found its way to the cabinet. (interview, March 2001)

The governments that followed Klaus were inhibited in their efforts to reform the structure of central administration by their political weakness. Under the caretaker Tošovsky government in 1998, a reform program was developed, but it only covered local self-government and local state administration. The program was discussed in the government, and general guidelines were produced, but the elections of May–June 1998 cut short the life of that reform (interview, March 2001). The Zeman government was the first to identify public administration reform as a political priority. In May 1999, it submitted to parliament a conceptual framework for the reform, and almost 75 percent of members of parliament were in favor (interview, March 2001). The reforms covered both local and central government structures. The Zeman government made relatively quick progress with local government reform, but as of March 2001, the central administration reform was still "being prepared" (interview, March 2001). By that point, the following concepts had been prepared: the structure of the government office, unification of the internal structure of the ministries, financial accountability, and efficiency in the public sector. As the deputy minister who spearheaded the reform drive noted, however, "there is only slim chance that the reform will be implemented by this government" (interview, March 2001).

THE POLITICS-ADMINISTRATION NEXUS

In the course of the 1990s, Czech governments have exhibited a remarkable reluctance to grasp the nettle of civil service reform. This is all the more interesting, given the steady growth of public administration: staff numbers in central and local administration have increased by almost 50 percent, from 123,000 in 1992 to 180,000 in 2000, while the percentage share of government employees in the total employment has nearly doubled, from

2.5 percent in 1992 to 3.9 percent in 2000 (International Monetary Fund 1998, 1999, 2000, 2001).

A more desegregated analysis, based on data provided by the Czech Finance Ministry's Department for the Financing of the Nonprofit Sector, shows, however, that employment in the Czech central bureaucracy has been fairly stable, with only a slight increase in the last two years. Total employment in the central bureaucracy has risen from 12,924 in 1996 to 15,329 in 2000. A closer analysis of the data also suggests that between 1996 and 1998, total employment in central administration was fairly constant and stood at around thirteen thousand employees. During that period employment in ministries fell slightly while it rose in central agencies, which may—but does not necessarily—suggest staff flows between these two domains of central government. A sharp increase in central staff levels came between 1998 and 2000, when they rose by more than twenty-four hundred employees. In contrast to the previous period, a rise was recorded both in ministries (by about fourteen hundred) and central agencies (by about one thousand).

A slower growth in ministerial staff numbers until 1998 could be attributed to Vaclav Klaus's strong antibureaucratic bias. A slight fall in the total figure for 1998 is probably a result of budget cuts in the wake of the 1997 budget crisis. A sharp rise in employment under the Zeman government is likely to have been provoked, at least in part, by a need to beef up administrative capacity after accession to NATO and before accession to the EU. The latter hypothesis seems to be confirmed by the fact that the biggest increases in staff numbers have been recorded in new central agencies (about a thousand) and those parts of the administration that are important for the EU and NATO accession (a rise by two hundred in the Agriculture Ministry between 1998 and 2000 and by the same number in the Defense Ministry).

Until the passage of a civil service law in 2002, Czech government employees did not enjoy a special legal status, and personnel policy in central administration continued to be governed by the general provisions of the labor code. While the pre-2002 regulatory framework provided that government employees "must act and take decisions in an impartial manner and refrain from any actions that may undermine the political impartiality of their work and decisions" (art. 73.2–5, labor code), it stopped well short of establishing a single framework for meritocratic recruitment and promotion of permanent civil servants. This is not to say that attempts have not been made to pass a comprehensive civil service legislation. On the contrary, work on such a law had been under way at least since late 1992. The Office for Legislation and Public Administration was the first to prepare a draft law, which although discussed in parliament, was not formally adopted by the Klaus government. The main reason for the delay was the unwillingness of Prime Minister Klaus, the head of the ODS (a party that dominated the

Czech party system in 1992–1996), to bind his hands with depoliticization legislation. As a close observer noted, "the Klaus government was content with the possibility to appoint people who were loyal to it" (interview, June 2000). The granting of responsibility for civil service reform to a line ministry—and an inappropriate one at that (Social Affairs)—underlined the prime minister's indifference. The Social Affairs Ministry proved incapable of pursuing the reform, not least because it was actively attacked by the Home Affairs Ministry, which perceived itself to be better placed to spearhead the process (interview, March 2001). The one reform measure that Klaus was prepared to support—the "lustration" legislation—fitted in with his preference for limited politicization of the civil service. The legislation provided for the screening of public employees for their collaboration with the communist regime, though it did not address directly the qualitative aspect of personnel recruitment and training (Hesse and Goetz 1993b; Pomahac 1993, 63). The adoption of the Federal Law on the Conditions of Admission to Certain Offices in State Organs and State Enterprises in October 1991 made it incumbent on all existing holders of senior posts in public administration and prospective candidates to submit a certificate issued by the Interior Ministry affirming that they had not worked as informers for the secret service or secretaries of the Communist Party at district level or higher (Kritz 1995). For example, at the Finance Ministry around 15 percent of high-level staff had to leave the administration due to lustration. While, originally, the law was envisaged to operate for five years, its validity has been extended twice, more recently until the new civil service law had been adopted.

Progress toward the adoption of civil service legislation only began under the Zeman government, partly in response to EU pressure. The government became the first cabinet since the start of transition to formally adopt a civil service law, but disagreements between the CSSD and the ODS delayed its passage through parliament, and it was only approved in 2002.

The 2002 law aims at separating the professional civil service from the political leadership functions. It proposes to introduce the position of a state secretary as the top-level civil servant in ministries, charged with the task of directing the heads of divisions and coordinating the civil service tasks entrusted to him by the minister. Professional criteria of human resource management within a ministry are to be ensured by personnel directors (*personální reditel*), who would be responsible for organizational, payment, and personnel matters. The law tries to protect the recruitment of leading civil servants from political interference by entrusting the director-general of the Office for the Civil Service within the Office of Government with the responsibility of appointing and dismissing state secretaries and personnel directors of the ministries. The personnel directors can make decisions, together with the minister, on important personnel issues—that is, the appointment, dismissal, and remuneration of civil servants. If the personnel director and the minister do not agree on an issue, the personnel director may, through the director-general for the civil service, submit his objection to the prime minister, who takes a final decision. The director-general for the civil service is appointed and dismissed by the prime minister. In other central organs of state administration, which are not headed by a government minister, the directors/presidents exercise personnel management powers. The draft civil service law tries not only to establish common rules for civil servants but also to homogenize the internal structure of ministries.

The framework for determining wages in state administration is provided by a special parliamentary act on salaries and remuneration for work in budgetary and certain other organizations (143/1992). While the law lays down the general principles, the government is authorized to regulate detailed issues by secondary regulations. These include, inter alia, job descriptions with required qualifications and salary scales, as well as conditions for awarding additional salaries, extra pay, and bonuses. Although strictly regulated, the system allows a fair degree of flexibility in determining individual salaries. For example, a personal evaluation bonus may constitute up to 100 percent of one's salary (National Training Fund 1998). Average earnings in public administration have tended to be slightly higher than for the economy as a whole, with average earnings in central government administration more than 50 percent higher in most years—in 1995, gross average monthly earnings in central government administration amounted to CZK 13,832, compared to CZK 8,172 for the economy as a whole; in 1996, CZK 15,089 and CZK 9,676; and in 1997, CZK 16,017 and CZK 10,695, respectively (Nunberg 2000).

Despite the absence of a formal law establishing a permanent civil service, the available evidence suggests that, in practice, the low and middle levels of the Czech bureaucracy benefit from a fairly stable employment environment in which overtly "political" interventions are rather rare. According to a report of the World Bank (1998) on public administration in the Czech Republic, explicitly political appointments tend to be restricted to the levels of ministers, deputy ministers, and one or two levels below. The report concluded that "average turnover below the director level appears, from anecdotal evidence, not to be extraordinarily high. Many staff have apparently held public positions for decades. It is also acknowledged that informal norms discourage dismissal except in cases of clear misconduct" (18). Our own observations corroborate such conclusions. In general, the Czech bureaucracy has been characterized by a relatively high degree of personnel continuity. At the Ministry of Finance, while between 1990 and 1991 Vaclav Klaus replaced around 70 percent of all top-level staff (deputies and directors), there was almost no staff turnover at low and medium levels. Since the beginning of the 1990s, the budgetary process has been managed at the Finance Ministry by a stable cadre of officials in the Budget and Financial

Policy Department. Similarly, key positions at the Government Office (e.g., in the Agenda Department and the Legislative Council) have been held by the same officials since the early 1990s.

The absence of civil service legislation has meant that the Czech government employees have not been vetted for their skills and expertise according to a common set of criteria. They also do not benefit from a comprehensive national training program. Training lies within the responsibilities of each ministry. The level of training expenditure varies across the administration but on average totals 1–2 percent of the wage expenditure (Nunberg 2000, 97). Training courses are run in-house or contracted to local and international suppliers and are mostly concerned with information technology and language skills. Since the mid-1990s qualitative change in the expertise of the Czech bureaucrats has been the focus of the PHARE program and bilateral cooperation with the British Know How Fund, the Ecole National d'Administration, SIGMA/OECD, and TAIEX (Organization for Economic Co-operation and Development 2000). In December 2000 the government adopted a comprehensive blueprint for training civil servants. In early 2001, a new department was established within the Government Office that is responsible for the training and education of state personnel. At the same time, the government agreed to establish an Institute of State Administration for the education of top-level officials.

To summarize, the relationship between ministers and civil servants in the Czech Republic in the 1990s presents an ambiguous picture. On the one hand, the politicization of the Czech bureaucracy, measured by the degree of turnover, was limited to the top echelons of the state employees. While such politicization may be functional, by facilitating the government in the exercise of its coordinating functions, the fact that it had not been legally regulated produced uncertainty and blurred boundaries. The delay in the passage of civil service legislation also meant that the depoliticization of the low- and middle-level civil service, while largely occurring in practice, has not been institutionalized, thus leaving the door open to potential political interference.

CONCLUSION

The Czech executive has enjoyed a clear dominance over the presidency and parliament. The basic institutional choices made at the start of transition, and then largely repeated at the time of the creation of the Czech Republic in 1993, have persisted until today, and there has not been any major proposals for reform in this area. This said, however, it must be recognized that relations with presidency have been influenced by the long-standing incumbent of the office, Vaclav Havel, who held this post between 1993

Table 5.7. Types of Government, Core Executives, and Centers of Government in the Czech Republic, 1993–2002

Type of Government	Type of Core Executive	Type of Center of Government

1993–2002:
  Cabinet
	1993–1997:
	  Centralized prime ministerial
	1997–2002:
	  Decentralized ministerial
		1993–2002:
		  Government registrar

and 2003, and it remains to be seen how these will fare under Havel's successor. The institutionalization of the internal organization of the Czech core executive offers a more complex picture (see table 5.7). For one thing, the horizontal structure of the Czech central administration seems to have entered a period of consolidation, with the overall structure having remained unchanged under three successive governments. In contrast, vertical boundaries have continued to be adjusted in recent years. This trend is likely to continue, as agencies are merged and demerged from ministries, in particular in the process of adapting to the *acquis communauitaire* of the EU. The formal-legal type of government has shown remarkable stability. The communist-era mode has survived without any significant changes until the early twenty-first century, combining as it does some formal recognition of the collective nature of the cabinet with an unusually strong emphasis on the ministers' authority within their own departments. Under Prime Minister Klaus, however, and especially during his first government (June 1992 to July 1996), his personalist hold over his ministers and his party gave the core executive a strongly prime ministerial flavor; under Prime Minister Zeman neither prime ministerial authority nor collective responsibility was strong enough to prevent a trend toward ministerial government. Klaus's strong reliance on party-based coordination meant that the core executive operated as a centralized prime ministerial core, albeit one that largely bypassed the formal channels of government and, crucially, parts of the ministerial administration. It was because of the existence of such mechanisms that the center of government itself was left largely untouched. However, Zeman could not rely on the effectiveness of such channels; at the same time, his position in the government was too embattled to allow for a redirection of the center of government. The prime ministerialization of the core executive has been undermined by the failure to move ahead with civil service reform. Neither politicians seem to have made a sustained effort at imposing tight controls over the bureaucracy, nor have the public officials moved to assert their role through higher professionalism. The Czech case demonstrates both the positive and the negative role that party-political mechanisms could play in relation to the development of coordinating institutions within the core executive: while party-political instruments could compensate for the weakness of such institutions and produce a relatively effective centralization of power in the hands of a politically powerful prime minister, they could also inhibit the development of such institutions, with debilitating long-term consequences.

NOTES

1. This committee and the folowing commission, although not ministries in name, were headed by cabinet ministers and should be regarded as such.
2. The diagram shows year-on-year changes in aggregate numbers and does not reflect fluctuations during the year.
3. The data for 2001.

6

Bulgaria: A Core against the Odds

Vesselin Dimitrov

This chapter analyzes the development of core executive institutions in Bulgaria from 1989 to 2001. It starts with a brief overview of the development of the Bulgarian party system and its effect on government formation and then proceeds to map the executive's relationship with the presidency, parliament, and political parties. The following sections give an overview of the institutional changes in central governmental administration and focus on the evolution of the prime minister's position. The chapter then turns to the development of the cabinet and party-based political coordination mechanisms, before examining the evolving powers of the center of government. Finally, the chapter analyzes the politics–administration nexus and accounts for the rather tardy progress of civil service reform.

THE DEVELOPMENT OF THE PARTY SYSTEM AND GOVERNMENT FORMATION, 1989-2001

On 10 November 1989, as a result of an internal coup by reformers within the leadership of the Bulgarian Communist Party (BCP), the aging Todor Zhivkov was removed from his positions as general secretary of the BCP and chairman of the State Council. Both posts were assumed by Petur Mladenov, a long-serving foreign minister who had disassociated himself from Zhivkov in the eleventh hour. In the spirit of Gorbachev's perestroika, the BCP reformers intended to liberalize the communist system, without challenging its fundamental principles. The reformers moved quickly to consolidate their control of the party's decision-making bodies, pushing Zhivkov's old guard out of the Politburo and the Central Committee by early December

1989. They soon discovered, however, much to their surprise, that control of the party was no longer sufficient for controlling developments in the country. On 7 December 1989, thirteen opposition groups came together to form the Union of Democratic Forces (UDF). They soon demonstrated their determination to challenge BCP's dominant position by organizing a mass demonstration in Sofia on 14 December 1989. In order to preempt the radicalization of the protests, the BCP leadership proposed to the UDF the holding of roundtable talks, a device that had already proved its worth in Poland in enabling the Communist Party to retain a degree of influence over the process of systemic change (Dimitrov 2001). In spite of the occasional histrionics, the roundtable functioned relatively smoothly and in less than three months, produced a number of agreements that established the basic parameters of the transition to democracy. One pivotal decision was to use the first democratic elections to elect a constitutional assembly rather than an ordinary parliament. This ensured that the agenda of the first democratically elected parliament, and of Bulgarian politics as a whole in the first period of democratic transition, would be dominated by problems of system design rather than economic reform.

In parallel with the reshaping of the political system, the communist reformers also remolded their own party in order to make it capable of surviving in the more competitive political environment. At the BCP's Fourteenth Congress, on 30 January–2 February 1990, the party shifted its ideological stance to "democratic socialism," a change symbolized three months later with the rebranding of the party from "communist" to "socialist." The influence of the party vis-à-vis the government was subtly downgraded, as indicated by the decisions of the key reformers, Mladenov and Lukanov, to assume state rather than party positions, the former as president and the latter as prime minister. The party leadership went to the relatively marginal figure of Lilov, who had been in the political wilderness since his dismissal by Zhivkov in 1984.

The electoral system for the first democratic elections had provoked a fierce conflict between the BCP and the UDF, with the former favoring a majoritarian system—which it hoped would work to the benefit of the better-known communist leaders, especially in the small towns and villages—and with the latter pushing for proportional representation. Ultimately, a compromise was reached, with half of the members elected on a majoritarian basis and half by proportional representation.

The elections were won convincingly by the Bulgarian Socialist Party (BSP), whose 47 percent of the popular vote was transformed by the electoral system into an absolute majority of seats (52.75 percent). The UDF won 36 percent of the vote and the same share of seats, with the remainder going to the agrarian party and the Turkish minority party—the Movement for Rights and Freedoms (MRF; Dimitrov 2001). The results of the elections produced a political deadlock. In spite of its majority, the BSP was unwilling to assume sole responsibility for government, largely because it did not wish to be saddled with the onus of launching the "shock therapy" that the country's unsustainable macroeconomic situation clearly called for. The UDF was willing, indeed eager, to get into power but lacked the institutional capacity to do so. Its solution was to launch street protests in June and July 1990, which succeeded in forcing president Mladenov to submit his resignation. After several rounds of negotiations, the BSP agreed to allow the UDF leader Zhelev to be elected president by the constitutional assembly, in exchange for his promise to work with the BSP on the adoption of a new constitution. Zhelev was unable or unwilling, however, to bring the UDF into a coalition government with the BSP, as Prime Minister Lukanov was hoping he would be able to do. Lukanov was thus forced to form a single-party BSP government on 22 September 1990. He soon entered into conflict with the party leader Lilov over the launch of radical economic reform and was forced to resign at the end of November 1990. This opened the way for a new round of negotiations between the BSP and the UDF, which resulted in the ingenious solution of a government headed by a nonparty prime minister, Dimitur Popov, with deputy prime ministers from the BSP, the UDF, and the agrarian party. The nominally expert cabinet allowed both the major parties to absolve themselves of responsibility for the "shock therapy" that the government launched on 1 February 1991.

The spring of 1991 was dominated by an intense and sometimes acrimonious debate on the new constitution. The UDF party leadership, taken over by radicals following Zhelev's departure to the presidency, challenged the legitimacy of the constitutional assembly and called for new elections. The submission of the constitutional draft to the assembly precipitated the conflict, and on 14 May 1991, thirty-nine UDF deputies left the assembly in protest. Most of the UDF deputies, however, remained inside, thus splitting the opposition. The new constitution was nevertheless adopted by the assembly on 12 July 1991 with the support of 309 out of 400 deputies, considerably more than the necessary two-thirds majority of 267 votes.

Having adopted a new constitution, the constitutional assembly fulfilled its task, and new parliamentary elections were held in October 1991. The electoral law was changed to pure proportional representation, as the BSP expected to lose the elections and wished to minimize its losses. In this, it was eminently successful, polling just 1 percent less than the UDF (33 percent vs. 34 percent), and taking 2 percent fewer parliamentary seats (44 percent vs. 46 percent). The split in the UDF in May 1991 produced a multitude of parties. It was the thirty-nine radicals who had refused to support the constitution who were able to assume the mantle of the official UDF and get into parliament. All of their rivals were kept out by the 4 percent threshold. The agrarians also fell by the wayside, leaving in parliament only the UDF, the BSP, and the MRF, which was able to rely on its solid ethnic constituency. One quarter of voters failed to gain representation (Dimitrov 2001).

On 8 November 1991, the UDF leader Philip Dimitrov formed a one-party government. The MRF supported the government in parliament but did not take part in it. The newly formed National Assembly operated in a mood of confrontation that resembled the experience of the previous year. One could nevertheless observe a move toward the consolidation of the parliamentary system, as the electoral victory persuaded the UDF radicals to give up their nonparliamentary ways, and the BSP, adequately represented in parliament, had no reason to resort to them itself.

The government of Philip Dimitrov attempted to accomplish a "change of the system" and to speed up the economic reform. The government's political ineptitude, however, soon brought it into conflict with part of its own parliamentary group; with its informal ally, the MRF; and with President Zhelev, the trade unions, and the media. On 28 October 1992, the government resigned, after failing to win a vote of confidence in parliament.

The nominees for prime minister submitted by UDF (Svetoslav Luchnikov) and BSP (Petur Boiadzhiev) failed to gain the necessary majority. This left the president and the MRF as the only viable actors on the Bulgarian scene, and after complex negotiations, they succeeded in persuading most of the BSP deputies to back a government nominally under a MRF mandate and headed by professor Liuben Berov, a respected economic historian and advisor to the president. The BSP was thus back in the position it had achieved with the Popov government, being able to pull the government's strings from parliament while avoiding responsibility for its actions.

The Berov government managed to survive for nearly two years, getting through seven votes of no-confidence. It was able to accomplish little else. The conflict between its UDF-inspired economic program and socialist parliamentary support made it impossible for it to proceed with economic reform. The BSP managed to avoid being tarred with the government's failures and, under a forceful new leader, Zhan Videnov, began thirsting for direct power. In September 1994, encouraged by its lead in the opinion polls, the BSP brought the government down. On 17 October 1994, the president appointed a caretaker government, led by Reneta Indzhova, to prepare new elections.

The third democratic elections since the start of the democratic transition in Bulgaria marked an important new departure. For the first time, the elections were won with an absolute majority by a party that intended to exercise its mandate. The BSP gained 125 of 240 seats, with the UDF coming in a poor second with 69 seats (Dimitrov 2001). The BSP leader Videnov became prime minister and, in contrast to the socialist leaders in 1990, was fully prepared to assume responsibility for governing. His determination belied the fact that his party still did not have a clear policy program, torn as it was between the desire to turn the clock back to an idealized pre-1989 past and a recognition of the irreversibility of the transition to market economy. Ultimately, the government's hesitations brought the worst of both worlds. It failed to establish discipline over the loss-making state enterprises, either by time-honored administrative methods or by market discipline, and while increasing welfare payments and wages in an attempt to reward its core constituency, it failed to achieve a corresponding rise in taxation revenues. The result was the country's worst economic crisis since the start of transition, with hyperinflation, a paralysis of the banking system, and falls of the gross domestic product of 11 percent in 1996 and 7 percent in 1997.

The BSP's debacle provided an opportunity for the UDF, which had achieved internal consolidation under the leadership of Ivan Kostov. The UDF's first success was the election of Stefan Sofianski as mayor of Sofia, followed by the victory of its nominee Petur Stoianov in the presidential elections in October–November 1996, with 60 percent of the vote. The UDF combined its success at the ballot box with a reversion to its 1990 tactics of street demonstrations, culminating in the siege of the parliament building on 10–11 January 1997. On 4 February 1997, the BSP recognized its inability to control the situation in the country and agreed to the formation of a caretaker government under Sofianski, opening the way for early parliamentary elections. The elections were held on 19 April 1997 and resulted in a decisive victory for the UDF, with 57 percent of the seats (Dimitrov 2001). Kostov became the prime minister of a government, which was the first one since 1989 to enjoy strong parliamentary backing for an explicitly reformist program. A currency board was adopted in July 1997, and the subsequent implementation of austere macroeconomic policies succeeded in abating inflation and improving public and investor confidence, if not in restoring growth. The government also scored important foreign policy successes, the most significant of which was perhaps the invitation to begin accession negotiations with the EU in March 2000.

THE LOCATION OF THE EXECUTIVE IN THE POLITICAL SYSTEM

In the initial stages of the transition to democracy, Bulgaria seemed headed for a semipresidential system, where executive authority is shared between the president and the government. As in Poland, the communist leaders argued at the roundtable for the creation of a powerful presidency, which they saw as a means of guaranteeing their power in the face of a possibly hostile parliament. The UDF was opposed to what it saw as a device for perpetuating communist hegemony, and as a result, the roundtable agreements signed in March 1990 did not contain a clear formulation of the powers of the presidency.

The lack of codification of presidential powers at the onset of democracy meant that they would be shaped by the course of political events. Initially, it seemed that the presidency might emerge as the dominant executive institution. The Communist Party leader Mladenov certainly thought so and was prepared to cede his party position in order to be elected as Bulgaria's first president in April 1990. Within four months, however, Mladenov was forced to resign in humiliating circumstances. An amateur video recording was found showing him uttering the words "It is better for the tanks to come" when faced with the first mass anticommunist demonstration on 14 December 1989. Mladenov should have been able to shrug this off as an unfortunate remark made in the heat of the moment, as he had not actually ordered the tanks to disperse the demonstrators. He decided, however, to declare publicly the recording to be a fake and accuse the UDF of conducting a smear campaign against him. A commission of experts was appointed and, much to the surprise of Mladenov, found that the recording was authentic. The opposition immediately demanded the resignation of a president who had been shown to be a liar. They were backed by a sit-in student strike and a wave of street protests. Mladenov's colleagues in the BSP, disappointed by his political ineptitude, were also inclined to let him go, and on 6 July 1990 he submitted his resignation.

The second president, Zhelev, also found himself isolated from his party, the UDF. As noted, to be elected as Mladenov's successor in August 1990, Zhelev had been prepared to strike a deal with the BSP, which held a majority in the constitutional assembly. By the spring of 1991, this had turned the radicals in his own party against him, which meant that in the drafting of the constitution, he could not rely on unreserved UDF support for the strengthening of the powers of the presidency. The BSP, having conceded the presidency to Zhelev, also had no reason to work for the empowerment of his office. The two major parties thus found themselves opposed to a powerful presidency, and this was duly reflected in the provisions of the constitution adopted in July 1991.

The constitution focused executive power virtually exclusively in the hands of the government. The president was left only with the vague function of exercising "neutral authority," mediating between the political institutions to secure the preservation of the constitutional system. The president's role in forming the government is of rather limited significance, reduced to a largely autonomous reflection of the party composition of parliament. According to the constitution, in nominating the prime minister, the president should start by proposing a candidate from the party holding the highest number of seats in parliament. If the prime minister–designate fails to form a government within seven days, the president has to entrust this task to a candidate nominated by the second largest parliamentary group. Should the new prime minister–designate also fail to form a government within seven days, the president should entrust the task to a candidate nominated by one of the minor parliamentary groups. If the groups in the parliament fail to form a government, the president can engage in "active intermediation" for the formation of a new parliamentary majority. If no government can be formed, the president appoints a caretaker government, dissolves the National Assembly, and schedules new elections within two months. In normal circumstances, the president's influence on government formation is minimal. In crisis situations, however, he could play quite a significant role, as Zhelev did in the creation of the Berov government in December 1992, following the failure of both the UDF and BSP candidates for prime minister to gain parliamentary support, and as did Stoianov, in negotiating the peaceful transfer of power from the collapsing BSP government to a caretaker administration in February 1997.

The 1991 constitution places parliament in a relatively strong institutional position vis-à-vis the government, by providing for a negative vote of confidence, whereby members of parliament could bring down a government without having to vote for a successor at the same time. The executive's ability to control parliament is also undermined by the incompatibility of the mandate of members of parliament with ministerial mandate, a provision unique among the four CEE countries under examination. This rather strict interpretation of separation of powers, a reaction against the merging of executive and legislative functions under communism, means that the government cannot rely on its own "block vote," which in some parliamentary systems, such as the British one, can be quite considerable. On the other hand, members of parliament have few effective means of controlling the executive. Ministers are held generally responsible to parliament for their activities, but the mechanisms for ensuring accountability are not given a specific definition. At most, members of parliament may address questions and interpellations to the council of ministers and to individual ministers, who are obliged to respond, but for a debate to take place on the responses, there has to be a proposal by one-fifth of the members of parliament, which indicates that this is not envisaged as a usual procedure.

The executive's influence over parliament was undermined in the early years of democratic transition by the low degree of party discipline. Party leaders often found themselves defied by a substantial minority and, on occasion, even a majority, of their members of parliament. The most notable example was the decision of the majority of UDF members of parliament in the constitutional assembly to vote for the 1991 constitution, in spite of the contrary decision of the UDF party leadership. Following the fall of the UDF government of Philip Dimitrov, a substantial proportion of UDF members of parliament defied their party leadership to vote for the formation of the Berov government in December 1992. The BSP had fewer problems with party discipline, benefiting from the communist traditions of unity and loyalty, although on occasion substantial minorities of its members of parliament refused to follow the party leadership, especially when it engaged in behind-the-scenes dealings with the UDF and the MRF, as in the election of Zhelev as president in August 1990. Party discipline improved substantially in the latter stages of transition, with the 1994–1997 parliament marking a turning point. The most important change came in the UDF, where Kostov was able to create a united party from a motley of bickering groups. The improvement in party discipline proved difficult to sustain, however, following the unexpected victory of a party formed by the former king Simeon, the National Movement for Simeon II, in the 2001 general election. The movement found it extremely difficult to maintain discipline within its own ranks, hardly surprising in what is largely a personal and ephemeral organization. Defections from the party led to a loss of its parliamentary majority (it had gained 120 out of 240 seats) and forced the government to rely for its survival on the minor coalition partner, the MRF.

THE OUTLINES OF THE EXECUTIVE TERRAIN

In contrast to the pre–World War II Bulgarian constitution and the first communist constitution adopted in 1947, the second communist constitution—adopted in 1971 and thus representing the theory and practice of "mature socialism"—did not specify the number of ministries. The 1971 constitution remained in force until 13 July 1991. In that twenty-year period, there were numerous changes in the number and competencies of the ministries. Perhaps the most intriguing was the fact that between 1987 and 1989, Bulgaria became one of the few countries in the world to make do without a Ministry of Finance. The decision to close down the ministry was taken in August 1987 by the BCP Politburo, which apparently attached more importance to the Ministry of Economy and Planning, the successor of the State Planning Committee.

Changes in the structure and designation of ministries continued to occur after 1989. Like the 1971 constitution, the constitution adopted in 1991 does not specify the number of ministries. The law on the administration, adopted in 1998, in spite of its express intention to rationalize administrative structures, does not stipulate the allocation of task areas to ministries. This has made it possible for each incoming government to restructure ministries and other executive bodies virtually at will.

The most extensive changes have occurred in the ministries dealing with economic policy. Some of these transformations can be seen as a rational response to the withdrawal of the state from the economy, such as the redesignation of the Ministry of Domestic Trade into a Ministry of Trade and Services on 8 February 1990 and its abolition by the expert government of Dimitur Popov on 20 December 1990. The abolition of the Ministry of Foreign Economic Relations by the UDF government of Philip Dimitrov on 8 November 1991 falls in the same category. On a more positive note, the Dimitrov government established a unified economic ministry, the Ministry of Industry and Trade, which was intended to mark a shift from a direc- tive to a regulatory approach to the economy. The importance of rational considerations in the restructuring of ministries should not, however, be overemphasized. The very same Dimitrov government decided to split the unified economic ministry into separate ministries for industry and trade in July 1992, barely eight months after it had established it, largely because of political conflicts between the minister and his colleagues. In May 1997, the second UDF government headed by Ivan Kostov transformed the Ministry of Trade and Foreign Economic Cooperation into a Ministry of Trade and Tourism, and in December 1999, that ministry was merged with the Ministry of Industry to form a Ministry of Economy, thus coming full circle to 1991.

There have also been substantial changes in the ministries dealing with social policy, largely because the transfer of responsibility for social provi- sion from enterprises to the state, combined with the sharply increased level of social deprivation after 1989, created the need for a significant expansion in social administration. In the last years of communism, social policy was handled by the Ministry of Public Health. In January 1990, an independent Committee for Labor and Social Insurance was created, attached to the coun- cil of ministers. In September 1990, the committee was elevated to ministerial rank as the Ministry of Employment and Social Care. This ministry under- went two changes in name—Ministry of Labor and Social Care and Ministry of Labor and Social Policy—without a change in its task profile.

Finally, there has been continuous succession of fusions and splits in the ministries dealing with education and culture, as governments tried to find administrative solutions for the accumulating problems of these sectors. In the late 1980s, there existed a National Council for Education, Science, and Culture, which included the Ministry of Public Education, the Commit- tee for Culture, and the Committee for Science and Higher Education. On 24 November 1989, in the flurry of reorganization that followed the down- fall of Zhivkov, the National Council was closed down, and the three bodies became independent. In 1990, the Committee for Science and Education was transformed into a ministry, as was the Committee for Culture, while the Ministry of Public Education was renamed Ministry of Education. On 15 November 1991, the newly elected UDF government of Philip Dimitrov closed down the Ministry of Science and Higher Education and created a Ministry of Education and Science. In the beginning of 1993, the Ministry of Education and Science and the Ministry of Culture were united into a Ministry of Education, Science, and Culture but after six months were split again into two separate ministries—Ministry of Culture and Ministry of Science and Education (in order to be distinguished from the former Ministry of Education and Science).

There has also been considerable variation in the size of the government since 1989, although one can observe a tendency toward smaller cabinets. The last communist government of Georgi Atanasov (19 June 1986–8 February 1990) had thirty-two members, with as many as seven deputy prime ministers. A sharp reduction in the size of the government became evident as soon as the political transition began, with the first government of Andrei Lukanov (appointed on 8 February 1990) having twenty-four members, with four deputy prime ministers. The expert government of Dimitur Popov had twenty members, with three deputy prime ministers, and all subsequent governments have hovered around this size, including the last government included in our analysis, that of Ivan Kostov, elected on 21 May 1997 (see the chapter annex).

Successive governments since 1989 have failed to deal effectively with the problem inherited from the communist era of the existence of a myriad of agencies, with varying status and objectives, attached to the council of ministers. The council has virtually complete freedom to establish, change, and abolish administrative structures that are not determined by the constitution, do not have the status of ministries, and are subordinated to the central executive organs. The council has not been particularly economical in the exercise of that right. Even toward the end of the rationalizing Kostov government, in September 2000, there were as many as twenty-seven agencies, commissions, and other administrative units attached to the council of ministers.

These agencies do not even have to be created by law and can be brought into existence by a decree of the council of ministers. The agencies are considered to be organs of the executive, and as such, they may issue administrative acts. There is no clear classification scheme for the various types of agencies. The Public Administration Act of 1998 distinguishes between state agencies, state commissions, and executive agencies. State agencies are directly subordinated to the council of ministers and perform functions that have not been assigned to ministries. State commissions are collegiate bodies attached to the council of ministers or to individual ministers that perform control, registration, and approval functions in the implementation of a law or a decree of the council of ministers. Executive agencies provide administrative support to ministers in the implementation of their policies. The list of existing agencies, however, contains a number of other designations, such as *center, national agency,* and *committee,* which do not fit into the three legal categories.

There was also a rather slow progress in creating uniform administrative structures within the ministries. The degree of divergence was demonstrated by a report submitted to the council of ministers in May 1997 by the task team charged with the preparation of a new public administration law. The report indicated, for instance, that the position of secretary-general, the highest administrative authority, was present in most ministries but not in the Ministry of Defense. Furthermore, while the secretaries-general were intended to be politically neutral and to perform purely administrative functions, in a number of ministries, such as the Ministry of Trade and Foreign Economic Cooperation, the Ministry of Culture, and the Ministry of Environment, the secretaries-general were also holding the political position of deputy ministers. There was also lack of uniformity in administrative structures below the level of secretary-general. In most ministries, the highest positions after the secretary-general were those of heads of general directorates and of directorates, but in the Ministry of Interior, the second position in the hierarchy was that of head of service. The distinction between general directorates and directorates was not legally regulated, and it varied from one ministry to another. The fact that Bulgarian public administration had been influenced by the French system at its creation, in the late nineteenth century, and by the Soviet one after 1945 led to a lack of common criteria and to terminological confusion. Problems were also caused by the fact that different administrative institutions had been created by different normative acts, most of them by a governmental decree but others by a special law.

A shift toward more uniform structures came only with the adoption of the public administration law in 1998. The law developed a common model for the internal organization of ministries, based on directorates, departments, and sections. Overall responsibility for the administrative management of the ministry and for interministerial relations was vested in the hands of the secretary-general. The law also codified the functions and the structure of political coordination mechanisms, such as political *cabinets*. Political *cabinets* could be created by the prime minister, the deputy prime ministers, and the individual ministers. In the case of ministers, the political *cabinets* consist of the deputy ministers (usually three), the parliamentary secretary, the head of the *cabinet*, the head of the public relations unit, and a few political advisors (art. 28). The functions of the political *cabinet* were defined as supporting the minister in formulating and developing specific policy decisions and in representing these policies to the public. The support that the *cabinet* could give to a minister was, however, limited to consultation and analysis and did not include the power to issue directives to civil servants in the name of the minister. This limited the capacity of *cabinets* to perform coordinating functions.

In order to increase administrative capacity for managing EU accession, the public administration law provided for the creation of specialized EU integration units within each ministry. This structural change has had some positive effects, at least as measured by Bulgaria's rapid progress in closing chapters of the *acquis communautaire*. At the same time, the creation of specialized units has led to fragmentation within the ministries, as these units attracted more qualified staff and significantly greater resources than other ministerial departments.

THE POWERS OF THE PRIME MINISTER

Bulgaria, like the Czech Republic, has retained throughout the 1990s the formal-legal definition of cabinet government, dating back to the communist era. One interesting twist in the last era of communism, replicated in most East European countries, was the creation, by the 1971 constitution (Spasov 1977), of a State Council. The council, which was defined as standing secondary body of the National Assembly, had the task of ensuring the unity of legislative and executive activity, in accordance with the Marxist-Leninist postulate of the "unity of state power". The council was able to govern by decrees, legalized by incidental sessions of the National Assembly. The existence of the State Council severely reduced the significance of the council of ministers. The 1971 constitution defined the council of ministers as the "superior executive body of state authority," but due to the presumption of sovereignty of parliament, vested in the State Council as its standing body, the State Council was given the right to "exercise general guidance and control over the activity of the Council of Ministers." The council of ministers was thus turned into little more than a subsidiary body for implementing the policy of the Communist Party. The fact that Zhivkov, the party leader, chose to occupy the position of chairman of the State Council and sent relatively secondary party figures to be prime ministers further underlined the prime minister's inferior position in the communist hierarchy.

The conditions under which the 1991 constitution was being drafted were not propitious for augmenting the position of the prime minister. The political changes after 1989 did not significantly strengthen the prime minister's role in the government (for Bulgaria's postcommunist prime ministers, see table 6.1), as the executive was still subordinate to the communist—later socialist—party leadership. Prime Minister Lukanov found himself fighting a losing battle for supremacy with the party leadership, most notably over economic reform. The party leader Lilov refused to support Lukanov's program for a Balcerowicz-style shock therapy and forced him to resign in November 1990. The subsequent expert government of Dimitur Popov had a figurehead prime minister whose role was confined to providing a suitably legalistic veneer for the deals cut between the BSP parliamentary majority and the UDF.

The political circumstances under which the constitution was created largely shaped its provisions. It provided for a relatively weak role of the prime minister in government formation. As the first stage in government

Table 6.1. Bulgarian Prime Ministers, 1989–2001

Prime Minister	Period
Georgi Atanasov	19 June 1986–3 February 1990
Andrei Lukanov	8 February 1990–22 September 1990
Andrei Lukanov	22 September 1990–19 December 1990
Dimitur Popov	20 December 1990–7 November 1991
Philip Dimitrov	8 November 1991–29 December 1992
Liuben Berov	30 December 1992–17 October 1994
Reneta Indzhova (caretaker government)	17 October 1994–24 January 1995
Zhan Videnov	25 January 1995–11 February 1997
Stefan Sofianski (caretaker government)	12 February 1997–20 May 1997
Ivan Kostov	21 May 1997–24 July 2001

formation, parliament votes for a prime minister and then, at his proposal, for members of the government. The prime minister can propose changes of ministers, but they have to be approved by parliament. This seriously restricts the ability of the prime minister to undertake changes in the government's composition. The prime minister does have the power to appoint and dismiss deputy ministers in his own authority (art. 108), but as our interviews have indicated, this power is usually exercised in consultation with the relevant ministers.

The constitution's provisions also severely limit the prime minister's power to direct and coordinate the work of his ministerial colleagues, thus making it difficult for him to establish a centralized core executive. According to the constitution (art. 105), it is the council of ministers as a collective body that decides and implements domestic and foreign policy, ensures public order and national security, and exercises overall guidance over the state administration and the armed forces. The prime minister is given the power to lead and coordinate the overall policy of the government, and bears responsibility for it (art. 108.2), but at the same time ministers have the power to lead their own ministries and bear responsibility for them (art. 108.3). The constitutional definition of the prime minister's competencies implies that he may not use his leading position in the government to issue instructions to the other members of the council of ministers in their areas of responsibility. Indeed, the official Commentary on the Bulgarian Constitution—far from seeing the prime minister as representing an officeholder with a role distinct from, and superior to, that of the cabinet—interprets his role as the guardian of collectivity in the government.

The weak institutional position of the prime minister under the 1991 constitution has not been strengthened to any considerable extent in the course of the following decade. The public administration law adopted in 1998— under what was generally recognized to be the most politically powerful prime minister since the start of the democratic transition, Ivan Kostov—still defined the council of ministers as "the central collegiate, general competence body of the executive" (art. 20.1). A slight augmentation in the status of the prime minister was noticeable only with regard to deputy ministers. The prime minister was given the power not only to appoint and dismiss them but also to determine their powers and portfolios (art. 23.4) and coordinate their work (art. 23.5–6). Even under Kostov, however, deputy ministers worked largely under the guidance of their ministers rather than that of the prime minister, and their contact with the latter was incidental.

One other area in which the public administration law did try, albeit rather cautiously, to strengthen the prime minister was by granting him the power to propose to the council of ministers the abolition of acts that he considers illegitimate or improper (art. 20.6). This provision had to be deleted in 1999, as it was declared unconstitutional by the constitutional court. According to the court, article 20.6 gave the prime minister the sole right to refer illegal or wrongful acts for revocation to the council of ministers. The court decided that that was not in accordance with article 107 of the constitution, which envisages that the council of ministers must act as a collective body in rescinding any illegitimate or improper act issued by a minister. Members of the council have equal rights, and decisions should therefore be taken collectively. The court declared that any other institutional mechanism would lead to a restriction of the ministers' competencies and be contrary to the constitution.

In its ruling on the public administration law, the constitutional court also rejected two provisions that enabled the prime minister to appoint regional governors and to control their activities (art. 29). According to the court, the constitutional text explicitly states that regional governors are to be appointed by the council of ministers. According to article 143.2 of the constitution, the council of ministers appoints (not only proposes) regional governors, and the appointment is legal only by virtue of a decree issued by the council of ministers. Article 29.5, on controlling the work of regional governors, was declared unconstitutional for the same reasons. The court considered that control over the activity of certain bodies is to be exercised by the institution that has appointed them. Since the regional governors are appointed by the council of ministers, this institution, and not the prime minister, must control their activity.

PATTERNS OF CABINET COORDINATION

The 1991 constitution emphasizes the government's function of exercising political leadership, in contrast to the communist system, in which the council of ministers was confined to executing the policy of the party leadership.

The new principle has not, however, been fully translated into reality, partly because of the continuing strength of the perception of the government as an administrative body. The two functions are, of course, linked. The "political" function of the government, or conceptual policy formulation, implies that the government should also create the organization and find the means by which policies can become reality. The political competence of the government has, however, been institutionalized to a significantly lesser extent than its administrative powers. The constitution provides only a general list of the political powers of the government, such as the right for legislative initiative (art. 87.1); the right to draw up and present the annual budget law (art. 87.2); and the right to conclude, confirm, or denounce international treaties (art. 106).

The administrative powers of the government are set out much more extensively in chapter 5 of the constitution and in the 1998 public administration law. The council of ministers directs and coordinates the work of the ministers. It can determine the powers of ministers by a decree, except those powers that are stipulated by law. The council of ministers may create, change, or abolish administrative structures that do not have the status of a ministry and are not defined by the constitution. On the basis of a law and for the implementation of a law, the council of ministers may adopt decrees (*postanovleniia*), ordinances (*razporezhdaniia*), and resolutions (*resheniia*). Based upon a decree, the council of ministers may also adopt standing orders (*pravilnitsi*) and administrative directives (*naredbi*). The status of decrees and ordinances is left rather open, enabling the council of ministers to resolve substantive political questions by administrative fiat.

The main institutional mechanism operating within the council of ministers is the weekly meeting of the cabinet. The evolution of cabinet procedures over the course of the 1990s can be followed through an analysis of the standing orders for the operation of the council of ministers, adopted by successive governments.

The first standing order was adopted by the Berov government in 1993. According to the standing order, a cabinet meeting could only be called by the prime minister. All cabinet meetings had to have an agenda that was prepared by the secretary-general of the council of ministers. Points for the agenda could be proposed by members of the council of ministers, by the secretary-general, and by central state organs whose heads were not members of the council of ministers. Proposals for the agenda could be accepted only if an opinion on them had been provided by the functional departments of the council of ministers' administration and if they had been finalized on time. The council of ministers discussed only the points of the agenda; the agenda could be changed only exceptionally and with the assent of the prime minister. The council of ministers could add supplementary topics to the agenda only if it adopted a resolution on the topic.

The powers of ministers were safeguarded by the provision that ministers could not allow the council of ministers to discuss and decide issues belonging to their own areas of responsibility and by the mainly interministerial process by which submissions to the cabinet were prepared. Draft laws could be discussed and approved by the council of ministers only after all interested organs and organizations had taken a position on the draft. If no agreement had been reached, the submitting body had to add the opinions of other organs to its submission. There were only limited coordination mechanisms that counterbalanced the interministerial nature of the preparation process. Some of these mechanisms were essentially formal, such as the need to ensure the legality of the proposed legislation. This function was discharged by the Legislative Council at the Ministry of Justice, rather than by the legal department of the council of ministers' administration, thus reducing the center of government's coordination capacity. The superfluous role of the council of ministers' legal department was underlined by the provision that if the department did not have remarks concerning the legality of a proposal, it did not need to prepare a position. The requirement to seek the opinion of the Ministry of Finance on the financial implications of the proposal could have substantive consequences, but its effectiveness was constrained by the inability of the Ministry of Finance to veto proposals with which it disagreed.

The discussion of each topic on the agenda commenced with the submitter's presentation, which contained an oral report and a brief account of the comments received. The prime minister then invited contributions from members of the council of ministers who wished to express an opinion. If the debate pointed to a rejection of the proposal, the issue had to be postponed for a supplementary voting. The council of ministers voted on its acts openly and adopted them with a simple majority of the members present at the meeting. A final requirement, once again underlying the collective nature of the cabinet, was that for an act to become valid, it had to be signed by all the members of the council of ministers. If a member of the cabinet refused to do so, the prime minister had to postpone the matter until the following cabinet meeting.

The 1993 standing order was modified by the caretaker government of Reneta Indzhova in November 1994. While some of the provisions added to the powers of the prime minister, this was done primarily to improve efficiency rather than strengthen the prime minister's ability to provide political steerage. The prime minister was given the power to confirm the agenda for the council of ministers' meeting prepared by the secretary-general. The enhancement of the prime minister's power as agenda setter was partly counterbalanced by enabling the council of ministers as a whole to add supplementary topics to the agenda without adopting a special resolution. In an attempt to streamline the cumbersome submission procedure, the range of organizations that needed to be consulted was restricted, and those organizations were obliged to express an opinion within seven days. In addition, the prime minister was empowered to set a deadline for preparation of positions by the council of ministers' administration departments. A final efficiency measure was the provision that proposals on which a negative opinion had emerged in the course of the debate could simply be rejected rather than postponed for supplementary voting.

Some limited strengthening of the prime minister's powers took place under the BSP government in 1995–1997, the first one since the start of transition, in which the party leader held the position of prime minister. The standing order of 1995—through its interpretation of the vague constitutional provision regarding the prime minister's power to head and coordinate the general policy of the government—empowered him to coordinate the work of *individual* ministers, without, however, specifying the mechanism for doing so. The standing order of 1996 enabled the prime minister to establish working groups headed by deputy prime ministers or ministers in order to deal with specific issues. This measure—largely a response to the accumulating problems of 1996, which were soon to engulf the socialist government—did not become a precursor to more permanent cabinet committees. The trend toward the limited strengthening of the cabinet coordination capacity continued under the UDF government of Ivan Kostov, but once again this did not take the form of the creation of institutional mechanisms within the cabinet. Secure in his political dominance, Kostov did little to strengthen formal cabinet coordination. While the standing order of 1999 did empower the council of ministers to establish standing cabinet committees, Kostov was reluctant to use that right. No formal cabinet committees were established, and while the cabinet was supported by a Council of Structural Reform and a Council of Education, Science, Culture, Health, and Social Reform, both of these councils were purely advisory. The most extensive structure was developed in the area of EU integration. The prime minister chaired a Council on European Integration at ministerial level. Below this, a Coordination Council chaired by a deputy foreign minister brought together the chairmen of thirty working groups (each dealing with a chapter of the *acquis*), generally at the level of deputy minister. In addition, a Directorate for EU Integration and Relations with International Financial Institutions was created within the council of ministers' administration to support this process.

To the extent that the cabinet under Kostov became more efficient, this improvement was due largely to the better use of existing procedures. As noted by the head of the Economic Policy Directorate of the council of ministers' administration,

> The preparation of cabinet meetings has improved considerably since 1997. The cabinet agenda is divided into three parts: items on which there is an agreement, items on which there are relatively few differences, and items on which there are substantial disagreements. By going quickly through the first two categories, the cabinet frees up time for the more important third category and can cope with an agenda of considerable size, up to thirty items, in a single meeting. There has also been a clear tendency for the cabinet meetings to be less of a forum for discussion between ministers, who initially considered them almost as party political meetings, and become more businesslike and focused. (interview, September 2000)

As the head of the prime minister's political *cabinet* observed, the requirement that all interministerial consultations have to be completed ten days before discussion in cabinet had become an "iron rule" (interview, September 2000), a point confirmed by the secretary-general of the council of ministers' administration, who noted that "the current procedure [the ten-day term] brings us very much under control, and we have succeeded in applying it for two to three years already" (interview, March 2001).

PARTY-BASED POLITICAL COORDINATION DEVICES

The use of party-based, rather than executive-based, coordination mechanisms has been an enduring feature of the Bulgarian transition. The pattern was set in the communist era, when party institutions such as the Politburo, the secretariat, and the sectoral departments of the Central Committee were largely responsible for policymaking and for holding together an institutionally highly fragmented central government system. The domination of the former Communist Party in the early stages of the transition to democracy meant that the party leadership continued to make the key policy choices and to resolve policy conflicts. The fact that the BSP leaders deliberately stayed out of the government until 1994 meant that the prime minister was reduced to a rather marginal role. Even when Videnov took over as prime minister following BSP's emphatic victory in the 1994 elections, he preferred to coordinate the work of his colleagues relying on his position as party leader rather than as prime minister. Ministers who did not enjoy a strong standing within the party found it rather difficult to even see the prime minister, as happened to finance minister Dimitur Kostov in 1996. The BSP's dominance of the Bulgarian party system was succeeded by the supremacy of the UDF, following the humiliating collapse of the BSP government in the midst of hyperinflation and street demonstrations in January–February 1997.

The delayed nature of the Bulgarian transition meant that the UDF's victory in the April 1997 elections was not a normal swing of the political pendulum but rather an equivalent to the Civic Forum–Public against Violence's overthrow of communism in Czechoslovakia in 1989. Prime minister Ivan Kostov enjoyed a virtually complete political preeminence over his cabinet, based on his position as UDF party leader—a preeminence demonstrated dramatically in December 1999, when he was able to dismiss two-thirds of his ministers without calling into question his own position. Kostov was able to use his political dominance to achieve relatively effective coordination, even within the decentralized institutional setup of the council of ministers, by speeding up the process of preparation of proposals and their discussion in cabinet. In particular, he made extensive use of preparatory meetings to discuss and resolve problems over proposed agenda items in advance of the formal cabinet meeting. Two types of such meetings have been used. The first is codified in article 97.2 of the standing order for the operation of the council of ministers and is defined as a "working meeting." It takes place at least three days before the formal meeting of the council of ministers and has the task of working out the agenda for that meeting. The working meeting is chaired by the minister of state administration, a new position created by Kostov, and it includes the head of the prime minister's political *cabinet* and the heads of departments of the council of ministers' administration. If necessary, the minister of state administration can also invite the secretaries-general of the ministries and/or the heads of the political cabinets to the ministers. The second type of preparatory meeting is not formalized. It is usually attended by the prime minister, the deputy prime ministers, the head of the prime minister's political cabinet, and the head of the Government Information Service, and it meets just before the formal meeting of the cabinet. This meeting functions as an inner cabinet, although the term is not used explicitly. The operation of these mechanisms depended greatly on Kostov's political leverage, directly in the case of the inner cabinet and indirectly in the case of the minister of state administration, a position to which Kostov appointed a thrusting UDF party activist. In December 1999, following his drastic reshuffle, Kostov himself took over the post of minister of state administration.

THE POWERS AND ORGANIZATION OF THE
CENTER OF GOVERNMENT

Under communism, the council of ministers' administration was geared largely to the implementation of the decisions of the Communist Party's policymaking bodies. This meant that the administration, while relatively competent in the tasks of oversight and control, did not concern itself overtly with the legal status of the acts that it was implementing and lacked the capacity to initiate and develop policies. While relatively good progress has been made in the course of the 1990s toward the overcoming of the first deficiency, the administration's policymaking capacity has remained rather rudimentary. The council of ministers' administration has thus failed to become a true center of government.

We can follow the evolution of the council of ministers' administration by analyzing the successive standing orders that determine its structure and organization. The standing order issued by the Berov government in March 1993 defined the task of the administration as that of supporting the council of ministers by means of functional and service departments. The administration was expected to give an opinion on the legality and expediency of submissions to the council of ministers; participate in the finalization of acts adopted by the council, the prime minister, or the deputy prime ministers; and participate in the drafting of submissions to the council if expressly requested by the proposing department. The prime minister approved the structure and composition of the administration, of his own personal *cabinet*, and of those of the deputy prime ministers. The administration had four functional departments: legal; social and economic affairs; local administration; and social order, responsible for relations with trade unions and employers. The administration was headed by a secretary-general, who distributed administrative tasks between the departments, managed the work of the heads of departments, and controlled the implementation of tasks resulting from acts of the council of ministers, the prime minister, and the deputy prime ministers. The secretary-general was accountable to the prime minister and the deputy prime ministers in their areas of responsibility. The prime minister also had the power to appoint the heads of departments of the council of ministers' administration upon the proposal of the secretary-general. The activities of these departments were regulated by a standing order confirmed by the prime minister. While the list of prime ministerial powers may seem extensive, they related primarily to the appointment of officeholders and the formal determination of the activities of the administration. The prime minister did not have the power to direct the activities of the administration on a day-to-day basis, as the administration's main function was to serve the council of ministers as a collective body.

The modifications adopted by the Indzhova government in November 1994 had the effect of weakening the powers of the prime minister over the council of ministers' administration. While in the 1993 order it was the prime minister who made decisions on the creation, abolition, and transformation of the functional departments of the council of ministers, the 1994 revision transferred that responsibility to the council of ministers. In determining the basic duties of the functional departments, the prime minister now had to coordinate with the secretary-general. The prime minister continued to approve the structure and staff plan of the council of ministers' administration, but his decision had to be based upon a proposal from the secretary-general. Finally, the prime minister could no longer approve the personal *cabinets* of the deputy prime ministers. The ultimate effect of the 1994 standing order was therefore to strengthen the powers of the deputy prime ministers and the council of ministers vis-à-vis those of the prime minister.

The standing orders issued by the socialist government in 1994–1997 went in the opposite direction and resulted in the partial strengthening of the powers of the prime minister. In the 1995 standing order, the prime minister regained the right to determine, without recourse to the council of ministers, the establishment, transformation, and abolition of the functional departments of the administration and the right to appoint and dismiss members of the political *cabinets* of the deputy prime ministers, although that had to take place on their motion. The prime minister's power was also enhanced by a new provision that, in absence of the secretary-general, his tasks were to be performed by an official appointed by the prime minister.

The 1996 standing order was the first one since the start of transition to at least attempt to address the lack of policymaking capacity within the council of ministers' administration. The order tried to resolve the problem by establishing target (*tselevi*) directorates dealing with specific policy areas, such as international integration, research, and public relations. The target directorates were developed further in the standing order issued by the Kostov government in 1999. The government not only established new target directorates dealing with European integration, state administration, and economic policy but also provided them with significantly increased staff and resources. The organization and personnel of the council of ministers' administration in March 2001, the high point of the expansion, is shown in table 6.2.

The Kostov government sought to increase the coordinating capacity at the center of government by the introduction of a minister for state administration. The minister displaced the secretary-general as the chief of the council of ministers' administration, the first time since the start of transition that the administration was given a political head, and one of ministerial rank. The minister was also given the task of coordinating and controlling the activities of the secretaries-general of the line ministries, thus creating a potentially powerful coordination network. Kostov's assumption of the position of minister of state administration in December 1999 was an indication of the importance that the prime minister attached to it.

The reforms undertaken by Kostov increased the efficiency of the operation of the council of ministers' administration. The specialized directorates of the administration played an important role in reviewing submissions from the line ministries to the cabinet. The main contribution of the directorates, however, came less in terms of substance than in terms of ensuring

Table 6.2. Organization and Personnel of the Council of Ministers' Administration, March 2001

Administrative body	Personnel (no.)
General Administration	
Directorate "Governmental Chancellery"	60
Organization of Sittings Department	39
Records and Archive Department	11
Protocol Department	9
Directorate "Financial and Economic Activity"	108
Budget, Bookkeeping and Human Resources Department	14
Management of Ownership Department	7
Technical Service and Supply Department	74
Representative and Repose Activities Department	5
Specialized Administration[a]	
Law Directorate	27
State Administration Directorate	11
Regional Coordination Directorate	9
Public Procurement Directorate	10
Economic Policy Directorate	20
National Economy Department	7
Investments and Concessions Department	9
Directorate for Information and Public Relations	29
Information Department	10
Analysis, Public Relations and European Integration Department	10
Reception Department	6
Information Technology and Communication Directorate	19
Television Studio Department	5
Directorate for Ecclesiastical Matters	4
Directorate of European Integration and Relations with International Financial Institutions	25
International Financial Institutions Department	6
European Integration Department	15
Administration of Councils Attached to the Council of Ministers	
Administration of the Council for Security	10
Secretariat of the National Council for Tripartite Cooperation	2
Secretary and Liaison Unit (*zveno*) of the Interadministrative Council for Questions of the Military-Industrial Complex and Mobilization Capacity	4
Secretary and Liaison Unit of the National Council for Ethnic and Demographic Questions	4
Total	387

[a]The competence of the directorates in the specialized administration of the Council of Ministers is specified in detail in section 2, articles 99–107, of the standing order of the Council of Ministers (*State Gazette*, no. 103, 1999).

that submissions to the cabinet were presented in the appropriate format. The head of the Economic Policy Directorate noted that

> many of the proposals that are produced in the ministries are unfinished, and there is therefore considerable scope for the [Economic Policy] Directorate's intervention. It is not that the ministries lack substantive expertise but rather experience in drafting documents in an effective format. The ministries have their own legal departments, and they are reasonably effective in purely legal terms. They miss quite a lot, however, on the methodological level. For example, when there is a request for extra spending, there is no framework for evaluating results. In some cases the directorate has had virtually to rewrite the ministries' proposals. In order not to take too much time with correspondence going to and fro, the directorate often prefers to invite experts from the ministry concerned and sort out the problems in one meeting.... While the opinions of the directorate have no binding force, they are respected both by the ministries and by the cabinet, which recognize its administrative competence, especially in drafting documents and its unique position to oversee the entire national economy and thus be aware of problems that may escape the attention of the sectoral ministries or even the Ministry of Finance. Indeed, the ministries actively seek out the directorate's involvement because they think that if a draft law has been revised by the directorate, it is almost certain to pass through the cabinet.... Disagreements are very few, especially as the directorate's recommendations are on the expert level. (interview, September 2000)

While the specialized departments were relatively successful in improving the quality of submissions coming to the cabinet, they were not involved extensively in policy coordination, largely because of a lack of hierarchical powers vis-à-vis the ministries. They could, however, provide some administrative support to the head of prime minister's political *cabinet*, who could exercise some direct control over the ministries on a political basis (more on this later). The Economic Policy Directorate, for instance, reviewed the economic program of the government and helped the head of the prime minister's *cabinet* to oversee its implementation but in a strictly expert role:

> The government's program is a political document, and the directorate treats it as a given. [Its] task, which [it] will do for any incoming government, is to translate the political commitments into the language of administration. After the review, the directorate makes a list of the administrative tasks that would need to be done to put the program into effect and then sends it to the head of the prime minister's political cabinet. Of course, in the course of a government's life, the program may be revised, and at these points the directorate is brought in as [an expert].... [It hosts] meetings of economic experts from the ministries. The ministries recognize the directorate's expertise, especially in terms of administrative competence, and are willing to send their experts. After these meetings, the directorate prepares an expert document, which is sent to

the head of the prime minister's political cabinet and the political cabinet of the respective minister. (interview, September 2000)

Under Kostov, the prime minister's political *cabinet* played an active role in coordinating the work of ministries. This was done through a number of devices. The most well-established mechanism involved a weekly meeting on Monday morning between the prime minister, the deputy prime minister for economic policy, the head of the prime minister's political *cabinet*, the secretary-general of the council of ministers' administration, and the head of the Public Relations Directorate of the council of ministers' administration. The latter is a civil servant, but by a provision of the law on public administration she is also a member of the prime minister's *cabinet*. The meeting considered the tasks for the coming week and lasted for about half an hour. This meeting was followed by a meeting between the head of the prime minister's political *cabinet* and the heads of political *cabinets* of all the ministries. At this meeting, the heads of the political *cabinets* reported on the work of their ministries in the past week, while the head of the prime minister's *cabinet* "instructed" them on the tasks for the coming week (interview, September 2000).

In addition to this regular mechanism, the head of the prime minister's political *cabinet* often acted as a "transmitter" of the prime minister's wishes (interview, September 2000). He did not have formal hierarchical powers vis-à-vis the ministers, but his closeness to the prime minister usually meant that the messages he passed on were difficult to ignore. The coordinating capacity of the prime minister's political *cabinet* was restricted, however, by its very limited resources. The head of the *cabinet* and the parliamentary secretary were the only political appointees, and the *cabinet* contained no economic experts. The head of the *cabinet* recognized clearly the institutional deficiencies:

> The political cabinet should become a mirror image of the government, with an advisor responsible for each ministry. Ideally, on each question, there should be a confrontation between the cabinet advisor and the minister involved, with the prime minister acting as an arbiter. At the moment, to solve any question, the prime minister has to do everything himself from A to Z, and he has to do that dozens of times a day. He is extremely productive; he does the work of a thousand people, but this is wearing him down and it is not a durable system. (interview, September 2000)

While the institutional arrangements put in place under Kostov succeeded in creating, through the specialized directorates of the council of ministers' administration, a relatively effective control mechanism over the submissions coming to the cabinet from the line ministries, the council of ministers' administration did not acquire policymaking capability sufficient to offer a substantive challenge to the proposals put forward by line ministries. The prime minister's political *cabinet*, or rather its head, played an important coordinating role but on the basis of rather meager resources. Attempts to strengthen the coordinating capacity of the Bulgarian center of government ran counter to the deeply entrenched traditions of ministerial autonomy, and that limited their chances of success.

THE POLITICS–ADMINISTRATION NEXUS

Postcommunist governments in Bulgaria have found it difficult to strike a balance between the twin imperatives of depoliticization of the low- and middle-level civil service and the regulated politicization of a top layer of administrative positions, which could help the executive in the exercise of its coordinating functions. Prior to the adoption of a Civil Service Act by the Kostov government in 1999, no general regulation of the civil service existed. Civil servants were treated as ordinary employees under the labor code, which provided no protection against dismissal on political grounds. Before 1989, the leading administrative personnel were closely linked to the Communist Party through the *nomenklatura* system. The first two governments of the Bulgarian Socialist Party after 1989 confined themselves to dismissing old political cadres from the military and intelligence services. In 1991, the UDF government led by Philip Dimitrov launched a comprehensive decommunization campaign. The government dismissed 260 employees, approximately half of the staff, in the administration of the council of ministers. In the Ministry of Foreign Affairs, 320 employees were dismissed, as were a large number of generals and about one thousand officers from the Ministry of Defense. While no detailed information is available with respect to the extent of personnel changes under the Berov, Indzhova, and Videnov governments, there are some indications that they carried out less-radical changes than those of the Dimitrov government. None of these governments, however, showed any willingness to regulate the status of civil servants (Georgiev 1999).

The Kostov government has been the first one to make a determined effort at public administration reform. This has been due largely to the realization that continuing delay in this area might have a serious negative impact on Bulgaria's chances of EU accession (European Commission 1997, 1999a). Once Kostov realized the problem, he provided strong and consistent political leadership, helped by the newly created minister for state administration, the building of an active reform team, and the subsequent establishment of an effective Directorate for State Administration in the council of ministers' administration. These efforts bore fruit with the adoption of a public administration law in 1998 and a civil service law in 1999.

Under the public administration law, the administrative guidance of ministries is performed by secretaries-general, who are appointed by the relevant minister. The secretary-general is responsible for the implementation of the instructions of the relevant minister and for coordinating and controlling the work of the ministry's administration. While the legal description of the secretary-general's functions assigns him to a strictly administrative role, there are also elements of political discretion and control, since he is appointed by the minister and his appointment is limited to a period of five years. The secretary-general is subject to dual supervision: first, by his own minister and, second, by the minister for state administration, who coordinates and controls the activities of secretaries-general throughout the government. Apart from the secretary-general heading the administration, ministries also have a parliamentary secretary and a deputy minister, who are considered to be political staff. The administrative guidance of units within the ministerial administration is performed by directors-general (directorate-general), directors (directorate), heads (department), and heads (section). Administrative staff are appointed by the ministry, by the head of the relevant administration, or by a deputy authorized by the head of the administration.

The Kostov government also made progress with the regulation of the status of civil servants. The civil service law of 21 July 1999 is intended to establish a "corps" of professional civil servants. Based on a traditional threefold distinction made already by the precommunist civil service legislation, the law differentiates between leadership, expert, and technical functions and posts. Among these categories, the law confines the civil servant status to those employees who perform leading functions or provide expert services. Persons who are concerned with technical functions in the administration are excluded from becoming civil servants (Bozhidarova, Kolcheva, and Velinova 1999). The law thus reverses the equalization of civil servants and ordinary public employees that was introduced by the labor code of 1951. The law follows the "classic" civil service model by providing for the political neutrality of low and middle-ranking civil servants. A civil servant's employment relationship may not be changed unilaterally, although the law opens up a loophole by providing that the relationship may be terminated by the appointing authority if the authority abolishes the post or if there is an "objective impossibility" of fulfilling the civil servant's duties. Recognizing the functional need of governments to be supported in their executive role by politically reliable civil servants, the law also creates a category of politically appointable civil servants, which includes secretaries-general, the chairmen of state agencies and state commissions, and the directors of executive agencies. The law also provides for the creation of political *cabinets*, the members of which, however, are not given civil service status. Experts and technical staff of the political *cabinets* may not perform administrative functions, and the expenditure for the *cabinets* and their staff constitute a separate budget item.

The civil service law was not put into effect immediately, since the government needed to implement several preparatory measures. A regulation on the office of the civil service, a uniform classification of positions in public administration, and a regulation on its application have been adopted. Following the commitment to establish a State Administration Commission to control the observation of the status of the state servant and to enact rules of procedure for it, a process of consultation is under way to prepare a draft for these rules. A draft of a civil service code of conduct has been developed. In meeting the commitment to introduce a general system for the development of professional skills and training of state servants, an Institute of Public Administration and European Integration has been set up, attached to the council of ministers.

In the initial formulation of the civil service law, the government tried to exclude members of the former Bulgarian Communist Party *nomenklatura* and the state security service from occupying leading functions in the state administration for five years. The constitutional court rejected this provision as contradicting the constitutional principle of equality and the right of work.

While the Kostov government has shown admirable energy in preparing and adopting the acts on public administration and the civil service, it is too early to assess whether they mark a genuine departure from the time-honored tradition of unregulated politicization. The implementation of these laws is at such an early stage that it is premature to judge to what extent the new legal framework would be put into practice. The real test would come with a change of government. For Kostov, one of the reasons for the consolidation of the status of civil servants was the wish to entrench in their positions the large number of UDF-sponsored appointees who colonized the administration, down to the level of head of department or even lower, following the UDF's overwhelming victory in the 1997 general elections. A successor government may not look favorably at these appointees, and its reaction to them will be critical in determining the prospects for the consolidation of a civil service system that combines legally regulated politicization at the top, with the depoliticization and professionalization of the mid- and lower-level administrators.

CONCLUSION

After a brief period in the early democratic transition, when the powers of the president were left deliberately undefined, the 1991 constitution put in place a semipresidential presidential system in which the president has virtually no executive powers. While presidents have played an important

**Table 6.3.   Types of Government, Core Executives, and Centers of Government in
Bulgaria, 1989–2001**

Type of Government	Type of Core Executive	Type of Center of Government
1989–2001: Cabinet	1989–1997: Decentralized ministerial 1997–2001: Centralized prime ministerial	1989–2001: Government registrar

role in government formation in crisis situations, they have usually taken a
backseat and have rarely challenged the authority of the government. By
contrast, the executive's relationship with parliament continues to evolve,
driven largely by the fluctuating degree of party discipline. The institutionalization of the internal organization offers a similarly complex picture. Some
progress has been made toward reducing the excessively high number of
ministries inherited from the communist period, but the division of labor
between ministries remains driven by political contingency rather than functional rationale. Some progress has also been made toward the creation of
a uniform template for the internal organization of the ministries, although
the split between high-status and well-resourced departments, such as those
dealing with EU accession, and the rest of the ministerial administration has
created potential for fragmentation and conflict. The type of government
has remained in the cabinet mode throughout, but as in the Czech Republic, a prime minister who could exercise personal and party-political
dominance over his ministerial colleagues, as was the case with Kostov
in 1997–2001, could create a centralized prime ministerial core executive
(see table 6.3).

Kostov's reliance of party-political mechanisms meant, however, that he
was uninterested in the strengthening of coordinating institutions within the
executive. Prime ministers who could not command Kostov's political authority found themselves virtually powerless, a weakness reinforced by the
incapacity of the center of government, which has retained its communist-
era role of government registrar to provide policymaking support to the
prime minister. The domination of the Bulgarian party system by one party,
the BSP in 1989–1997 and the UDF in 1997–2001, and the extensive reliance
on party-political mechanisms have created rather unfavorable conditions
not only for the depoliticization of the bulk of administrative personnel but
also for the structured and effective politicization of top-level civil servants.
The case of Bulgaria, like that of the Czech Republic, demonstrates both the
usefulness of party-political mechanisms in compensating for the weakness
of centralizing institutions within the executive and their pernicious effect
in preventing the development of such institutions.

ANNEX

Table 6.4.   Composition of Bulgarian Cabinets, 1986–2001
Table 6.4a Georgi Atanasov Cabinet, 19/6/1986–8/2/1990

Chairman of the Council of Ministers (Prime Minister) Georgi Atanasov (19/6/1986[a]–8/2/1990[b])	
First Dept. Chairman of the CoM:	Andrei Lukanov, 19/6/1986–19/8/1987
Chairman of State Council for Research and Technologies	Stoian Markov, 19/6/1986–19/8/1987
Dept. Chairman of CoM and Chairman of the Council for Economy	Ognian Doinov, 19/6/1986–19/8/1987
Dept. Chairman of CoM and Chairman of the Social Council	Georgi Karamanev, 19/6/1986–19/8/1987
Dept. Chairman of CoM and Chairman of the Council for Ecclesiastical Development	Georgi Yordanov, 19/6/1986–19/8/1987
Dept. Chairman of CoM and Chairman of the State Commission for Planning	Ivan Iliev, 19/6/1986–19/8/1987
Dept. Chairman of CoM and Chairman of the Council for Urban and Forestry Economy	Alexi Ivanov, 26/12/1986–19/8/1987
Deputy Chairmen of CoM	Grigor Stoichkov, 19/6/1986–18/12/1989
	Kiril Zarev, 19/6/1986–18/8/1987
	Georgi Yordanov, 4/8/1989–18/8/1987
	Petko Danchev, 4/8/1989–17/11/1989
	Georgi Pirinski, 17/11/1989–8/2/1990
	Kiril Zarev, 17/11/1989–8/2/1990
	Mincho Yovchev, 17/11/1989–8/2/1990
	Stoian Mihailov, 17/11/1989–8/2/1990
	Nadia Asparuhova, 18/12/1989–8/2/1990
Ministry of Foreign Affairs	Petur Mladenov, 19/6/1986–17/11/1989
	Boiko Dimitrov, 17/11/1989–8/2/1990
Ministry of Interior	Dimitur Stoianov, 19/6/1986–19/12/1989
	Georgi Tanev, 19/12/1989–27/12/1989
	Atanas Semerdzhiev, 27/12/1989–8/2/1990
Ministry of People's Education[c]	Ilcho Dimitrov, 19/6/1986–19/8/1987
Ministry of People's Education[d]	Assen Hadzhiolov, 4/7/1989–8/2/1990
Ministry of Finance	Belcho Belchev, 19/6/1986–19/8/1987
Ministry of Finance[e]	Belcho Belchev, 17/11/1989–8/02/90

(Continued)

Tabel 6.4a *Continued*

Ministry of Justice	Svetla Daskalova, 19/6/1986–8/02/90
Ministry of Defense	Dobri Dzhurov, 19/6/1986–8/02/90
Ministry of Trade	Hristo Hristov, 19/6/1986–19/8/1987
Ministry of Transport	Vassil Tsanov, 19/6/1986–22/11/1988
	Georgi Tanev, 22/11/1988–19/12/1988
	Trifon Pashov, 19/12/1988–8/2/1990
Ministry of Agriculture and Forestry	Alexi Ivanov, 19/8/1987–19/12/1988
	Georgi Menov, 19/12/1988–8/2/1990
Ministry of People's Health[f]	Radoi Popivanov, 19/6/1986–19/8/1987
Ministry of People's Health and Social Care	Mincho Neichev, 19/8/1987–8/2/1990
Ministry of Foreign Trade Relations[g]	Andrei Lukanov, 19/8/1987–17/11/1989
	Hristo Hristov, 17/11/1989–8/2/1990
Ministry of Economic Planning	Stoian Ovcharov, 19/8/1987–17/11/1989
	Kiril Zarev, 17/11/1989–8/2/1990
	First deputy Petur Balevski,
	17/11/1989–8/2/1990[h]
Ministry of Industry and Technologies	Mincho Yovchev, 17/11/1989–8/2/1990
Ministry of Internal Trade	Ivan Shiativ, 17/11/1989–8/2/1990
Ministry of Construction and Public Works	Petur Petrov, 17/11/1989–8/2/1990
State Committee for Environment	Nikolai Diulgerov, 20/11/1989–22/11/1989
Ministry of Culture, Science, and Education	Georgi Yordanov, 19/8/1987–4/7/1989
National Council for Education, Science and Culture[i]	Alexandur Fol, 4/7/1989–17/11/1989
Committee for Science and Higher Education	Alexandur Iankov, 28/7/1989–8/2/1990
Committee for State Control	Georgi Georgiev, 19/6/1986–8/2/1990

[a]Acts 2046 and 2048 (*State Gazette* [*SG*], no. 49, 1986).
[b]Act 160 (*SG*, no. 12, 1990).
[c]Closed down by act 2656, from 19/8/1987.
[d]Created by act 1321, from 4/7/1989.
[e]Created by act 2556, from 20/11/1989.
[f]Ministry of People's Health was transformed into the Ministry of People's Health and Social Care on 19/8/1987.
[g]Created by act 2656, from 19/8/1987.
[h]With ministerial rank.
[i]The Ministry of Culture, Science, and Education was transformed into the National Council for Education, Science, and Culture on 4/8/1989, which was closed down by act 2556, from 20/11/1989.

Table 6.4b Cabinets (Excluding Caretaker Cabinets), 8/2/1990–12/2/1997

Andrei Lukanov 8/2/1990[a]– 22/9/1990[b]	Andrei Lukanov 22/9/1990[c]– 19/12/1990[d]	Dimitur Popov 20/12/1990[e]– 8/11/1991[f]	Philip Dimitrov 8/11/1991[g]– 29/12/1992[h]	Liuben Berov 30/12/1992[i]– 17/10/1994[j]	Zhan Videnov 26/1/1995[k]– 12/2/1997[l]
Dept. Chairmen of CoM:	**Dept. Chairmen of CoM:**	**Dept. Chairmen of CoM:**	**Dept. Chairmen of CoM:**	**Dept. Chairmen of CoM:**	**Deputy Prime Ministers:**
Chudomir Alexandrov, 8/2/1990– 22/9/1990;	Georgi Pirinski, 22/9/1990– 20/12/1990;	Alexandur Tomov, 20/12/1990– 8/11/1991;	Nikolai Vassilev, 8/11/1991– 30/12/1992;	Valentin Karabashev, 30/12/1992– 15/4/1994;	Doncho Konakchiev, 26/1/1995– 12/2/1997;
Belcho Belchev, 8/2/1990– 22/9/1990;	Belcho Belchev, 22/9/1990– 20/12/1990;	Viktor Vulkov, 20/12/1990– 8/11/1991;	Stoian Ganev, 8/11/1991– 20/5/1992;	Neicho Neev, 30/12/1992– 8/9/1993;	Kiril Tsochev, 26/1/1995– 23/7/1996;
Konstantin Kosev, 8/2/1990– 22/9/1990	Nora Ananieva, 22/9/1990– 20/12/1990	Dimitur Ludzhev, 20/12/1990– 8/11/1991	Svetoslav Luchnikov, 20/5/1992– 30/12/1992;	Evgeni Matinchev, 30/12/1992– 17/10/1994;	Rumen Gechev, 26/1/1995– 12/2/1997;
Nora Ananieva, 8/2/1990– 22/9/1990			Ilko Eskenasi, 20/5/1992– 30/12/1992;	Kiril Tsochev, 15/6/1994– 17/10/1994	Svetoslav Shivarov, 26/1/1995– 12/2/1997
			Nikola Bozhilov, 20/5/1992– 30/12/1992		

(Continued)

Table 6.4b   Cabinets (Excluding Caretaker Cabinets), 8/2/1990–12/2/1997 (Continued)

Ministry of Foreign Affairs	Ministry of Foreign Affairs	Ministry of Foreign Affairs	Ministry of Foreign Affairs	Ministry of Foreign Affairs	Ministry of Foreign Affairs
Boiko Dimitrov, 8/2/1990– 22/9/1990	Liuben Gotzev, 22/9/1990– 20/12/1990	Viktor Vulkov, 20/12/1990– 8/11/1991	Stoian Ganev, 8/11/1991– 30/12/1992	Liuben Berov, 30/12/1992– 23/6/1993; Stanislav Daskalov, 23/6/1993– 17/10/1994	Georgi Pirinski, 26/1/1995– 13/11/1996; Irina Bokova, 14/11/1996– 12/2/1997
Ministry of Interior	**Ministry of Interior**	**Ministry of Interior**	**Ministry of Interior**	**Ministry of Interior**	**Ministry of Interior**
Atanas Semerdzhiev, 8/2/1990–2/8/1990; Stoian Stoianov, 2/8/1990–5/9/1990; Pencho Penev, 5/9/1990– 22/9/1990	Pencho Penev, 22/9/1990– 20/12/1990	Hristo Danov, 20/12/1990– 8/11/1991	Yordan Sokolov, 8/11/1991– 30/12/1992	Viktor Michailov, 30/12/1992– 17/10/1994	Liubomir Nachev, 26/1/1995– 10/5/1996; Nikolai Dobrev, 10/5/1996– 12/2/1997
Ministry of People's Education	**Ministry of People's Education**	**Ministry of People's Education**[m]			
Konstantin Kossev, 8/2/1990– 22/9/1990	Matei Mateev, 22/9/1990– 20/12/1990	Matei Mateev, 20/12/1990– 8/11/1991			

Ministry of Finance
Belcho Belchev,
8/2/1990–
22/9/1990

Ministry of Justice
Pencho Penev,
8/2/1990–
5/19/1990;
Angel Dzhambazov,
5/9/1990–
22/9/1990

Ministry of People's Defense
Dobri Dzhurov,
8/2/1990–
22/9/1990

Ministry of Economic Planning
Ivan Tenev,
8/2/1990–
22/9/1990

Ministry of Finance
Belcho Belchev,
22/9/1990–
20/12/1990

Ministry of Justice
Angel Dzhambazov,
22/9/1990–
20/12/1990

Ministry of People's Defense
Yordan Mutafchiev,
22/9/1990–
20/12/1990

Ministry of Economic Planning[o]

Ministry of Finance
Ivan Kostov,
20/12/1990–
8/11/1991

Ministry of Justice
Pencho Penev,
20/12/1990–
8/11/1991

Ministry of Defense[n]
Yordan Mutafchiev,
20/12/1990–
8/11/1991

Ministry of Finance
Ivan Kostov,
8/11/1991–
30/12/1992

Ministry of Justice
Svetoslav Luchnikov,
8/11/1991–
30/12/1992

Ministry of Defense
Dimitur Ludzhev,
8/11/1991–
20/5/1992;
Alexandur Staliiski,
20/5/1992–
30/12/1992

Ministry of Finance
Stoian Alexandrov,
30/12/1992–
17/10/1994

Ministry of Justice
Misho Vulchev,
30/12/1992–
15/5/1993;
Petur Kornadzhev,
23/6/1993–
17/10/1994

Ministry of Defense
Valentin Alexandrov,
23/6/1993–
17/10/1994

Ministry of Finance
Dimitur Kostov,
26/1/1995–
12/2/1997

Ministry of Justice
Mladen Cherveniakov,
26/1/1995–
12/2/1997

Ministry of Defense
Dimitur Pavlov,
26/1/1995–
12/2/1997

Ministry of Economic Development
Rumen Gechev,
26/2/1995–
12/2/1997

(Continued)

Table 6.4b   Cabinets (Excluding Caretaker Cabinets), 8/2/1990–12/2/1997 (*Continued*)

Ministry of Industry and Technology	Ministry of Industry and Technology[p]	Ministry of Industry and Trade[q]	Ministry of Trade	Ministry of Industry
Krustio Stanilov, 8/2/1990– 22/9/1990		Ivan Pushkarov, 15/11/1991– 20/5/1992	Valentin Karabashev, 23/6/1993– 15/6/1994; Kiril Tsochev, 15/6/1994– 17/10/1994	Kliment Vuchev, 26/1/1995– 10/6/1996; Liubomir Dachev, 10/6/1996– 12/2/1997

Ministry of Trade and Services	Ministry of Trade and Services	Ministry of Industry, Trade, and Services[r]	Ministry of Trade[s]	Ministry of Industry
Ekaterina Marinova, 8/2/1990– 22/9/1990	Valeri Tsekov, 22/9/1990– 20/12/1990	Ivan Pushkarov, 20/12/1990– 8/11/1991	Alexandur Pramatarski, 20/5/1992– 30/12/1992	Rumen Bikov, 30/12/1992– 17/10/1994

				Ministry of Industry
				Rumen Bikov, 20/5/1992– 30/12/1992

Ministry of Foreign Economic Relations Petur Bashikarov, 8/2/1990– 22/9/1990	**Ministry of Foreign Economic Relations** Atanas Paparizov, 22/9/1990– 20/12/1990	**Ministry of Foreign Economic Relations** Atanas Paparizov, 20/12/1990– 8/11/1991			**Ministry of Trade and Foreign Economic Cooperation** Kiril Tsochev, 26/1/1995– 23/1/1996; Atanas Paparizov, 23/1/1996– 12/2/1997
Ministry of Science and Higher Education Assen Hadzhiolov, 8/2/1990– 22/9/1990	**Ministry of Science and Higher Education** Ilia Konev, 22/9/1990– 20/12/1990	**Ministry of Science and Higher Education** Georgi Fotev, 20/12/1990– 8/11/1991	**Ministry of Education and Science** Nikolai K. Vassilev, 8/11/1991– 30/12/1992	**Ministry of Science and Education[1]** Marko Todorov, 23/6/1993– 17/10/1994	**Ministry of Education, Science, and Technologies** Ilcho Dimitrov, 26/1/1995– 12/2/1997
Ministry of People's Health and Social Wealth Ivan Chernozemski, 8/2/1990– 22/9/1990	**Ministry of Health** Ivan Chernozemski, 22/9/1990– 20/12/1990	**Ministry of Health** Ivan Chernozemski, 20/12/1990– 8/11/1991	**Ministry of Health** Nikola Bozhilov, 8/11/1991– 30/12/1992	**Ministry of Health** Tancho Gulakov, 23/6/1993– 17/10/1994	**Ministry of Health** Mimi Vitkova, 26/1/1995– 12/2/1997

(*Continued*)

Table 6.4b   Cabinets (Excluding Caretaker Cabinets), 8/2/1990–12/2/1997 (Continued)

Ministry of Agriculture and Food Industry	Ministry of Agriculture and Food Industry	Ministry of Agriculture and Food Industry	Ministry of Agriculture[u]	Ministry of Agriculture	Ministry of Agriculture and Food Industry
Todor Pandov, 8/2/1990– 22/9/1990	Todor Pandov, 22/9/1990– 20/12/1990	Boris Spirov, 20/12/1990– 8/11/1991	Stanislav Dimitrov, 8/11/1991– 20/5/1992	Georgi Tanev, 23/6/1993– 17/10/1994	Vassil Chichibaba, 26/1/1995– 23/1/1996; Svetoslav Shivarov, 23/1/1996– 10/6/1996; Krustio Trendafilov, 10/6/1996– 12/2/1997
			Ministry of Agricultural Development, Land Use, and Restitution of Land Property Georgi Stoianov, 20/5/1992– 30/12/1992		

Ministry of Construction, Architecture, and Public Works Ivan Kamenov, 8/2/1990– 22/9/1990	**Ministry of Construction, Architecture, and Public Works** Ivan Kamenov, 22/9/1990– 20/12/1990	**Ministry of Construction, Architecture, and Public Works[v]** Liubomir Pelovski, 23/03/1991– 8/11/1991	**Ministry of Territorial Development, Housing Policy, and Construction[w]** Nikolai Karadimov, 20/5/1992– 30/12/1992	**Ministry of Territorial Development and Construction** Hristo Toshev, 23/6/1993– 17/10/1994	**Ministry of Territorial Development and Construction** Doncho Konakchiev, 26/1/1995– 12/2/1997
Ministry of Transport Vesselin Pavlov, 8/2/1990– 22/9/1990	**Ministry of Transport and Communications** Atanas Popov, 22/9/1990– 20/12/1990	**Ministry of Transport[x]** Vesselin Popov, 20/12/1990– 8/11/1991	**Ministry of Transport** Alexandur Alexandrov, 20/5/1992– 30/12/1992	**Ministry of Transport** Neicho Neev, 30/12/1992– 23/6/1993; Kiril Ermenkov, 23/6/1993– 17/10/1994	**Ministry of Transport** Stamen Stamenov, 26/1/1995– 12/2/1997

(Continued)

Table 6.4b Cabinets (Excluding Caretaker Cabinets), 8/2/1990–12/2/1997 (*Continued*)

Committee for State and People's Control
Georgi Georgiev,
8/2/1990–
22/9/1990

Minister without Portfolio
Stefan Stoilov,
8/2/1990–
22/9/1990

Ministry of Environment
Alexandur Haralanov,
8/2/1990–
22/9/1990

Ministry of Culture
Krustio Goranov,
8/2/1990–
22/9/1990

Ministry of Environment
Alexandur Haralanov,
22/9/1990–
20/12/1990

Ministry of Culture
Dimo Dimov,
22/9/1990–
20/12/1990

Ministry of Environment
Dimitur Vodenicharov,
20/12/1990–
8/11/1991

Ministry of Culture
Dimo Dimov
20/12/1990–
8/11/1991

Ministry of Environment
Valentin Vassilev,
20/5/1992–
30/12/1990

Ministry of Culture
Elka Konstantinova,
20/5/1992–
30/12/1992

Ministry of Environment
Valentin Bossevski,
30/12/1992–
17/10/1994

Ministry of Culture[y]
Ivailo Znepolski,
23/6/1993–
17/10/1994

Ministry of Environment
Georgi Georgiev,
26/1/1995–
12/2/1997

Ministry of Culture
Georgi Kostov,
26/1/1995–
10/6/1996;
Ivan Marazov,
10/6/1996–
12/2/1997

Ministry of Employment and Social Care[z]	Ministry of Labor and Social Care[aa]	Ministry of Labor and Social Welfare	Ministry of Labor and Social Welfare	Ministry of Labor and Social Welfare	Ministry of Energy and Energy Resources[bb]
Emilia Maslarova, 22/9/1990–20/12/1990	Emilia Maslarova, 20/12/1990–8/11/1991	Vassil Vanov, 20/5/1992–30/12/1992	Evgeni Matinchev, 30/12/1992–17/10/1994	Mincho Koralski, 26/1/1995–12/2/1997	Rumen Ovcharov, 10/6/1996–12/2/1997

[a] Decision of the Eleventh National Assembly, from 8/2/90 (State Gazette [SG], no. 14, 1990).

[b] On 22/8/90 the government resigned but continued to act until the election of a new council of ministers, on 22/9/90 (SG, no. 77, 1990).

[c] Andrei Lukanov was elected chairman of the council of ministers on 20/9/90 with decision of the Seventh Grand National Assembly. The ministers were elected on 22/9/90 (SG, no. 77, 1990).

[d] On 30/9/90 the government resigned but continued to act until the election of a new council of ministers, on 20/12/90.

[e] Decision 168 (SG, no. 1, 1991).

[f] Decision of the Thirty-sixth National Assembly (SG, no. 92, 1991).

[g] Decision of the Thirty-sixth National Assembly (SG, no. 94, 1991).

[h] On 28/10/92 the government lost a vote of confidence in parliament but continued to act until the election of a new council of ministers, on 30/12/92.

[i] Decision of the Thirty-sixth National Assembly (SG, no. 1, 1993).

[j] On 2/9/94 the government resigned but continued to act until the election of a new council of ministers, on 17/10/94.

[k] Decision of the Thirty-sixth National Assembly, from 26/1/95 (SG, no. 10, 1995).

[l] On 28/12/96 the government resigned but continued to act until the election of a new council of ministers, on 12/2/97.

[m] Closed by a decision of the National Assembly (SG, no. 94, 15/11/91).

[n] The Ministry of People's Defense was transformed into the Ministry of Defense with a decision of the Thirty-sixth National Assembly, from 20/12/90.

[o] The ministry was expected to be restructured; therefore, no ministers were elected but only deputy ministers.

[p] The ministry was expected to be restructured; therefore, no ministers were elected but only deputy ministers.

[q] Created by a decision of the Thirty-sixth National Assembly (SG, no. 94, 15/11/91).

[r] Created by a decision of the Thirty-sixth National Assembly, from 20/3/90.

[s] Created by a decision of the Thirty-sixth National Assembly, from 20/5/91.

[t] The Ministry of Education, Science, and Culture was transformed into the Ministry of Science and Education and the Ministry of Culture on 23/6/93.

[u] The Ministry of Agriculture was closed down, and the Ministry of Agricultural Development, Land Use, and Restitution of Land Property was established on 20/5/92.

[v] Recreated by decree 106, from 23/3/92.

[w] Created by a decision of the Thirty-sixth National Assembly, from 20/5/91.

[x] The Ministry of Transport and Communications was transformed into the Ministry of Transport with a decision of the Thirty-sixth National Assembly, from 20/12/90.

[y] The Ministry of Education, Science, and Culture was transformed into the Ministry of Science and Education and the Ministry of Culture on 23/6/93.

[z] Created by a decision of the Seventh Grand National Assembly, from 21/9/90.

[aa] The Ministry of Employment and Social Care was transformed into the Ministry of Labor and Social Care with a decision of the Thirty-sixth National Assembly, from 20/12/90.

[bb] Created by a decision of the Thirty-eighth National Assembly, from 10/6/96.

Table 6.4c Composition of Caretaker Cabinets

	Caretaker Government with Prime Minister Reneta Indzhova 17/10/1994[a]–26/1/1995[b]	Caretaker Government with Prime Minister Stefan Sofianski 12/2/1997[c]–21/5/1997[d]
Deputy prime ministers	Hristina Vucheva, 17/10/1994–26/1/1995 Ivailo Trifonov, 17/10/1994–26/1/1995 Nikola Vassilev, 17/10/1994–26/1/1995	Alexandur Bozhkov, 12/2/1997–21/5/1997 Haralambi Anchev, 12/2/1997–21/5/1997
Ministry of Foreign Affairs	Ivan Stanchov, 21/10/1994–26/1/1995	Stoian Stalev, 12/2/1997–21/5/1997
Ministry of Interior	Chavdar Chervenkov, 17/10/1994–26/1/1995	Bogomil Bonev, 12/2/1997–21/5/1997
Ministry of Defense	Boiko Noev, 17/10/1994–26/1/1995	Georgi Ananiev, 12/2/1997–21/5/1997
Ministry of Finance	Hristina Vucheva, 17/10/1994–26/1/1995	Svetoslav Gavriiski, 12/2/1997–21/5/1997
Ministry of Transport	Milcho Kovachev, 17/10/1994–26/1/1995	Vilhelm Kraus, 12/2/1997–21/5/1997
Ministry of Environment	Valentin Bossevski, 17/10/1994–26/1/1995	Ivan Philipov, 12/2/1997–21/5/1997
Ministry of Health	Nikola Vassilev, 17/10/1994–26/1/1995	Emil Takov, 12/2/1997–21/5/1997
Ministry of Culture	Ivailo Znepolski, 17/10/1994–26/1/1995	Emil Tabakov, 12/2/1997–21/5/1997
Ministry of Science and Education	Marko Todorov, 17/10/1994–26/1/1995	Ivan Lalov, 12/2/1997–21/5/1997
Ministry of Education, Science, and Technology		
Ministry of Justice	Teodor Chipev, 17/10/1994–26/1/1995	Haralambi Anchev, 12/2/1997–21/5/1997

Ministry of Agriculture	Rumen Hristov, 17/10/1994–26/1/1995	Ministry of Agriculture and Food Industry	Rumen Hristov, 12/2/1997–21/5/1997
Ministry of Industry	Vitko Elenkov, 17/10/1994–26/1/1995	Ministry of Industry	Alexandur Bozhkov, 12/2/1997–21/5/1997
Ministry of Trade	Kiril Velev, 17/10/1994–26/1/1995	Ministry of Trade and Foreign Economic Cooperation	Daniela Bobeva, 12/2/1997–21/5/1997
Ministry of Labor and Social Care	Yordan Hristoskov, 17/10/1994–26/1/1995	Ministry of Labor and Social Care	Ivan Neikov, 12/2/1997–21/5/1997
Ministry of Territorial Development and Construction	Daniel Leviev, 17/10/1994–26/1/1995	Ministry of Territorial Development and Construction	Nikola Karadimov, 12/2/1997–21/5/1997
		Ministry of Economic Policy	Krassimir Angarski, 23/3/1997–21/5/1997
		Ministry of Energy	Georgi Stoilov, 23/3/1997–21/5/1997

[a] Decree 210, from 17/10/94 (*State Gazette* [*SG*], no. 85, 1994).
[b] Decision of the Thirty-eighth National Assembly, from 26/1/95 (*SG*, no. 10, 1995).
[c] Decree 100, from 12/2/97 (*SG*, no. 15, 1997).
[d] Decision of the Thirty-eighth National Assembly, from 21/5/97 (*SG*, no. 41, 1997).

Table 6.4d Ivan Kostov Cabinets, 21/5/1997–24/7/2001

Position	First Kostov Cabinet 21/5/1997–21/12/1999	Second Kostov Cabinet 21/12/1999–24/7/2001
Prime Minister	Ivan Kostov	Ivan Kostov
Deputy prime ministers	Alexandur Bozhkov	Petur Zhotev
	Evgeni Bakurdzhiev	
	Vesselin Metodiev	
Ministry of Foreign Affairs	Nadezhda Mihailova	Nadezhda Mihailova
Ministry of Interior	Bogomil Bonev	Emanuil Yordanov
Ministry of Defense	Georgi Ananiev	Boiko Noev
Ministry of Finance	Muravei Radev	Muravei Radev
Ministry of Justice and Legal European Integration[a]	Vassil Gotsev	
Ministry of Justice[b]		Teodossi Simeonov
Ministry of Agriculture, Forestry, and Agrarian Reform[c]	Ventsislav Vurbanov	
Ministry of Agriculture and Forestry[d]		Ventsislav Vurbanov
Ministry of Trade and Tourism[e]	Valentin Vassilev	
Ministry of Transport	Vilhelm Kraus	
Ministry of Transport and Communications[f]		Antoni Slavinski
Ministry of Industry	Alexandur Bozhkov	
Ministry of Economy[g]		Petur Zhotev
Ministry of Energy[h]		
Ministry of Regional Development and Public Works[i]	Evgeni Bakurdzhiev	Evgeni Chachev
Ministry of Labor and Social Policy[j]	Ivan Neikov	Ivan Neikov
Ministry of Health	Petur Boiadzhiev	Ilko Semerdzhiev
Ministry of Culture	Emma Moskova	Emma Moskova

Ministry of Education and Science[k]
Ministry of Environment and Waters[l]
Minister of State Administration
Minister without portfolio

Vesselin Metodiev
Evdokia Maneva
Mario Tagarinki

Dimitur Dimitrov
Evdokia Maneva
Ivan Kostov
Alexandur Pramatarski

[a] The Ministry of Justice was transformed into the Ministry of Justice and Legal European Integration with a decision of the National Assembly from 21/05/97 (*State Gazette* [*SG*], no. 41, 1997).

[b] The Ministry of Justice and Legal European Integration was transformed into the Ministry of Justice with a decision of the Thirty-eighth National Assembly, from 21/12/99 (*SG*, no. 112, 1999).

[c] The Ministry of Agriculture and Food Industry was transformed into the Ministry of Agriculture, Forestry, and Agrarian Reform, with a decision of the National Assembly from 21/05/97 (*SG*, no. 41, 1997).

[d] The Ministry of Agriculture, Forestry, and Agrarian Reform was transformed into the Ministry of Agriculture and Forestry with a decision of the Thirty-eighth National Assembly, from 21/12/99 (*SG*, no. 112, 1999).

[e] The Ministry of Trade and Foreign Economic Cooperation was transformed into the Ministry of Trade and Tourism with a decision of the National Assembly from 21/05/97 (*SG*, no. 41, 1997).

[f] The Ministry of Transport was transformed into the Ministry of Transport and Communications with a decision of the Thirty-eighth National Assembly, from 21/12/99 (*SG*, no. 112, 1999).

[g] The Ministry of Industry and the Ministry of Trade and Tourism were transformed into the Ministry of Economy with a decision of the Thirty-eighth National Assembly, from 21/12/99 (*SG*, no. 112, 1999).

[h] The Ministry of Energy was closed down with a decision of the National Assembly from 21/05/97 (*SG*, no. 41, 1997).

[i] The Ministry of Territorial Development and Construction was transformed into the Ministry of Regional Development and Public Works with a decision of the National Assembly from 21/05/97 (*SG*, no. 41, 1997).

[j] The Ministry of Trade and Social Care was transformed into the Ministry of Labor and Social Policy with a decision of the National Assembly from 21/05/97 (*SG*, no. 41, 1997).

[k] The Ministry of Education, Science, and Technologies was transformed into the Ministry of Education and Science with a decision of the National Assembly from 21/05/97 (*SG*, no. 41, 1997).

[l] The Ministry of Environment was transformed into the Ministry of Environment and Waters with a decision of the National Assembly from 21/05/97 (*SG*, no. 41, 1997).

III

COMPARATIVE ASSESSMENTS

7

Executive Trajectories Compared

This chapter summarizes the main empirical findings of chapters 3 to 6 by comparing and contrasting institutional trajectories and outcomes; it interprets the emergent types of government, core executives, and centers of government; it accounts for the cross-country differences found with reference to institutional legacies, critical junctures, and party–actor constellations and choices; and, by way of concluding, it discusses some of the implications of the institutional disjunctures revealed in the empirical analysis.

FROM SUBORDINATED ADMINISTRATION TO CORE EXECUTIVE

The evolution of postcommunist core executives between 1989 and the early twenty-first century can be understood as a succession of more or less successful attempts at transforming a subordinated and fragmented administration into a cohesive government. Such efforts implied the creation of governments endowed with a capacity for the consideration of policy alternatives, making policy choices, and implementing them, and of core executives capable of coordination and arbitration.

Under communism, political decision taking was the prerogative of the Communist Party, which enforced its domination through its formations that run parallel to, and penetrated, all state, economic, and societal institutions. In a double structure, party units virtually duplicated the organizations of the state and were sometimes placed side by side within the same organization. Hence, the state apparatus—including the central government, its ministries, and agencies—had an essentially instrumental function in the execution and implementation of the policies decided by the party

Politburo and the party bureaucracy as the real center of political power. In this sense, one may describe the communist central state executive as being "under-politicized" (Goetz and Wollmann 2001, 865). In addition, at least three further institutional features of the central executive under communism deserve highlighting:

- The central state administration consisted of a multitude of ministries and other central agencies, the majority of which were charged with directing the various industrial branches and subbranches of the state economy under the overarching influence and control of the party. This made for a high degree of organizational fragmentation and sectorization of the central government.
- The council of ministers was formally guided by the principle of collective deliberation and decision taking. Collectivity was formally enshrined, despite the limited autonomous decision-making powers of the council of ministers and its fragmentation into a large number of ministries and central agencies. In practice, the council of ministers functioned as a ministerial rather than a cabinet government, with individual ministers responsible for their actions to the party rather than to their government colleagues.
- Reflecting the ministerial nature of the government, the administration of the council of ministers as the center of government acted largely as the government registrar rather than as a guardian of collective responsibility or vanguard of the chairman of the council of ministers.

The contrast of this model of a subordinated central administration to the position of governments in liberal democratic systems scarcely needs elaborating. Regardless of whether the executive operates in a presidential, semipresidential, or parliamentary system, it regularly acts as a powerful center of political agenda setting, policy initiation, authoritative decision taking, and control over implementation. The government's powers are primary rather than merely the result of delegation by other political institutions, and although political parties influence, and reach into, the state executive, the party bureaucracy does not rival or overshadow the state bureaucracy. The government thus has the role of political leadership. This political leadership function may be concentrated in the office of a directly elected president (presidential government); it may be divided, and often contested, between the president and the government (semipresidential government); it may be focused on the office of a prime minister who dominates within the government (prime ministerial government); it may be vested into the cabinet as a collective and collegiate body (cabinet government); or it may be dispersed amongst ministers (ministerial government).

The postcommunist transformation of central government has thus required the creation of institutions capable of taking on the tasks of governing and the creation of a coordinating machinery capable of supporting this governmental role. Chapter 2 sets out the eight dimensions along which we have examined this transformation, including the location of the core executive in the political system; the outlines of the executive terrain; the powers of the head of government (the prime minister); the powers of the minister of finance (discussed at length in chapter 8); patterns of cabinet decision making; party-based political coordination devices; the powers and organization of the center of government; and the politics–administration nexus. As already noted, some of these dimensions point beyond problems of core executive building. This is particularly the case for the politics–administration nexus, understood here to concern, in particular, the professionalization of the civil service personnel system. Professionalization at the top level of the ministerial administration does not equal straightforward depoliticization. Rather, the policymaking capacity of the executive requires a complex mixture of professionalization and depoliticization of the bulk of administrative personnel, which provides for long-term administrative competence, while the politicization of a layer of top administrative and advisory positions allows the executive to exercise its political-governmental functions. One of the main issues discussed here is, accordingly, how the tensions between professionalization, depoliticization, and politicization have been addressed and what institutional forms attempts at their resolution have taken.

CRITICAL JUNCTURE I: THE DEMISE OF COMMUNISM

The Executive

Hungary

Starting in the 1970s, Hungary became increasingly differentiated from the other CEE countries under communist rule, notably through the softening of the centralist state command economy and the loosening of the centralist grip of the Communist Party on both central and local governments. Following the ousting of Janos Kadar in 1988, the reform communist government under Prime Minister Nemeth (1988–1990) gradually distanced itself from the Communist Party (Vass 2001, 154). During the 1980s, quite vigorous debates were conducted within the academic and professional elites about the reform of political and administrative institutions; these discussions were accompanied by expanding exchanges of ideas with Western experts. The staff and graduates of the National School of Public Administration, which had been established in 1977, were active contributors to the reform discourse of the 1980s, during which the conceptual bases for much subsequent institution building were laid.

Hungary's political and institutional transformation in 1989 followed the pattern of a "negotiated transition" (Batt 1991, 566ff.) based on roundtable talks between reformist communist leaders and a score of opposition parties. The adoption of a semipresidential system was a "dilatory power compromise" typical of such a transition. The postcommunist MSZP insisted on introducing a directly elected president with substantive powers, apparently in the hope of seeing the election of a president close to their political cause, while the opposition groups, particularly the MDF preferred a weaker president, as it expected to dominate a democratically elected parliament (see chapter 3). The constitutional amendments enacted in 1989 mirrored the underlying compromise. The anticommunist camp prevailed in having the president elected by parliament, rather than by popular vote, but the ex-communists succeeded in endowing the presidency with significant powers, such as the right to "petition parliament to take action," to initiate national referendums, to veto bills (a veto that parliament can overrule by majority vote), and to refer bills to the constitutional court for constitutional review. All this made for a moderate semipresidential system.

Almost at once, political tensions arising from "cohabitation" emerged. The first parliamentary elections of April–May 1990 led a center-right coalition of the MDF, the KDNP, and the FKGP, while president Arpad Göncz had an affiliation with the liberal SZDSZ. The president lost no time in his attempt to make extensive use of his constitutional prerogatives, for instance, by refusing to sign bills enacted by parliament. He was, however, rebuffed by the constitutional court, which rejected the notion of a division of the executive power between the government and the president and established a restrictive interpretation of the powers of the presidency (Körösenyi 1999, 423). This early confrontation ended by placing Hungary on a constitutional path toward a parliamentary system of government. In regulating the relations between parliament, the government, and the prime minister, Hungary's founding constitution differed significantly from the postcommunist constitutional arrangements of other CEE countries, most notably by emphasising the leadership of the prime minister both within the cabinet and vis-à-vis parliament. The prime minister is elected by an absolute majority of the members of parliament. The position of the prime minister was further strengthened by the introduction of a constructive vote of no-confidence that could only be directed against the head of the government but not the cabinet, a provision reminiscent of Germany's constructive vote of no-confidence aimed at the chancellor. The leadership role of the prime minister within the cabinet is buttressed by his power to appoint and dismiss ministers.

In line with the constitutional logic of having a strong prime minister, the Office of Government, which during the communist era was subordinated to the council of ministers, was turned into the Prime Minister's Office, again drawing on the German example. The Antall government introduced the term *government* instead of *council of ministers* in order to emphasize the shift from sectoral to functional integration and from fragmentation to political control. Whereas the standing orders of the last state socialist governments had mentioned sixteen central agencies and institutions supervised by the council of ministers, the Antall government first reduced and, in 1991, deleted all references to such institutions. They were either dissolved or subordinated to ministries in an attempt to further streamline the core executive.

Hungary's early transition to prime ministerial government can be explained both by the institutional legacy of communism and by the party composition of the first democratic government. As noted, the government under Prime Minister Nemeth had already begun to dissociate itself from the Communist Party during the last years of communism and had sought to strengthen its own governmental capacities. The dominant role played by the MDF in the first democratic government allowed the party, and especially its leader, Josef Antall, to push for a wide range of prime ministerial prerogatives. Indeed, so strong was MDF's position that it did not hesitate to conclude an agreement with the opposition SZDSZ in May 1990 to secure the necessary support for these institutional changes. Antall's effective personal exercise of these powers, until his death in December 1993, contributed to their broad acceptance. Prime ministerialization was accompanied by the early strengthening of a centralized core executive, which relied, in particular, on a center of government that functioned as a Prime Minister's Office.

Poland

Poland's transition to democracy was shaped by constitutional arrangements hammered out between Solidarity and the Communist Party in their roundtable negotiations of February–March 1989. These arrangements remained in force until they were replaced by the Small Constitution of October 1992. The semipresidential system that emerged from these talks was a compromise. The communists insisted on having a strong president through whom they hoped to retain a share of power. The president was to be directly elected and endowed with significant powers, such as a legislative veto that could not be overruled by parliament and the right to appoint the ministers responsible for security matters. By contrast, Solidarity was eager to secure the rights of parliament and to institutionalize a cabinet that would be fully accountable to parliament.

The semipresidential system rapidly led to conflicts between the president and the government. Until the first direct presidential election in December 1990, there was a cohabitation between the communist president Jaruzelski and a government led by Solidarity under Prime Minister Mazowiecki. Perhaps surprisingly, given Jaruzelski's role in the suppression of Solidarity following the proclamation of martial law in 1981, this cohabitation passed off relatively peacefully. When the Solidarity leader Lech Walesa was elected president in December 1990 for a five-year term, he dominated the all-Solidarity cabinet under the politically weak Prime Minister Bielecki to the point that Poland came "closest ever to having a presidential government" (Zubek 2001).

In the Small Constitution of October 1992, which was adopted under a center-right multiparty cabinet headed by prime minister Hanna Suchocka, the Polish government system remained on the bipolar semipresidential track. Although the incumbent president, Walesa, succeeded in preserving most of his presidential prerogatives unimpaired, some of the powers of the presidency were trimmed, ushering in a more moderate variant of a semipresidential system. The president continued to be directly elected. While he retained his veto power over legislation, parliament could now reject his veto with a two-thirds majority of its members. The president's former prerogative of appointing security ministers was watered down to a right "to appoint ministers of state to represent him in matters related to the exercise of his powers" (art. 48.1). The president was given the right to "nominate the prime minister and, on his motion, the Council of Ministers" (art. 57.1), but his nominations had to be confirmed by parliament.

The 1992 constitution continued the communist practice of defining the council of ministers as a collective body. Although it stipulated that the premier "shall direct the work of the Council of Ministers and shall coordinate and control the work of individual ministers" (art. 55.1), he was scarcely more than an "equal among equals"—with the ministers claiming and exerting operational autonomy. Thus, "the government . . . acted like a loose federation of ministries" (Nunberg 1997, 5). In line with the emphasis on the collective nature of the council of ministers, the Office of Government continued to be subordinated to cabinet as a collective body and possessed few effective coordinating powers. In short, semipresidentialism coexisted with a cabinet type of government, and the core executive was decentralized in character (with the exception of the period immediately following the transition to democracy, when the unique cohesion of Solidarity made it possible for the government to function as a centralized cabinet executive).

The institutional weakness of the prime minister and the lack of a core executive that would have acted to support the chief executive can in large part be attributed to the very heterogeneous party composition of successive governments. In the first fully democratic parliamentary elections of 1991 (the election of 1989 had opened only one-third of the seats in the more important lower house of parliament, the Sejm, to democratic contestation, reserving the rest for the Communist Party and its allies), as many as twenty-nine parties entered the Sejm, with no one party commanding more than 13 percent of the seats. This multitude of political parties made the formation of stable coalition governments almost impossible. The Olszewski government, formed in December 1991, consisted of four parties and lasted only until June 1992. Another coalition government, led by Hanna Suchocka, was appointed in July 1992 and had to rely on the support of seven parties. After numerous crises, the government was finally brought down in May 1993. The parties' rapidly shifting fortunes made it impossible to predict which parties would survive to fight the next general election. Indeed, most of the parties represented in the 1991 parliament failed to secure a place in parliament in 1993. There were, therefore, few incentives for parties to agree to the creation of centralized executive institutions.

Czech Republic

The sudden collapse of the politically orthodox and repressive communist regime in Czechoslovakia in November–December 1989 initially left the anticommunist umbrella movements—the Civic Forum in the Czech Republic and Public against Violence in Slovakia—in a position of unchallenged dominance. In the Czech Republic, Vaclav Klaus succeeded in replacing the Civic Forum as the dominant party with his own liberal party, the ODS. The ODS not only won the Czech 1992 parliamentary elections, leading to the formation of a new Czech government under Klaus, but was also largely responsible for the creation of an independent Czech state in 1993.

The constitution of the Czech Republic of December 1992, the discussion and enactment of which were overshadowed by the conflict over the dissolution of the Czechoslovak federation, was strongly influenced by the anticommunist forces. It provides for a president who is elected by parliament at a joint session of the two chambers and is endowed with a number of substantive powers, such as the right of a suspensory veto over legislative bills, which can be overruled by an absolute majority in the Chamber of Deputies (between 1992 and 1996, four out of seven presidential vetoes were rejected by parliament; see Kopecký 2001, 156–57). In the process of government formation, the president has the right to appoint the prime minister and, upon the suggestion of the prime minister, the ministers. Perhaps the most significant lever of informal power available to the Czech president has been his ability to enter and shape the political debate by directly appealing to the general public, political parties, and organized interests (Wolchik 1997, 184–87).

The newly appointed government requires the approval of the Chamber of Deputies. The government can be brought down at any time by a negative vote of no-confidence, requiring the absolute majority of all deputies. The constitutional provisions define the government—the council of ministers—as a collective and collegiate body, with the prime minister as an "equal among equals." Accordingly, the Office of Government is subordinated as a support unit to the council of ministers and not to the prime minister.

The formally weak position of the prime minister may be explained with reference to the mode of the demise of the communist regime, the state of the emergent party system at the time, but also Vaclav Klaus's personal leadership. As the founding father both of ODS—as the dominant party-political force in the early transition period—as well as of the new Czech state, Klaus proved highly skillful in building up his own party and a strong parliamentary majority during the first legislative period of the Czech parliament (1992–1996). His strong personal leadership allowed him to make good for the constitutional weakness of the prime ministerial position. Yet, in the longer term, this institutional weakness proved an onerous legacy under conditions when the parliamentary majorities should become less secure and personalist power resources weakened. Thus, as early as, and during, his albeit short-lived second prime ministerial term, from July 1996 to November 1997, Klaus had to face up to the consequences of a formally weak premiership.

Bulgaria

To understand institution building in Bulgaria after 1989, the mode of the transition to postcommunism proves crucial. This transition took the form of the ousting of the orthodox communist leader Zhivkov in November 1989 by his reformist colleagues in the Politburo of Bulgarian Communist Party and the subsequent transformation of the party into the BSP, dedicated to democratic socialism. The BSP was able to remain the leading political party and power in the country well into the mid-1990s. Similar to that of Poland, the introduction of a semipresidential system was the outcome of roundtable negotiations in 1990 between the postcommunist BSP and the anticommunist UDF. Reflecting the underlying "dilatory power compromise," the temporary constitutional settlement agreed at the roundtable did not contain a clear definition of the powers of the president, a reflection of the BSP's hopes of retaining a share of power through a potentially strong presidency.

In the constitution adopted in July 1991 by the constitutional assembly—in which the BSP held 53 percent of the seats and the UDF 36 percent—the powers of the president were given a clearer definition that stressed his limited political role. By that time, the BSP, contrary to its expectations, had lost the presidency to the UDF leader Zhelev but dominated the constitutional assembly and no longer wished to endow the president with extensive prerogatives. Thus, the president is directly elected but has few executive powers.

The 1991 constitution gives parliament a comparatively strong position vis-à-vis the government. Parliament elects both the prime minister and, upon his motion, the ministers and can force the government to resign by a negative vote of confidence, directed either against the council of ministers as a collective body or against the prime minister. In a provision that is exceptional among CEE countries, the constitution stipulates that "a member of the National Assembly elected as a minister shall cease to serve as a Member during his term of office as a minister" (art. 68.2). This rigorous interpretation of the separation of powers may be seen as a reaction against the merging of executive and legislative functions under communism. However, the fact that government does not have a personal power base within parliament deprives it of a forceful influence over parliamentary business; it has also encouraged parties in parliament to regard themselves as being distinct from the parties in government.

The 1991 constitution defines the council of ministers as a collective body, with the prime minister being merely an "equal among equals." The collective responsibility of the council of ministers surfaces also in the constitutional provision that "the council of ministers shall rescind any illegitimate or improper act issued by a minister" (art. 107). In line with the primacy of collective responsibility of the council of ministers, the Office of Government is subordinated to it. However, its ability to serve as a guardian of collective responsibility has remained strictly limited throughout the period under investigation, and its predominant nature has been that of a government registrar.

The institutionally weak leadership role of the Bulgarian prime minister can be explained with reference to both the institutional legacy of communism and the party composition of the first democratic governments. Under the last communist constitution of 1971, the council of ministers was subordinated not only to the Communist Party but also to a State Council, which combined legislative and executive functions. The low political status of the council of ministers was indicated by the fact that the party leader Zhivkov took for himself the chairmanship of the State Council and appointed secondary political figures to be prime minister. The ex-communist BSP dominated the first democratic governments after 1989. While the BSP party leadership was prepared to accept a partial transfer of policymaking responsibilities to the government, as part of an attempt to safeguard at least some of its powers, it continued to insist on the primacy of the party over the government. This meant that it was not prepared to agree to the centralization of power in the hands of the prime minister or the creation of a prime minister's office. The executive's influence over parliament was further undermined in the early transition years by the low degree of party discipline. The ensuing political instability of the core executive meant that between April 1990 and January 1995, Bulgaria saw not less than six governments.

An Interim Summary

The four countries under review shared important features of the system change of 1989–1990. When the late-authoritarian one-party rule of the Communist Party—around which the entire decision-making and governing system had previously revolved—was brought down, the new political leaders were confronted with the task of building up political and administrative institutions that would be capable of assuming the policymaking and governing functions associated with executives under the conditions of pluralist party democracy. Yet, from the very beginning of system change, the countries showed significant differences in the range, depth, and pace of executive institution building.

As regards the trajectories of executive development as set by the critical juncture that the demise of communism represented, one can identify an early common trend to opt for a bipolar semipresidential system with a form of power sharing between the president and the government. This created the potential for two institutional paths—presidentialism versus parliamentary government—and for fractious cohabitation in political and executive leadership. In Hungary, such a possibility was rapidly ruled out following decisions of the constitutional court so that the country emerged from the critical juncture set on the path to a parliamentary system. By contrast, Poland went through several variants of semipresidentialism—of which the earlier one, agreed at the roundtable in 1989—came close to strong semipresidential system. The Small Constitution of 1992 retained an important presidential role, which—due to President Walesa's personal grip on the Solidarity movement and its majority in the Sejm—brought post-1989 Poland temporarily close to a presidential system. Both in the Czech Republic and in Bulgaria, developments after 1989 made for a weak presidency, for structurally similar but politically opposite reasons. While the Czech Republic was dominated by a fervently anti–Communist Party constellation under the strong leadership of Prime Minister Klaus, who opposed the idea of a strong presidency as a possible challenge to parliamentary rule, in Bulgaria it was the postcommunist Bulgarian Socialist Party that rejected a strong presidency as a possible rival to the hoped-for continuation of the party's strong position inside and outside parliament.

In executive-legislative relations, Hungary went furthest in strengthening the government and, within the government, the political leadership of the prime minister, by introducing from the outset the constructive vote of no-confidence, under which parliament can bring down the government only if and when it elects, by majority vote, a new prime minister. By contrast, in the other three countries, procedural provisions for a negative vote of no-confidence were adopted, which placed governments in a much more precarious position vis-à-vis the legislature. Executive-legislative relations were critically shaped by the evolution of the country-specific pluralist political party systems, which affected the stability of the incumbent governments and their dependence on often conflict-torn political coalitions. Thus, while Hungary immediately embarked on course of stable party governments— each of which has subsequently lasted for the entire legislative term—both Poland and Bulgarian experienced seven governments each between 1989 and 1997.

Turning to power relations within the government, the council of ministers continued to be perceived primarily as a collective actor in the Czech Republic and Bulgaria, and also in Poland, for as long as the 1992 constitution remained in force. The concept of collective cabinet responsibility of the government vis-à-vis parliament was enshrined in the Czech constitutional provision of a negative vote of no-confidence, which permit parliament to oust the council of ministers as a collective body. A similar provision could be found in the Polish 1992 constitution. In Bulgaria, a negative vote can be turned against both the council of ministers and the prime minister. The Hungarian constitution was the only one to make the prime minister the sole addressee of the constructive parliamentary vote of no-confidence, thus buttressing his prominent position within the cabinet and favoring a prime ministerial type of government.

The core executive proper and the organization of the center of government also showed divergent paths. In Hungary, a congruent pattern of development took shape early on, so that a prime ministerial type of government became underpinned by a centralized prime ministerial core executive and a center of government that was turned early on into a Prime Minister's Office, thus reinforcing prime ministerialization. By contrast, in Poland, a centralized cabinet-type core executive existed in the first years after the fall of communism, supported by the internal coherence of the Solidarity government, but over time it increasingly gave way to a decentralized ministerial pattern, in which ministers enjoyed considerable discretion. The center of government acted as a government registrar, unable to ensure cabinet responsibility. By contrast, in the Czech Republic, Prime Minister Klaus relied on party-based political coordination mechanisms in particular, thus establishing a core executive that was centralized prime ministerial in character. But this core operated to a large extent outside the formal channels of government and the ministerial administration. The center of government itself was left largely untouched. Finally, in Bulgaria, the forms of cabinet government were observed, but there, no core executive emerged that could have effectively supported cabinet coordination, and the center of government retained its character as a government registrar.

The Politics–Administration Nexus

As noted in chapter 2, the reform of the politics–administration nexus, as one of the eight dimensions of executive development that we have investigated, takes us into the broader terrain of postcommunist state building. In a summary assessment, it does, therefore, warrant some more detailed discussion.

After the communist takeover, in Hungary, as in the other communist CEE countries, a personnel system was put in place in which the employment of state sector personnel was regulated by a unitary labor code. The Communist Party controlled the key administrative positions through the *nomenklatura* system. However, from the 1970s on, the Hungarian communist regime began to ascribe growing importance to professional competence in the recruitment and promotion of state employees. In 1977, a National School of Public Administration was founded; under the leadership of reform-minded academics, administrative reforms—including civil service legislation—began to be prepared (Meyer-Sahling 2001, 2003). The call for professionalization was based both on the rediscovery of Hungarian state and administrative traditions and on the references to the experiences of Western European countries.

Following the democratic elections of May 1990, one of the very first legislative initiatives was to draw a clear legal distinction between the political and administrative functions and position holders in state administration, particularly in the government ministries. The law on state secretaries, which was enacted in 1990, dealt with only part of this issue. It covered the top positions in the executive—that is, ministers, political state secretaries, and administrative state secretaries. While the appointment and dismissal of ministers and political state secretaries were to follow a purely political logic, the administrative state secretaries, as top positions in the line ministries, were given a hybrid status. On the one hand, they were granted the status of civil servants, including tenure; on the other hand, the minister could remove them from their positions at any time, without, however, their ceasing to be civil servants. In legally recognizing the right of the government to treat the administrative state secretary as a political appointee, the Hungarian legislation borrowed from the German model of the *politische Beamte*.

The civil service bill that regulated the general administrative personnel underwent a more protracted legislative process and was finally passed in March 1992 (Meyer-Sahling 2001, 971ff.). It introduced the distinction between civil servants and public employees. The former were to be appointed and engaged in executive activities in state and municipal administration, while the latter group, working on a contractual basis, encompassed service-related activities and positions, including those of teachers (György 1999, 2).

The legal regulation of the civil servants followed the classical career-based civil service principles (Bossaert and Demmke 2002, 9), premised on tenure and political neutrality, and it distinguished four career groups, each with different entry requirements (György 1999, 40ff.; Hazafi and Czoma 1999). In an additional legal provision, the 1992 civil service legislation expanded the scope of political appointees by extending the possibility of "political appointment and removal" to the department and division heads in ministries. In total, the group of politically appointed civil servants now amounted to between 15 percent and 20 percent of the entire ministerial personnel (Meyer-Sahling 2001, 96). From the outset, the prime minister and the ministers also surrounded themselves with French-type *cabinets*, consisting of political confidants and personal advisors, who were not given civil service status but were on the government payroll.

In Poland, too, the communist regime introduced a unitary labor code in the 1950s. In 1982, however, legislation was enacted that stipulated special provisions for government employees, including tenured positions for some occupational categories. Following the collapse of the communist regime, the Solidarity-led government of Prime Minister Bielecki (January 1991–October 1991) first introduced a civil service bill in parliament but failed to find a parliamentary majority. Another bill was tabled by the center-right Suchocka government (August 1992–May 1993). The draft stipulated that all current public service employees, including those holding tenured positions under the 1982 act, should undergo a qualification test procedure before being appointed as civil servants under the new act. With the resignation of the Suchocka government in May 1993, the bill lapsed. In practice, incoming governments regularly changed all top officials at the central level. The instability of coalitions provided strong incentives to the political parties to resort to a spoils system in order to exploit what they expected to be a narrow window of opportunity. The prospect of frequent staff replacements engendered unresponsiveness among government employees, who tended to frustrate new government programs lest the next government punish them for collaboration with its predecessor.

Following the collapse of the communist regime, the Czechoslovak parliament, which was dominated by the anticommunist umbrella movement, passed a "lustration law" (Federal Law on the Conditions of Admission to Certain Offices in State Organs and State Enterprises) in October 1991, which excluded all former members of the State Security Service and active members of the Communist Party from senior positions in public administration. After 1 January 1993, this federal act remained in force in the Czech Republic, and it has been repeatedly extended since. Apart from the anti-Stasi legislation put in effect in East Germany, the Czech Republic has been the only postcommunist country to try to cleanse its public administration of *nomenklaturists* of the communist era.

The constitution of the Czech Republic of December 1992 explicitly stipulates that the public service shall be regulated by law (art. 79.2). Furthermore, the labor code (art. 73.2–5) lays down that government employees "must act and take decisions in an impartial manner and refrain from any actions that may undermine the political impartiality of their work and decisions." Yet, early attempts undertaken by the Czech government to get civil service legislation through parliament failed (Vidláková 1999). Despite the absence of a formal law establishing a permanent civil service, the available evidence suggests that, in practice, the lower and middle levels of the Czech bureaucracy benefited from a fairly stable employment environment in which overtly political interventions were rather rare (World Bank 1998, 18).

Finally, Bulgaria, as most other CEE countries under communist rule, employed government personnel on the basis of a unitary labor law, which was amended by the labor code of 1986. The postcommunist constitution of July 1991 lays down that state employees "shall be guided solely by law and shall be politically neutral" (art. 116.1) and provides for the passage of a law that would "establish the conditions for appointment and dismissal of state employees and the conditions on which they shall be free to belong to political parties and trade unions, as well as to exercise their right to strike" (art. 116.2). Yet, during the communist-led early transition period into the mid-1990s, "no purposeful actions were put in place to create efficient administrative structures, and thus the process of disintegration of the administrative system continued" (Georgiev 1999, 25).

Once we add the dimension of civil service reform to the analysis of executive development, the differences between the four countries under consideration begin to emerge even more clearly. Again, legacies and party–political actor constellations proved decisive during this first critical juncture. In Hungary, transition took place through negotiations between the reform wing of the Communist Party and opposition groups, thus making it easier for the latter, when they won power, to agree to retain most of the communist-era administrators. The emphasis on the professionalization of the public service since the 1970s facilitated this choice. Moreover, the fact that the Hungarian party system rapidly took on bipolar character, with the Left and the Right succeeding each other in power, created incentives for the parties to lock in their successors by creating and preserving a career civil service.

In Poland, the end of communism took place through negotiations between the Communist Party and the opposition, but, in contrast to Hungary, its first fully democratic election created a party system composed of a multitude of weak and often ephemeral parties. The fact that most Polish governments in the early 1990s were coalitions with partners that did not expect to run together in the next elections created incentives for the politicization of the civil service.

In Czechoslovakia, the end of communism came as a result of the collapse of the regime, and the anticommunist umbrella movements that took over enjoyed a virtually unchallenged authority. The movements tended to view all communist-era administrators with profound distrust and were eager to push them out or keep them out by lustration legislation. They were also unwilling to adopt civil service legislation that might entrench these administrators in their posts. The political dominance of umbrella movements in Czechoslovakia was succeeded by the supremacy of Klaus's ODS in the Czech Republic. The domination over the political system by one party meant that the government had little incentive to adopt depoliticizing measures and preferred to keep open the possibility for political interference in the civil service. Furthermore, legislative resistance came from various angles. Civil service legislation met opposition from within the ranks of ODS, the senior coalition party chaired by Prime Minister Klaus. Among ODS adherents, legislation that would have opted for classical career-based civil service concepts found little sympathy, as more "liberal" contract-based concepts were preferred (Vidláková 1999).

Finally, in Bulgaria, the transition to democracy was dominated by the former Communist Party, which naturally had little wish to adopt legislation that might threaten the position of pre-1989 administrators. The fact that the Communist Party was able to control most of the governments in the early 1990s gave it an additional incentive for delaying the passage of depoliticization legislation.

CRITICAL JUNCTURE II: THE CRISIS OF GOVERNANCE OF THE MID-1990S

The institutional arrangements established at the critical juncture provided by the demise of communism in 1989 remained in place for the following few years. According to an institutionalist logic, the new institutions, once in place, can be expected to possess considerable inertia and persistence, which favor path dependencies. A departure from this developmental path was likely to require a new critical juncture and favorable actor constellations. Such a second critical juncture occurred in the four CEE countries with the crisis of governance in the mid-1990s. This crisis manifested itself primarily in fiscal terms. Escalating budget deficits provided a clear demonstration of the inability of governments to match their policy choices to budgetary resources. The fiscal crisis varied in depth: it was most severe in Bulgaria, grave in Hungary and Poland, and relatively modest in the Czech Republic (for details see chapter 8). At the same time, the EU accession context—with the conclusion of the Europe Agreements, the submission of membership applications, and, eventually, the opening of accession negotiations—further

helped to focus attention on the coordination capacities of central governments (Grabbe 2001). As the EU Commission and the council of ministers
made clear, both the accession negotiations and, in particular, the efficient
and effective transposition of the EU *acquis communautaire* into national
legislation and programs required a degree of coordination that had thus far
been absent in the weak core executives of most of the applicant countries.
The crisis of governance of mid-1990s then had the potential to act as a
catalyst that could set a new path for executive development, while the accession context helped to identify one of the key causes of the fiscal crisis,
namely, the relative weakness of coordinating devices within government.

The Executive

Hungary

Hungary's response to the fiscal crisis was shaped by the institutional
structures put in place in 1989–1990, in particular, prime ministerial leadership of the government. Once the depth of the fiscal crisis had become
clear to Prime Minister Horn in 1994–1995, he moved swiftly and resolutely
to support the austerity package proposed by Finance Minister Bokros. Such
was Horn's dominance of his cabinet that he was able to absorb the resignation of three cabinet ministers without suffering any serious political
damage. In spite of the fact that the austerity package antagonized many
key constituencies in Horn's Socialist Party, the party's parliamentary group
gave it virtually unanimous support. The resolution of the fiscal crisis gave
a further boost to the institutional powers of the prime minister, a trend
continued under Horn's center-right successor, Victor Orbán.

Under Orbán, the Prime Minister's Office was turned in a state "chancellery" (*kancellaria*) closely modeled to the German Chancellor's Office
(*Bundeskanzleramt*). The main structural change was to create three new
organizational units within the chancellery: a Communication Office, a Center for Strategic Analysis, and ministry desks. These desks were to shadow
the sectoral responsibilities of the ministries and monitor their activities,
thus enhancing the coordination capacity of the prime minister. As the
European Commission (1999b, 58) noted, "since July 1998 the role of the
Prime Minister's Office in the overall co-ordination between the Ministries
has significantly increased." The prime minister also acquired important prerogatives in the budgetary process, including the power to set spending caps
for the individual ministries (see chapter 8).

The importance of effective party control as a power resource was especially evident in the case of Prime Minister Orbán, whose control over
the ministers belonging to his own party—FIDESZ-MPP—was generally regarded as being very far-reaching. However, the norm of coalition politics

in postcommunist Hungary meant that his authority over the cabinet as a whole remained in check. Even Orbán, seen as the most prime ministerial of the Hungarian heads of government, had to accept that the ministries controlled by his main coalition partner, the FKGP, operated largely outside his control. Several Hungarian political scientists have stressed the marked concentration of power around the office of the prime minister that took place under the Orbán government and likened it to the creation of a chancellor democracy, as in Germany (Fricz 2000), or, even more strongly, as "a presidential-style democracy in parliamentary guise" (Ágh 2001, 101), with the prime minister as the supreme center of power.

Poland

While in Hungary the governance crisis reinforced the trend toward prime ministerial leadership, in Poland the crisis was to produce a significant shift in the trajectory of the central executive away from the cabinet-ministerial governments of the early 1990s and toward a substantial enhancement of the powers of the prime minister. The peak of the fiscal crisis occurred in 1992, but while the powers of the Ministry of Finance were strengthened already in 1993, the empowerment of the prime minister proved to be a longer process. While the first steps toward strengthening the position of the prime minister were taken in the Small Constitution of 1992, which recognized his right to "coordinate and control the work of individual ministers," the establishment of coordinating institutions, which would enable him to exercise this right, was difficult to achieve in the short-lived multiparty governments of the early 1990s. It was only under the relatively stable SLD-PSL coalition government of 1993–1997 and with the victory of the SLD candidate Alexander Kwasniewski in the 1995 presidential elections that the actor constellation became favorable to the concentration of power in the hands of the prime minister. There was also a growing realization by Poland's political elites that governance capacity needed to be radically improved to meet the demands of EU accession (Nunberg 1999). The dynamics of change surfaced, first of all, in the drafting of a new constitution to replace the Small Constitution of 1992. The new constitution was passed by parliament on April 2, 1997, and was approved in a national referendum in October 1997.

While the 1997 constitution retained a directly elected president, presidential executive powers were further reduced in favor of the government. Under the 1997 constitution, the president can still play an active role in government formation, as he nominates a prime minister, who in turn proposes the composition of the government. The president has the right to introduce legislative drafts in parliament, to refer bills passed by parliament to the constitutional court, or to veto them; in the last case, parliament may overrule the presidential veto with a three-fifths majority in the presence of at least half of the statutory number of deputies. The president has, however, been stripped of his earlier prerogative of appointing ministers. In assessing the impact of the constitutional reform on Poland's governmental system, some observers went as far as suggesting that the president had been reduced to a largely representational role (van der Meer Krok-Paszkowska 1999). But even if President Kwasniewski has shown restraint in the use of his powers, the president's prerogatives are still significant (see Millard 2000).

In its relation with parliament, the position of the government has been strengthened by the introduction of a constructive vote of no-confidence in place of the previous negative one. Once the program of the incoming government has been approved by parliament, it can be brought down only by a constructive vote of no-confidence, approved by a majority of the statutory number of deputies (art. 158.1). Regarding the position of the prime minister within the government, however, the new constitutional and legal provisions reveal some ambivalence. On the one hand, the constitution still focuses on primacy of the council of ministers as a collective organ (art. 197.1). On the other, the prime minister has been given a leading role in the formation of the government in that he can propose the composition of the council of ministers. In addition, the position of the premier has been markedly strengthened by legislation that was part of the reform package passed in August 1996 (Fidien 1996; Zubek 2001, 920ff.).

Through legislation of April 1999, the Office of Government, which had until then been subordinated to the council of ministers, was transformed into a chancellery, adding some organizational and personnel muscle to the prime minister in the exercise of executive leadership. An abortive attempt was made by Walendziak, who was appointed in 1997 to head the chancellery, to create a Prime Minister's Office capable of hierarchical coordination vis-à-vis the line ministries. This scheme encountered heavy opposition, not least from the ministries. The presence of numerous political appointees within the chancellery was widely criticized as excessive party politicization (Kublik and Wielowieyska 1997). With Walendziak's dismissal in 1999, this attempt to increase the control of the chancellery over the ministries remained an episode.

Czech Republic

In stark contrast to the whirl of institutional change that Poland experienced in 1996–1997, the Czech Republic's government structures—with its moderate semipresidential system and the formal focus on the council of ministers and its collective responsibility—remained unchanged. During his first term (1992–1996), Prime Minister Klaus compensated for the formal weakness of the prime ministerial position by skillfully employing the safe parliamentary majority of his government coalition and his strong personal leadership. But the problematic consequences of the institutional legacy of the founding period soon became increasingly apparent. During his short-lived second term (1996–1997), Klaus himself came to face the consequences of the institutional enfeeblement of the prime ministerial position. His successor, Milos Zeman, the social democratic prime minister of a tolerated minority government (1998–2002), was not able to rely on informal power resources of the type Klaus could use to bolster limited formal powers. As a result, Zeman's hold over the members of his government remained weak, and a centralized core executive failed to emerge.

Bulgaria

In 1996–1997, Bulgaria slid into its worst economic crisis since the beginning of the transition, with a drop in the gross domestic product of 11 percent in 1996 and another 7 percent in 1997. Against the backdrop of this dismal economic record, the democratic opposition party UDF, led by Ivan Kostov, won a landslide victory over the BSP in the parliamentary elections of April 1997. This victory was not a normal swing in the political pendulum but a political rupture. It established the UDF's supremacy within the Bulgarian party system, which was rather similar to the dominance that the BSP had enjoyed before 1997. Prime Minister Kostov made significant progress in reforming the government structure, notably though the Public Administration Act of 1998. For the first time, the act established a uniform organizational structure for central government. It emphasized the primacy of the council of ministers as "a central collective body of the executive power with a general competence" (art. 20.1), but it also aimed at cautiously upgrading the position of the prime minister by endowing him with the right to refer acts which he considers illegal or improper to the council of ministers (art. 20.6) and to appoint regional governors and to control their activities. It is revealing that all three provisions were later nullified by the constitutional court, on the grounds of violating the collective primacy of the council of ministers laid down in the constitution. Thus, notwithstanding the overwhelming majority of UDF in parliament and the political muscle of Kostov, the cabinet type of government continued to prevail. In the same vein, the Office of Government continued to be assigned and subordinated to the council of ministers. But centralization was modestly increased through the establishment of sectoral units mirroring policy fields and of horizontal units, including the "Chancellery Department," which were charged with providing administrative support to the council of ministers (SIGMA 1999). Kostov could, however, exercise personal and party-political dominance over his ministerial colleagues, and, thus, he created a centralized prime ministerial core executive that relied strongly on party-political coordination mechanisms.

An Interim Summary

Among the four countries examined, Hungary's trajectory stands out in that it was oriented, from the outset, toward an institutionally powerful position for the prime minister. Executive power was quickly centralized in the government, in which the prime minister took center stage, although his powers with regard to the smaller coalition partners remained limited. The prime ministerialization of executive leadership was reinforced by the impact of the governance crisis of the mid-1990s.

By contrast, Poland started out as a semipresidential system with strong presidential powers and early cohabitation struggles. The 1997 constitution marked a significant shift to a government system that, while still semipresidential, approached a parliamentary system. The standing of the government vis-à-vis parliament was augmented through the introduction of the constructive vote of no-confidence. The powers of the prime minister in determining the composition of the government were strengthened considerably, but the development of a centralized core executive was hampered by party-political problems and the limited capacity of the center of government to support prime ministerial leadership. In the Czech Republic, events during the mid-1990s did not lead to a formal reallocation of powers. In its relations with parliament, the government continued to face a negative vote of no-confidence, making it easy for parliament to threaten the government with dismissal. Within the government, the focus remained on the cabinet as a collective body, and the Office of Government continued to be subordinated to the council of ministers. The weakness of the prime minister came to the fore as soon as the prime minister's party position was challenged, as was the case during Zeman's premiership.

In Bulgaria, the mid-1990s crisis, while leading to centralization in the budgetary core executive (see chapter 8), did not set the country on a new path of executive development as far as the government in general and the core executive in particular were concerned. Parliament remained in a strong position vis-à-vis the government because of the negative vote of no-confidence and of the incompatibility principle, which meant that ministers could not be members of parliament. Constitutional provisions emphasized collective responsibility within the council of ministers. The landslide electoral victory of the anticommunist UDF in April 1997 signaled the end of postcommunist dominance and the end of the foundation period but had only very limited effects on the formal institutional arrangements of the executive government, including the position of the prime minister. However, Prime Minister Kostov could rely on a majority in parliament, allowing him to overcome, to some extent, the formal constraints put on a prime ministerial rule. Cautious steps to strengthen the prime minister were rebuffed by the constitutional court so that the predominance of the cabinet principle in the organization of the executive persisted.

The cross-country differences that emerged up to the early twenty-first century may be attributed to the differing impact of the governance crisis and the variable composition of governments at the critical juncture. In Hungary, the impact of the fiscal crisis was important in promoting the further strengthening of the prime minister and the minister of finance. The fact that Hungarian governments continued to be dominated by one party, in the context of a bipolar party system in which the Left and Right regularly succeeded each other in power, created further incentives for the empowerment of the prime minister. In Poland, the fact that, after 1993, Polish governments tended to be dominated by one party, with the Left and Right alternating in office, made it easier for all parties to accept a modicum of centralization in the hands of the prime minister. In the Czech Republic, the impact of the fiscal crisis was less severe, and the party composition of government was not conducive to the reform of executive structures. Given ODS's domination of the Czech party system until the mid-1990s and Klaus's supremacy within the ODS, Klaus found it easy to browbeat his ministerial colleagues and felt little need for a formal reinforcement of his executive powers. While weakened by the 1998 elections, the ODS retained sufficient residual power to ensure that the ensuing social democratic government would be critically dependent on its support. The weakness of his minority government made it difficult for Prime Minister Zeman to promote institutional reforms. Finally, in Bulgaria, the UDF's domination of the Bulgarian party system, following its landslide victory in April 1997, and Prime Minister Kostov's unchallenged position as UDF leader made it possible for Kostov to coordinate the work of the government using party-political instruments, thus reducing the incentive to develop executive coordination mechanisms.

The Politics–Administration Nexus

As noted earlier, EU accession, while not acting as a "critical juncture" in executive development in its own right, helped to focus attention on the need for improved policy coordination and increased the urgency of addressing the sometimes deep-seated problems of administrative performance. The growing relevance of the EU integration context from the mid-1990s onward is especially evident in the case of civil service reform (see also chapter 9).

As noted earlier, Hungary was a frontrunner among CEE countries by enacting civil service legislation in 1990 and 1992 (Meyer-Sahling 2001, 961). While drawing a clear dividing line between the political position holders in government—ministers and political state secretaries—and administrative staff, the introduction of political civil servants remained controversial, as it lead to a high rate of fluctuation and turnover in these positions.[1] To counteract this trend, the Civil Service Act was amended in May 2001 by introducing the concept of an elite corps of "senior civil servants"—with tenure and higher salaries than those at the low and middle levels—who should include administrative state secretaries and other top positions. The power to appoint these elite civil servants was to lie with the prime minister, thereby allowing him to fashion an elite corps that would be active throughout the ministerial administration. Moreover, under the 1997 amendment of the Civil Service Act, the prime minister was allowed to employ up to twenty-five—and each minister up to fifteen—political advisors, whose employment is tied to the tenure of the minister and whose salaries can be negotiated freely (Goetz and Wollmann 2001, 878). These staff form personal *cabinets* of political and personal confidants who serve as the "eyes and ears" of the prime minister and the ministers.

Hungary's civil service legislation, although inspired by Weberian notions of a career civil service and set in place for over a decade, appears to have had a limited effect on depoliticizing personnel policy in the sense of reducing the scope for political involvement in individual decisions on personnel policy. In fact, the May 2001 amendment in particular created a prime ministerial elite corps whose members, although enjoying full tenure, owe their post to the head of government personally. Not surprisingly, this reform immediately attracted public and academic criticism; it was also criticized by the EU. Yet, this initiative was entirely consistent with the development of a centralized core executive led by the prime minister, which we noted earlier.

In Poland, it was only in July 1996 that a Civil Service Act was finally passed (Torres-Bartyzel and Kacprowicz 1999). It envisaged the gradual phasing out of the provisions of the 1982 law on state employees. However, the implementation of this act was aborted by the incoming center-right coalition under Prime Minister Buzek (October 1997–June 2000). A new Public Service Act was passed in December 1998 and came into force in mid-1999. This law formally curbed political discretion in the appointment process in two important respects. First, it extended civil service status to all existing state employees working in ministries, central agencies, and regional *voivodship* offices. Within the comprehensive concept of civil service, a distinction was made between public employees engaged under contract and governed by the general labor law and civil servants awarded tenure under a special appointment procedure laid down in the act. Second, under the new law, tenure was to be granted according to the results of a formal written examination administered by the newly created Office of the Civil Service.

Under the center-right AWS-UW coalition, the implementation of the new act continued to be controversial, particularly because of what remained a politicized appointment procedure. In an attempt to place party-loyal activists in their administration, ministers resorted to circumventing the very provisions they had previously endorsed. A blatant example was the practice of making temporary appointments to senior director positions that later proved to be permanent. In December 2001, the center-left SLD-PSL-UP coalition under Prime Minister Miller moved to legalize this practice by an amendment to the Civil Service Act (art. 144a). This provision would have allowed ministers to recruit civil servants from outside the civil service for provisional appointments to senior positions. This article was, however, nullified by the constitutional court in December 2002.

As a result, despite a fairly stringent regulatory regime, the Polish civil service in the early twenty-first century still showed a high degree of politicization, mainly at the senior and middle levels. The formal selection and appointment process of civil servants proceeded quite slowly. Between 1997 and 2002, just 1,148 tenured civil service appointments were made (out of 118,000 public employees). For the highest career group, including department heads and division heads, some sixteen hundred positions were earmarked (European Commission 2000, 16), but by September 2001, only half had been filled (European Commission 2001b, 18).

Civil service development proved even more protracted in the Czech Republic. Although the constitution of the Czech Republic of 1992 envisaged that the public service should be regulated by law, repeated attempts throughout the 1990s remained unsuccessful (Strecková 1998; Vidláková 1999). The Social Democrat minority government under Prime Minister Zeman eventually adopted a civil service draft, but disagreements between the government and the oppositional ODS delayed the legislative process. The law was finally passed in May 2002 "after difficult discussions and a close vote in Parliament" (European Commission 2002b, 13) and, after another delay, signed into law by the president on 20 August 2003. Following the floods of 2003, the implementation of the law was further postponed to 2005. In its *Public Service and Administrative Framework Assessment* for the Czech Republic of 2003, SIGMA (in collaboration with the Organization for Economic Co-operation and Development) noted that it was "unlikely that civil servants as defined by this law" would be in place before 2008.

Finally, in Bulgaria, there, too, the road to professionalization and the depoliticization of personnel policy proved more tortuous than had been envisaged. Although the Bulgarian constitution of 1991 prescribes that a law on "the conditions for the appointment and dismissal of state employees" (art. 116.2) should be adopted, no serious legislative moves were undertaken until 1997. It was only after the UDF came into power in spring 1997 that an actor constellation emerged that was able to overcome resistance to a civil service law. The new government's resolve to improve Bulgaria's prospects of EU accession in the face of harsh criticism of institutional deficiencies further spurred reform. Parliament finally enacted the Law on Administration in October 1998 and the Civil Service Act on 21 July 1999, designed to restructure the administrative apparatus and the administrative personnel system.

The new Bulgarian legislation made a clear distinction between politically appointed positions and the ordinary administrative personnel. Regarding the politically appointed officials, there were different categories. First, a number of civil service positions were enumerated that could be politically appointed and dismissed. These included the secretaries-general in the ministries, the chairmen of state agencies, and the directors of executive agencies. Second, the new law recognized the creation of political *cabinets* (which had existed for years). Members of such personal *cabinets* must not be civil servants and may not perform administrative functions. In an amendment of the Law on Administration, adopted in November 2001, the strict separation between political appointees (including those working in *cabinets*) and politically neutral civil servants was somewhat blurred by permitting "the dismissal of certain senior officials and their deputies at the discretion of their appointing authority" (European Commission 2002a, 21).

Concerning the ordinary administrative personnel, the Civil Service Act of 1999 distinguished three functions: leadership/management, expert, and technical. Only the former two—leadership/management and expert—were granted civil service status by appointment, while the last was to be employed on a contractual basis. The legislation followed the classical career-based model, providing for professionalism, tenure, and political neutrality. By May 2002, the share of central government personnel with civil service status had reached about 33 percent (European Commission 2002a). While the recruitment into, and promotion to, civil service positions by way of competition was legally prescribed and mandatory, such competitive procedures were still "the exception rather than the rule," as noted by the European Commission (21).

It is indicative of Bulgaria's delayed transition that in an earlier draft of the Civil Service Act, the Kostov government had included a measure to prevent members of the former Communist Party *nomenklatura* and of the State Security Service from becoming civil servants. The constitutional court, however, rejected this provision as contradicting the constitutional principle of equality and the right to work (decree N2/21.01.1999). The court explicitly ruled that no restrictions of access to the civil service related to party affiliation prior to the democratic transition were to be imposed (see also Georgiev 1999, 4).

In summary of the legal regulations on administrative personnel, there emerges, first, a striking difference in the timing of civil service legislation, stretching from Hungary (1990–1992) to Poland (1996–1997), Bulgaria (1999), and the Czech Republic (2003). While the development of government structures was an indispensable part of institution building and was, in its basic elements, laid down in the early founding constitutions, the latter addressed the personnel aspects of the executive transformation only in the most general terms. The legislation that was adopted uniformly introduced a distinction between the ordinary civil servants on the one hand and the position holders on the other, particularly those in the highest administrative and advisory posts, who were seen as performing political functions and whose appointment and dismissal were, accordingly, treated as political decisions. In all of the four countries, it proved difficult to find a solution to the crucial task of ensuring a professional nonpolitical administrative staff as the foundation for a stable government while, at the same time, recognizing the political interest of the government of the day in having a number of senior administrators who enjoy its political confidence.

In recognizing political positions and staff in government service, essentially two strategies were pursued. In the first strategy, developed in early government practice and then acknowledged by legislation, groups of political advisors and aides were attached, in a staff function, to the prime minister and the ministers, respectively, borrowing from the French *cabinet ministeriel* tradition. From the outset, political aides and advisors were introduced as part of the governmental machinery in all four of the countries. They became increasingly legalized through subsequent legislation.

The second strategy, modeled to the German "political civil servant," regards the very top layers of ministerial officials as civil servants who must enjoy the political confidence of the executive leadership and may be removed from their positions by the minister at his discretion, without, however, losing their civil service status and privileges. This provision was first introduced in Hungary and, almost a decade later, also in Bulgaria.

FLUIDITY AND DISJUNCTURES IN EXECUTIVE DEVELOPMENT

Table 7.1 summarizes the institutional trajectories of our four countries between the late 1980s and the early twenty-first century with reference to types of government, types of core executives, and types of centers of government. Such a sweeping comparative classification is not, of course, without its problems. As we note in chapter 2, where the different types were briefly introduced, the distinction between them is continuous rather than dichotomous, and governments, core executives, and centers typically do not take pure forms but are typically approximations of one type or the other, with more or less pronounced traces of the others. The classifications in table 7.1 therefore represent our summary assessment of a complex reality that country experts may well wish to question. Moreover, change does not, of course, take place overnight, so that the dates given stand for the approximate time at which one type gave way to another.

These caveats notwithstanding, the summary overview highlights a number of important findings. First, following the initial regime change at the end of the 1980s and the early 1990s, only Poland experienced a subsequent

Table 7.1. Types of Government, Core Executives, and Centers of Government, Late 1980s to Early Twenty-First Century

Country	Type of Government	Type of Core Executive	Type of Center of Government
Hungary	1990–2002: Prime ministerial	1990–2002: Centralized prime ministerial	1990–2002: Prime minister's vanguard
Poland	1989–1997: Cabinet 1997–2003: Prime ministerial	1989–1991: Centralized cabinet 1991–2001: Decentralized ministerial 2001–2003: Centralized prime ministerial	1989–1997: Government registrar 1997–2001: Prime minister's vanguard—government registrar 2001–2003: Government registrar
Czech Republic	1993–2002: Cabinet	1993–1997: Centralized prime ministerial 1997–2002: Decentralized ministerial	1993–2002: Government registrar
Bulgaria	1989–2001: Cabinet	1989–1997: Decentralized ministerial 1997–2001: Centralized prime ministerial	1989–2001: Government registrar

change in the type of government, from a cabinet government with strong ministerial character to a prime ministerial type of government. As the type of government is typically grounded in the constitution—more so than the type of core executive and the center of government—the early decisions on the basic power relations within government proved remarkably durable. Put differently, the initial transition phase produced strong path dependencies.

Second, it is notable that only Hungary and, in somewhat weaker form, Poland have developed prime ministerial systems. This observation goes somewhat against the general perception of postcommunist politics that tends to emphasize the key role played by powerful and often ruthless "strongmen" (and the occasional "strongwoman"). What our research suggests is a somewhat more complex picture in which party-political and personalist power resources can be employed by skilled politicians—such as Prime Ministers Klaus and Kostov in the Czech Republic and Bulgaria, respectively—to overcome, albeit only temporarily, the restrictions that the type of government imposes on their authority and coordinative ability within the government. With the exception of the Hungarian case, the power of chief executives is thus built on rather precarious institutional foundations.

Third, and again with the exception of Hungary, we observe a good deal of change over time in the type of core executive. Fluidity was most pronounced in the Polish case but could also be observed in those of the Czech Republic and Bulgaria. Running contrary to common expectations about a general prime ministerialization of European politics, such a pattern is not borne out when we look at the core executive. In fact, the Czech Republic represents a case where a centralized prime ministerial core executive, once established, was later dismantled; if we had extended our analysis to the government of Simeon Saxe-Coburg-Gotha, which followed that of Kostov in 2001, it is likely that a similar observation would apply. This changeability underscores that the manner in which the core executive operates is highly sensitive to changes in party constellations and personal power relations.

Fourth, our analysis clearly demonstrates that cabinet government—with an emphasis on collegiality, collective decision taking, and collective responsibility—might be an attractive normative ideal (and one that the CEE countries inherited from the communist period), but it is exceedingly difficult to sustain in practice. Thus, our comparative overview only notes one case—in Poland, under the highly unusual circumstances produced by Solidarity's dominance of the country's party system in 1989–1991—where a centralized cabinet core executive was in operation, during which coordination was principally driven by considerations of effectiveness and efficiency in cabinet decision making and of ensuring that both the prime minister and the ministers adhered to the collective will of the government. Perhaps even more tellingly, we found no instance where the center of government functioned as a Cabinet Office, controlled by a powerful cabinet secretary or a minister of cabinet rank who, with his staff, could ensure the smooth operation of a collegiate and collective government and ensure its authority. Cabinet government and governmental institutions to underpin it effectively emerge as an especially demanding form of government.

Fifth, if, as often happens in the comparative literature on core executives, the organization and operation of center of the government are taken as proxy for the core executive as a whole, then our findings would indeed suggest that the "hollow crown" created by the fall of communism has not been replenished, with the notable exception of Hungary. But such a conclusion would be premature. Centers of government form an integral part of the core executive, but the latter regularly extends beyond the former. Efforts have been made to strengthen the core executive, but, in most of the cases and for most of the time, the center itself has not acted as a coordinating hub.

Sixth, and following from the last point, we observe frequent and, in the cases of the Czech Republic and Bulgaria, persistent disjunctures between types of government, core executive, and center. As we note in chapter 2, these three dimensions of executive development are logically linked, but only in the Hungarian case does one observe congruence over an extended period of time. The more prevalent pattern is, in fact, incongruence or disjunctures. In themselves, the latter should not, however, be read as evidence for failed or somehow dysfunctional or even "pathological" institutionalization. Rather, as pointed out in chapter 1, under conditions of considerable uncertainty, resource shortages, and attempts at external direction, "institutionalization for reversibility," which implies fluidity and opportunities for exploiting "loopholes," may constitute an appropriate strategy for institution building. Such patterns of "light" or "shallow" institutionalization are especially likely where political conflicts over institutional choices and external direction play a powerful role.

NOTE

1. The center-right Antall government (1990–1993) exchanged nine out of fourteen administrative state secretaries (from the preceding Nemeth government); the center-left Horn government (1994–1998), nine out of thirteen; and the center-right Orbán government (1998–2002), thirteen out of fifteen (Szente 1999).

8

Institutions and Their Effects: Budgetary Policymaking

The aim of this chapter is to examine how the trajectories in the development of core executive institutions analyzed in the previous chapter affect the policymaking process. Budgetary policy is a particularly appropriate area for the analysis of the effects of core executive institutions, given its central importance in the allocation of resources and policy coordination. This chapter builds on Brusis and Dimitrov (2001) but uses a different analytical framework developed from the typology of core executives put forward in chapter 2, and focuses on a narrower range of indicators. Based on this analytical framework, the hypothesis is put forward that centralized core executives achieve better budgetary performance, defined in terms of the level of the fiscal deficit, than do decentralized core executives. The hypothesis is then tested against empirical evidence for Hungary, Poland, the Czech Republic, and Bulgaria between the fall of communism and the early twenty-first century.

ANALYTICAL FRAMEWORK AND HYPOTHESIS

As discussed in chapter 2, Hallerberg and von Hagen's typology (1999) of intragovernmental institutional configurations can be reformulated on the basis of the threefold typology of core executives used in this book (centralized prime ministerial, centralized cabinet, and decentralized ministerial). A centralized prime ministerial executive involves, in the area of budgetary policy, the delegation of power to a strong prime minister and/or finance minister. In a centralized cabinet executive, coordination can be expected to be carried out through fiscal contracts, concluded between the parties participating in the governing coalition. In a decentralized ministerial executive, we are likely to see a decentralized configuration of budgetary institutions, with individual ministers advocating greater expenditure in their policy area with little if any constraint from either the prime minister or finance minister or the cabinet.

There are five main tasks in the budgetary process in which core executive institutions are likely to be involved:

1. Preparation of a medium-term fiscal framework
2. Determination of budget targets and guidelines
3. Preparation of the draft budget
4. Allocation of expenditure to the line ministries
5. Management of expenditure

The second, third, and fourth tasks are identified by von Hagen and Harden (1994). A medium-term fiscal framework can serve as an important mechanism for the centralization of the budgetary process, creating exogenous constraints for the spending ministries (Brusis and Dimitrov 2001). The management of the expenditure set out in the budget law can be centralized through the establishment of a single government account through which all payments must pass (Allen and Tommasi 2001; Brusis and Dimitrov 2001).

Depending on the type of core executive—centralized prime ministerial, centralized cabinet, or decentralized ministerial—these five tasks are likely to be undertaken by different institutions within the executive. Table 8.1 reflects, on the horizontal dimension, the main tasks involved in the budgetary process and, on the vertical dimension, the institutions performing each task, grouped under the three types of core executive.

To assess the impact of different types of core executive on budgetary performance, it would be useful to adopt a performance indicator that is both measurable in quantitative terms and capable of providing a basis for the assessment of the overall quality of the budgetary process. One such indicator is the level of fiscal deficit, which goes to the heart of the budgetary process, pointing to the ability of the executive to match resources to policy demands. In this chapter, *fiscal deficit* is defined as the general government fiscal deficit. The most important characteristic of the general government fiscal deficit is that it includes the deficits of both national and subnational governments.

Based on the outlined analytical framework, this chapter aims to test the hypothesis derived from Hallerberg (2000) that centralized core executives achieve lower fiscal deficits than do decentralized executives. As explained in chapter 2, the effect of the configuration of the core executive on the level of fiscal deficit is due to the fact that budgeting has the characteristics of a common pool resource problem. This problem can be overcome

Table 8.1. Types of Budgetary Tasks and Core Executives

	Core Executive		
Budgetary Tasks	*Centralized Prime Ministerial*	*Centralized Cabinet*	*Decentralized Ministerial*
Determination of medium-term fiscal framework	Determined by FM/PM	Medium-term fiscal framework included in coalition contract or determined by coalition summit, cabinet committee, and/or informal inner cabinet	No medium-term fiscal framework before the start of bilateral negotiations between FM/PM and individual ministers
Setting of budget targets and guidelines	Expenditure limits determined by FM/PM	Expenditure limits included in coalition contract or determined by coalition summit, cabinet committee and/or informal inner cabinet	No targets and guidelines before the start of bilateral negotiations between FM/PM and individual ministers
Preparation of draft budget	Prepared by FM, based on expenditure limits	Prepared by FM, based on expenditure limits	Prepared by FM, collecting bids from ministries
Allocation of expenditure to the line ministries	Determined by FM/PM	Determined by coalition summit, cabinet committee, and/or informal inner cabinet	Determined by cabinet on the basis of equal voting rights for all ministers
Management of expenditure	Single government account	Single government account	Individual ministry accounts

Source: Partly based on Brusis and Dimitrov (2001) and von Hagen (1998).
Note: FM: finance minister; PM: prime minister. An inner cabinet can consist of the prime minister and key ministers, such as deputy prime ministers and the finance minister, often with overarching responsibilities. A coalition summit usually involves a meeting of the leaders of the parties represented in the coalition (Müller and Strom 2000).

through delegation to the finance minister and/or prime minister within a centralized prime ministerial core executive or through the establishment of fiscal contracts within a centralized cabinet core executive (Hallerberg 2000; Hallerberg and von Hagen 1999; von Hagen 1998; von Hagen and Harden 1994).

EMPIRICAL RESULTS

This section presents our findings on the impact of the configuration of executive institutions on budgetary performance in Hungary, Poland, the Czech Republic and Bulgaria between the fall of communism and the early twenty-first century.

Hungary

The first postcommunist Hungarian government, formed after the elections of June 1990 and led by Prime Minister Antall, was a relatively unstable coalition of the MDF, KDNP, and FKGP. The coalition partners could not expect to run together in the following elections, as the MDF, the largest party in the coalition, experienced a process of disintegration. This ruled out delegation to a strong finance minister. Fiscal contracts could also not be applied, given that the parties in the coalition were still in the embryonic stage of their development and lacked clear programmatic identities, which made them unable or unwilling to commit themselves to explicit policy goals. In these circumstances, it is not surprising that the institutional configuration of the budgetary process remained largely decentralized in spite of some strengthening of the powers of the prime minister and the finance minister.

Constitutional changes introduced in 1990 gave the prime minister extensive powers in determining the composition of the government but did not enable him to intervene in the budgetary process on an institutional basis (Brusis and Dimitrov 2001). The finance minister was strengthened, albeit indirectly, by a number of institutional changes, some of which were initiated by the reform communist government led by Prime Minister Németh. The creation of an independent central bank in 1988 meant that budget deficits had to be financed at market interest rates. The president of the bank, György Surányi, who remained in office following the change of government in 1990, provided strong support to the finance minister in his efforts to stabilize the economy. The direct powers of the finance minister, however, were not significantly enhanced. While there were some changes, such as the introduction of a macroeconomic framework (Brusis and Dimitrov 2001), the budget preparation process was still largely based on the communist-era Act on the Financial Affairs of the State. Under this act, the finance minister was responsible for the preparation of the draft budget but only on the basis of project budgets prepared by ministries, national, and local authorities. Problems that could not be resolved between the finance minister and individual budget holders had to be sent to the council of ministers, where the finance minister was merely one minister among many (Brusis and Dimitrov 2001). The ambitious minister of finance Mihály

Kupa (1990–1993) attempted to undertake a comprehensive reform in the course of the preparation of the 1992 Public Finance Act but largely failed in his efforts due to lack of political support within the government (Brusis and Dimitrov 2001; Szántó 1992). Another reform attempt, undertaken with International Monetary Fund support in 1993, was also unsuccessful (Brusis and Dimitrov 2001).

The weak institutional position of the finance minister within the government—which meant, as finance minister Ferenc Rabár complained after his resignation in October 1990, that every single economic policy decision had to be voted in the cabinet—undermined the efforts of the successive officeholders (three in 1990–1994) to force their ministerial colleagues to make the necessary expenditure cuts to balance the budget during the recession induced by the transition from a centrally planned economy to a market economy and by the collapse of Hungary's trade with its eastern neighbors. The government expanded the competencies of the Tripartite Council, which provided a strong platform for trade union representation (Brusis and Dimitrov 2001). Decisions taken in this council—for instance, on the level of the minimum wage—had a negative impact on the budget deficit. The government's decision to strengthen the institutional independence of the social insurance system (Brusis and Dimitrov 2001)—while at the same time relieving it of responsibilities such as family allowance and child care subsidies, which were transferred to the state budget—had the same effect. The combination of these factors contributed to high and growing fiscal deficits: 7.8 percent of the gross domestic product (GDP) in 1992 and 9.2 percent in 1993 (World Bank 2000).

The party composition of the government changed for the better following the 1994 elections, which were won by an alliance of the postcommunist MSZP and the SZDSZ. The two parties formed a stable electoral bloc that could expect to stay together in the next elections—as it has indeed done in the 1998 and 2002 elections. Furthermore, Prime Minister Horn was the leader of the MSZP and was able to accept the resignations of his party colleagues with relatively little political damage. This party composition of the government created conditions for a change in the configuration of budgeting institutions toward delegation to a strong finance minister and prime minister. Such an institutional transformation did indeed occur in the course of 1995–1996. The first step toward the tackling of the mounting fiscal deficit was the so-called Bokros package, named after the minister of finance Lajos Bokros (1995–1996), which involved drastic tax increases and expenditure cuts. The package was decided on in seclusion by Horn and Bokros and then imposed by them on their cabinet colleagues at the expense of the resignation of three ministers (Greskovits 2001). The package succeeded in reducing the fiscal deficit to 6.2 percent of the GDP in 1995 and to 3.1 percent in 1996 (World Bank 2000).

Bokros was also successful in pushing through a comprehensive reform of the institutional framework for the budgetary process. The Public Finance Act was modified to include all off-budget liabilities into the general budget balance, introduce a multiyear budget plan, and create a State Treasury, which made it possible to centralize the financial management of the entire government (Brixi, Papp, and Schick 1999; Brusis and Dimitrov 2001; Thuma, Polackova, and Ferreira 1998). Before the establishment of the State Treasury, budgetary organs had operated their own accounts— approximately twelve hundred in total—which allowed them to take on payment obligations that exceeded their revenue estimates. The State Treasury operated a single account for all government payments, which made it possible to control ex-ante any such payments against budget estimates (Brixi, Papp, and Schick 1999).

The institutional changes undertaken by the Horn government were preserved and indeed taken forward under its successor, the government led by Prime Minister Orbán, a coalition of the FIDESZ-MPP, the MDF, and the FKGP. Orbán's position as party leader of the FIDESZ-MPP allowed him to dominate his ministerial colleagues and thus made possible a substantial delegation of power to the prime minister. In 2000, the prime minister acquired the right to set, on the proposal of the finance minister, the total expenditure limit and to inform each minister of the limit for his ministry (Brusis and Dimitrov 2001), through a letter, which is sent by the end of May and which specifies only the limit for the particular ministry, without indicating the limits for the other ministries. The more centralized institutional configuration led to a reduction in the fiscal deficit to 3.7 percent of the GDP in 1999, from 4.8 percent in 1998 (World Bank 2000).

Poland

The early years of Polish transition witnessed coalition governments that were even more unstable than their Hungarian counterparts. In the first fully democratic parliamentary election, in 1991 (the election of 1989 had opened only one-third of the seats in the more important lower house of parliament, the Sejm, to democratic contestation, reserving the rest for the Communist Party and its allies), as many as twenty-nine parties entered the Sejm, with no one party commanding more than 13 percent of the seats. The multitude of parties, most of which proved ephemeral and failed to get into parliament at the next election in 1993, made the formation of stable coalition governments almost impossible. The Olszewski government, formed in December 1991, consisted of five parties and lasted only until June 1992. Another coalition government, led by Hanna Suchocka, was appointed in July 1992 and after numerous crises was finally brought down in May 1993. The parties' rapidly shifting policy positions and bewildering changes of coalition partners ruled out fiscal contracts and made a decentralized configuration of budgeting institutions almost inevitable. The powers of the prime minister remained weak, as they had been in the communist period. The same was largely true of the institutional position of the finance minister. The success of finance minister Leszek Balcerowicz in cutting the fiscal deficit in 1990 and 1991 to a low point of 3.6 percent of the GDP (World Bank 2000) through painful expenditure cuts was due to the "extraordinary politics" of these years, in which Solidarity enjoyed the unqualified support of the population following its role in the collapse of the communist regime. Balcerowicz's success could not be sustained following the start of "normal" democratic politics with the 1991 elections. The decentralized institutional configuration of the budgetary process meant that the Finance Ministry could not impose effective controls in the course of the preparation of the budget (Brusis and Dimitrov 2001). This led to a rising fiscal deficit, up to 6.1 percent of the GDP in 1992 (World Bank 2000).

A turning point in the party composition of the government came with the 1993 elections, which were won by a coalition of the postcommunist SLD and the PSL. The two coalition partners formed a stable electoral bloc and stayed together in subsequent elections. The political cohesion of the SLD made it possible for SLD cabinet ministers to accept delegation to the finance minister, who was always an SLD member. The PSL ministers were not so tractable, but even they were forced to acquiesce in the delegation of power, given the SLD's dominance of the coalition, for which it supplied the bulk of parliamentary support. While the prime minister gained important new powers in determining the composition of the government, his powers in the budgetary process remained restricted (Brusis and Dimitrov 2001). The position of the Finance Ministry was strengthened considerably. The ministry gained a leading role in producing a three-year economic and fiscal framework (Brusis and Dimitrov 2001), which includes projections about the GDP, public debt, inflation, balance of payments, employment and unemployment rates, budget revenues, and budget deficit. While seemingly technocratic, the adoption of a particular framework is often a political rather than an economic decision. Based on the framework and on the task inventories it receives from the individual ministries, the Ministry of Finance then prepares budget guidelines. The budget guidelines contain a draft plan of budget revenues, expenditures and deficit/surplus, and, most important, spending caps for individual ministries (Brusis and Dimitrov 2001). This gives the finance minister an important advantage as an agenda setter. In principle, spending caps should be stated as simple figures without a detailed breakdown, but there are indications that they often come with further strings attached—for instance, caps on particular types of expenditures such as wages. The ministries can subsequently ask, in the drawing up of their own draft budgets, for spending caps to be increased—usually by

10–12 percent—but the Finance Ministry is free to reject demands that it considers unjustified. Based on the budgets presented to it by the ministries, the Ministry of Finance produces a draft state budget. In the discussion of the draft state budget in the cabinet, the minister of finance informs his ministerial colleagues of any adjustments in the economic forecast and their effect on the size of the budget envelope. This often produces a lump sum of uncommitted resources, which are then appropriated by the cabinet on the basis of a list of unresolved conflicts between the Ministry of Finance and individual ministries. The amounts involved are, however, insubstantial. The role of parliament in the budgetary process has been restricted by the 1997 constitution, which bars it from increasing the budget deficit, which has been proposed in the budget submitted to parliament by the government (Brusis and Dimitrov 2001). Any proposals for increased spending in one area have to indicate a corresponding reduction in expenditure in another area. Finally, the Ministry of Finance has gained the power to prepare, following the adoption of the budget by parliament and in consultation with the ministries, a revenue and expenditure implementation schedule. By law, ministries can undertake expenditure only in accordance with the implementation schedule. Ministries must seek the Ministry of Finance's approval for expenditures in excess of those foreseen in the schedule. The empowerment of the Finance Ministry has led to fiscal deficits below 3 percent of the GDP in the late 1990s: 2.7 percent in 1997, 2.4 percent in 1998, and 2.1 percent in 1999 (World Bank 2000).

Czech Republic

As in Poland, the early years of the transition to democracy in Czechoslovakia were a period of "extraordinary politics," in which the Czech Civic Forum and its Slovak counterpart, Public against Violence, enjoyed virtually unqualified support thanks to their role in the overthrow of communism. Their unchallenged domination made it possible for the federal finance minister Vaclav Klaus, a prominent member of Civic Forum, to push through a radical program of the economic reform, with strict fiscal discipline. These bold policy measures were not, however, accompanied by any significant centralization of the budgeting institutions. The weak position of the prime minister inherited from communism was preserved largely unchanged. The institutional position of the finance minister also remained relatively weak. Klaus's formal position within the government was rather marginal as one of nine deputy prime ministers in the first postcommunist government and one of four in the second.

In contrast to the situation in Poland, where the disintegration of Solidarity in 1990–1991 brought to an end Finance Minister Balcerowicz's political preeminence, the collapse of Civic Forum actually boosted Klaus's political ascendancy. Klaus played a leading role in the dissolution of Civic Forum, in a reaction against what he saw as its heterogeneous nature, with its uneasy combination of liberal and social democratic elements. The breakdown of Civic Forum was not, however, followed by the creation of an unstable party system composed of a multitude of weak parties, as in Poland. Instead, Klaus succeeded in replacing Civic Forum as the dominant party in the Czech Republic with his own explicitly liberal party, the ODS. The ODS not only won the 1992 parliamentary elections in the Czech Republic but was also largely responsible for the creation of an independent Czech state in 1993. Klaus's role as the founding father both of the ODS and of the new state made it possible for him to impose his preferences for a balanced budget on the spending ministers and give decisive support to the finance minister Ivan Kocarnik in 1993–1995. The Czech Republic had the unique distinction of being able to maintain a surplus budget for three successive years, between 1993 and 1995 (World Bank 2000).

Klaus's success in containing the fiscal deficit was not accompanied, however, by the centralization of budgeting institutions through delegation of power to the finance minister and the prime minister. He did not use his politically strong position as finance minister in 1989–1992 and as prime minister in 1992–1996 to increase the institutional powers of either the finance minister or the prime minister. With regard to the former, Klaus's reforms were limited to the removal of what he saw as remnants of communism, such as the State Planning Commission, but he was not concerned with putting anything positive in their place. The revision of the organic budget law in 1990 left the powers of the finance minister largely unchanged. Klaus's approach to the office of the Prime Minister was similar. While abolishing the positions of deputy prime ministers in 1992, which he saw as a survival from the communist system, he did nothing to increase the institutional powers of the prime minister. He also retained the existing structure of the Government Office, whereby the office served the cabinet as a whole rather than the prime minister.

The decentralized budgetary institutions began to exert their negative impact on the fiscal deficit, as Klaus's political dominance began to decline in the mid-1990s. As the impact from the transition from communism and the creation of the state faded, the Czech Republic began to see the development of a competitive party system. The 1996 election seriously weakened the ODS's position both within the parliament, where its minority government had to depend on the support of two opposition social democratic members of parliament, and within the cabinet, where the ODS controlled eight of the sixteen seats, in contrast to the ten of seventeen in the previous government. The ODS's constrained position meant that Klaus could no longer impose his preferences or give unqualified support to Finance Minister Kocarnik. In a crisis situation, as in the currency panic of May 1997,

Klaus and Kocarnik were able to act together and push drastic expenditure cuts through cabinet (7.7 percent of the original 1997 budget), but after the emergency had been overcome, the destabilizing forces reasserted themselves. Kocarnik was forced to resign as finance minister, and Klaus was so weakened that he was toppled from his position by a financial scandal in November 1997.

The parliamentary election of June 1998 brought to an end the ODS's dominance and created a balance of power between it and the CSSD. Each of the two parties, with 27.7 percent and 32.3 percent of the vote respectively, needed the other's support if it was to form a government. The fact that the two parties were indispensable to each other created the conditions for the conclusion of a fiscal contract. This took the form not of a grand coalition between the two parties but of an agreement by which the ODS agreed to tolerate a CSSD minority administration in return for specific policy commitments, including a restriction of the fiscal deficit to CZK 20 billion in 2001. The positive effect of the opposition agreement on fiscal performance was, however, weakened by the severe factional split within the CSSD, between advocates of higher social spending and those supporting fiscal responsibility. The CSSD leader Zeman found himself in the position of a mediator between the two factions and indeed was increasingly marginalized by the leftist faction, whose head, Špidla, eventually replaced him as party leader. The prime minister's weak position in his own party also meant that he could not force his cabinet colleagues to accept delegation of power to the finance minister or to himself. The ODS proved unable or rather unwilling to enforce the opposition agreement, fearful that pushing the CSSD into a corner might precipitate early elections in which the ODS's deficit-reduction stance would rebound to its disadvantage, as indeed proved to be the case when a fiscally expansionary CSSD under Špidla's leadership won the parliamentary election in 2002.

The unenforceability of the fiscal contract and the weakness of the minister of finance and the prime minister in the Zeman government were reflected in the prolonged failure to pass a new organic budget law, in spite of the need to integrate off-budget expenditures, to institutionalize the use of medium-term financial forecasts and to harmonize Czech law with that of the European Communities. It was only in 2000 that a new law replaced the 1990 law. It is significant that the new law did not make any significant changes to the bottom-up methodology of budget preparation, with ministries and lower-level government units coming up with spending claims without significant restrictions. The natural outcome has been that the total demands on the budget continue to exceed resources by a substantial margin, producing a growing fiscal deficit. While not high in nominal terms or as a proportion of the GDP in the first years after 1996, the deficit has been on a consistent upward trend. By 2001, the Czech Republic had reached a situation where it had the highest deficit of all the four countries under examination, at more than 8 percent of the GDP. As in 1997, the immediate crisis was likely to be resolved by temporary measures—in this case, privatization revenues, which were expected to amount to as much as 11.3 percent of the GDP in 2002 (*Financial Times* 2001), thus postponing the institutional reforms that alone could deal with the roots of the crisis.

Bulgaria

Unlike Hungary, Poland, and Czechoslovakia, Bulgaria did not witness the collapse of the ruling Communist Party in 1989. The party was able to preserve its power by removing the aging leader Zhivkov in November 1989 and winning the first democratic elections in June 1990. The Communist Party's dominance of the party system meant the retention of the pre-1989 configuration of budgeting institutions. Policymaking functions were still concentrated in the Politburo of the Communist Party (which underwent a nominal change of name in April 1990 to the BSP), with the role of the government being confined to the implementation of the Politburo's decisions. The centralization of government institutions was seen as unnecessary, as the government's work was organized by the Communist Party, and indeed dangerous, as it could create an alternative locus of power. One indication of the executive's low status in the political system was the fact that leaders of the Communist Party did not choose to become prime ministers. The prime minister's position remained institutionally weak, with few effective institutional powers vis-à-vis his ministerial colleagues. The finance minister fared even worse. Even in the best of times, the finance minister's role was confined to putting nominal financial values to the physical indicators of the five-year production plans determined by the Communist Party. In the last two years of communism, Bulgaria went even further and became one of the very few countries in the world to make do without a Ministry of Finance. Aware of the country's slide into deficit and debt, Zhivkov tried to resolve the problem by abolishing the institution that could remind him of it. While the reformers who brought Zhivkov down did restore the Ministry of Finance, with the veteran Belcho Belchev at the helm, the reconstituted ministry suffered from an acute shortage of analytical capacity.

A limited shift in the configuration of budgeting institutions only began in the autumn of 1990, when the BSP first conceded control of the presidency and then of the government. The BSP's willingness to do so was part of an attempt to save at least part of its power in what it recognized was an inevitable regime change by transferring competencies to the state apparatus. The transfer of competencies to the government was also facilitated by an emerging conflict between the socialist prime minister Lukanov and the BSP leader Lilov in September 1990. In a clear break with communist traditions, Lukanov attempted to assert the dominance of his office over that of the party leader. While Lukanov failed in his endeavor, the conflict was sufficient to demonstrate to the BSP leadership the problems of controlling the prime minister. Lilov's reaction to these problems was to shift to a more indirect method of controlling the executive, whereby the BSP would not provide the prime minister but would dominate the government by relying on the parliamentary majority that it had won in the June 1990 elections. Lilov accordingly allowed the Lukanov government to fall in November 1990 and engineered the appointment of an expert government headed by a nonparty prime minister in the following month.

The new view of the autonomous position of the executive vis-à-vis the party made it necessary to strengthen at least partially the policymaking capacity of the executive. The minister of finance was to benefit most, partly due to the imperatives of controlling the mushrooming budget deficit and repaying Bulgaria's foreign debt and partly because of his recognized leading role in the transition to a market economy. By contrast, the position of the prime minister was not strengthened, and he remained without any effective powers within the cabinet. This demonstrated the incompleteness of the transformation of the BSP's view of the executive. While the executive was to be allowed to develop a degree of autonomous capacity in the economic area, it was still considered to be ultimately subordinate to the party when it came to the overall coordination of public policy. The prime minister was therefore not allowed to develop overarching institutional powers and was expected to function under the political control of the party.

The strengthening of the minister of finance's position was also due to external factors, especially the role of the International Monetary Fund (IMF). Bulgaria joined the IMF in September 1990 and found itself in a position of heavy dependence on the fund, given the fact that it had declared a moratorium on its foreign debt repayments, thus closing off private sources of finance and making the fund the only available source of external credit. As part of its preparation for IMF membership, Bulgaria adopted a new budget classification, which made it possible to define the budget deficit clearly for the first time and to make a start with the preparation of macroeconomic forecasts. The dissolution of the State Planning Commission as part of the "big bang" liberalization of the economy in February 1991, undertaken by the expert government, also boosted the minister of finance's position. In 1991, Ivan Kostov, the finance minister in the expert government, was able to produce a budget that reversed the trend of rising deficits characteristic of the last years of communism, by cutting the deficit to 4.5 percent of the GDP and delivering expenditure cuts of 10.6 percent of the GDP (World Bank 2000). That was achieved largely through cuts in subsidies linked to the liberalization of prices and the higher-than-expected inflation of 1991. Once these easy resources had been exhausted, the fiscal deficit began to creep up. The finance minister was constrained by his weak institutional position vis-à-vis the line ministries. Most conflicts over expenditure could not be resolved through bilateral negotiations between the Ministry of Finance and the spending ministries and were catapulted into the cabinet, where they were endlessly rehashed and where the majority of his spending colleagues could outvote the finance minister. The prime minister was unable, given his weak institutional position, to provide effective support to the finance minister, either in the course of the bilateral discussions or in the cabinet meetings. Such a decentralized institutional configuration made it impossible to sustain Kostov's success in limiting the fiscal deficit, and the deficit climbed sharply after 1991, reaching a high of 12.1 percent of the GDP in 1993 (World Bank 2000).

In the years 1991–1994, the institutional decentralization of the government continued, driven by the underlying dominance of the BSP. The anticommunist UDF won the largest number of votes in the October 1991 elections, but the BSP fell short only by a whisker. The election result did not change the BSP's dominant position in the political system, as was demonstrated when the UDF government fell only after a year in office, to be succeeded by yet another expert government relying on the BSP's parliamentary support.

The BSP's hegemony was confirmed by its absolute victory in the November 1994 parliamentary elections. The victory encouraged the BSP leadership to undo even the limited strengthening of the position of the finance minister, which had been undertaken in 1991. The almost casual treatment of Finance Minister Dimitur Kostov by the party leader and Prime Minister Videnov was reminiscent of Zhivkov's denigration of Kostov's predecessors in the late 1980s. The finance minister could not even see the prime minister without waiting for weeks and was constantly outvoted in the cabinet by his colleagues. Another indication of the finance minister's diminished powers was the transfer of the Agency for Economic Forecasts, which had provided expert advice on the preparation of the macroeconomic forecasts since 1991, to the Ministry of the Economy. The finance minister could no longer rely on the IMF as a powerful external constraint, given the fact that the government believed that it could manage a state-led economic recovery on its own and regarded the IMF as an unwelcome interloper. The finance minister's weakness meant that he was unable to stop the prime minister and his colleagues from reflating the economy in 1995–1996. By late 1996, the government had lost control over the economy, and the country fell into hyperinflation and its most severe recession since the start of the transition. The fiscal deficit reached an incredible 15.4 percent of the GDP (World Bank 2000).

This debacle set the stage for a number of institutional changes. The most significant one was the introduction of a powerful exogenous constraint, a currency board, whereby the amount of Bulgarian lev in circulation could not exceed the country's foreign currency reserves at a fixed exchange rate. The board represented the ultimate recognition of the inability of Bulgarian governments to manage monetary policy and substantially restricted their discretion in fiscal policy by prohibiting the Bulgarian National Bank from lending to the government. The acceptance of such a constraint was made possible by the collapse of the BSP government in February 1997 and the appointment of a caretaker government with a mission to stabilize the economy by all possible means. Even the new government, however, found the currency board hard to stomach, and it initially argued that the board had to be introduced for a period of not more than six months and that the exchange rate was not to be regulated by law in order to leave room for more flexible policies. The IMF, by contrast, maintained that the currency board had to be introduced for a period of several years and that the exchange rate had to be fixed by law in order to enhance the credibility of the board. Its views ultimately prevailed.

The institutional changes implemented by the caretaker government were a reaction against the failure of party government. The absence of direct party involvement was, however, a mixed blessing. While a powerful external constraint was created in the form of the currency board, the internal configuration of government institutions could not be changed without a commitment by the political parties.

Such a commitment was not forthcoming in the following few years. The debacle of the BSP government paved the way for an overwhelming victory by the anticommunist United Democratic Forces, consisting of the UDF and allies, in the parliamentary elections held in April 1997. The delayed nature of the Bulgarian transition meant that the UDF's win was not a normal swing of the political pendulum but rather an equivalent to Solidarity's and Civic Forum's overthrow of communism in Poland and Czechoslovakia in 1989. The UDF therefore behaved much as Solidarity and Civic Forum did in the first few years after 1989, using its seemingly unassailable political dominance to push through painful reforms without showing any significant concern for the centralization of government institutions. Under the prime ministership of Ivan Kostov, who had been finance minister in the expert government in 1990–1991, and helped by the constraining effect of the currency board, the UDF government was able to achieve a dramatic improvement in fiscal performance: the 1997 and 1998 budgets were in surplus by 2.1 percent and 0.9 percent of the GDP, and the 1999 budget had a deficit of only 0.9 percent (World Bank 2000). Kostov's political preeminence, similar to the one enjoyed by Klaus in the Czech Republic in 1992–1996, made it unnecessary in his view to build up the institutional capacity of the Prime Minister's Office. The finance minister fared somewhat better. A new organic budget law adopted in 1995 gave him some powers, such as the ability to prepare a parallel budget on which to base his negotiations with the line ministries and the preparation of a medium-term macroeconomic framework. However, the law deliberately left vague the relationship between the Ministry of Finance and the spending ministries in the course of the bilateral negotiations preceding the submission of the budget to the cabinet. While substantial changes have been made in the budgetary system since 1997, such as the introduction of a single government account and the elimination of most of the extrabudgetary funds, they have not been incorporated into the organic budget law. Instead, they have been carried through the annual budget laws and could therefore in principle be reversed the following year. The institutional weakness of the Bulgarian prime minister and finance minister means that with a different party composition of the government, Bulgaria's fiscal performance could, as in the Czech Republic, take a downward turn.

CONCLUSION

The evidence presented in this chapter supports the hypothesis that centralized executives achieve lower fiscal deficits than do decentralized executives. In the first few years after the collapse of communism, the budgetary core executive institutions in all four countries in this study were decentralized. Neither finance ministers nor prime ministers gained any substantial institutional powers with respect to their ministerial colleagues. The decentralized institutions provided opportunities for the spending ministers to push for greater expenditure for their own departments without concern for the government as a whole, and high fiscal deficits (significantly above the Maastricht threshold of 3 percent of the GDP) were the inevitable result.

The shift to a centralized configuration of the budgetary core executive in Hungary and, to a lesser extent, in Poland after the early 1990s had a clear positive effect on the levels of their fiscal deficit. In both countries, prime ministers became more powerful, but while the Hungarian prime minister gained important powers in the budgetary process, including the setting of expenditure ceilings for the individual ministries, the powers of the Polish prime minister in the budgetary field remained relatively restricted. The powers of finance ministers were greatly extended in both countries. The Hungarian finance minister was strengthened by introduction of a multiyear budget plan, the inclusion of all off-budget liabilities into the general budget balance, and the creation of a State Treasury. The Polish finance minister gained a whole range of new powers, including the preparation of a three-year fiscal framework, the proposing of spending caps for individual ministries, and the drawing up of an implementation schedule obligatory for the ministries. The centralized executive institutions enabled Hungary and

Poland to achieve fiscal deficits of around 3 percent of the GDP in most years in the second half of the 1990s.

By contrast, the decentralized ministerial core executive institutions in the Czech Republic and Bulgaria proved unable to deliver a sustainable improvement in their fiscal deficits. In the Czech Republic, the weak position of the finance minister and prime minister and the unenforceability of the fiscal agreement between the social democratic minority government and the opposition ODS have led to a sharp deterioration in the fiscal balance, to a point where the country had the highest deficit of the four countries in the early twenty-first century. In Bulgaria, the finance minister and the prime minister have been equally weak in institutional terms vis-à-vis the spending ministers (although the introduction of a currency board has been an important positive influence), which is likely to spell danger once the period of "revolutionary" politics—which endowed the prime minister with unique political power—comes to an end.

NOTE

This chapter draws partly on Dimitrov (2005). Permission from PrAcademics Press.

9

Domestic Institutions and European Governance

DOMESTIC INSTITUTIONS IN CONTEXT

The research documented in the preceding chapters focuses on domestic executive institutions and emphasizes domestic factors—legacies, critical junctures, and actor constellations—in accounting for trajectories of core executive development. As noted in chapter 1, such a dual domestic focus differs, to some extent, from most empirical analyses of government, public administration, and public policy in postcommunist CEE. With few exceptions, such studies have been conducted from two closely related perspectives: EU enlargement and Europeanization. The enlargement perspective has principally inquired into the question of whether the new EU member states and accession states are "ready for Europe," in the sense that their governmental and administrative institutions comply with the accession criteria and are capable of implementing effectively and efficiently the EU's *acquis communautaire*. By contrast, studies of Europeanization have been interested more broadly in the institutional and policy effects of EU integration at the level of the new and likely future member states. Both perspectives give prominence to external drivers of institutional and policy change and regard domestic institutions primarily as the objects of reform attempts.

Our research has helped to highlight some of the specificities of institutions in the postcommunist settings that tend to be neglected in discussions of governance in CEE. These specificities relate both to institutional configurations and to forms and degrees of institutionalization. Thus, our discussion has noted that the empirical linkage between types of government, types of core executives, and types of centers of government is more ambiguous than comparative studies of executives typically imply. Configurations are more complex and, in some respects, less consistent than what students of Western executives might expect. Even more so than in Western Europe, executive institutions in CEE are often modeled around individuals, so that office and officeholder effectively merge; but we have also noted cases where personalist power resources have been strong enough so as to lead executive politicians to neglect formal institution building aimed at supporting their position. This oft-observed close identity between office and officeholder gives a fluidity to postcommunist institutions that can easily be mistaken for instability. As noted in chapter 1, there are good theoretical reasons to expect that degrees on institutionalization of postcommunist executives are lower than those in the case of Western Europe, as procedural routines have to become embedded, and individuals to be socialized, into the democratic institutions.

With their focus on domestic institutions and the specific conditions under which they operate, our findings on executive development and our attempt to account for executive trajectories over time may contribute useful insights to debates about the impact of enlargement, Europeanization, and, more broadly, the evolving patterns of European governance. In turn, these debates help to contextualize and interpret our findings and allow us to draw out some broader lessons. By way of concluding, we therefore want to put our case in the context of arguments about the changing landscape of governance in Europe. The three questions that we address are as follows:

- How do our findings and approach chime with arguments about CEE countries' "readiness for Europe"?
- How do our findings and approach chime with arguments about the Europeanization of institutions and public policy in the region?
- How do our findings and approach chime with arguments about the development of European governance?

READY FOR EUROPE?

From the mid-1990s, executive and administrative capacity building in the future EU member states began to be propagated by the EU institutions as a key precondition for accession. Regular calls on the part of the EU institutions for determined efforts at executive and administrative reform accompanied the accession negotiations; were reiterated in the last "progress reports" of November 2003 on the Czech Republic, Hungary, and Poland, which were issued prior to their accession to the EU in May 2004; and have continued to be issued since. The November 2003 reports—containing, as it were, the "final verdict" on more than a decade of integration-driven reform initiatives supported by the EU institutions and national governments—made uncomfortable reading. Across a raft of issues—including executive and administrative organization, policymaking procedures, financial management systems, the public personnel system, arrangements for ensuring administrative legality, and transparency and accountability—the reports highlighted significant shortcomings, with particularly trenchant criticisms reserved for Poland.

Academic comment and analysis from the enlargement perspective have concentrated, first, on providing assessments of domestic institutional capacity and, second, on charting the evolution of the EU approach to fostering domestic EU compatibility. As regards the former, attention has focused on governmental and administrative "linkage"—that is, "institutional arrangements that link national executives and EU authorities and the institutional practices that have evolved at the national level to support national-EU connections" (Goetz 2000, 212). In the CEE case, this has involved mapping the domestic setup for conducting and coordinating the accession negotiations and tracing the steps taken to ensure the transposition of the *acquis communautaire* into domestic law. There is already a good deal of research on this issue, with work on Hungary (Ágh 2003, 91ff.; 2004), Slovenia (Fink Hafner and Lajh 2003), Lithuania (Nakrosis 2003), Poland (Zubek 2005a, 2005b), and the Czech Republic (Kabele and Linek 2004); and with comparative studies covering a range of countries, including the Czech Republic, Estonia, Hungary, Poland, and Slovenia (Laffan 2003; Lippert, Umbach, and Wessels 2001; Lippert and Umbach 2005).

As in Western Europe (Kassim, Peters, and Wright 2000; Mittag and Wessels 2003), the new member states differ as regards the degree to which linkage functions have been concentrated within specialized units; patterns of interministerial coordination; and the role of the chief executive and his staff in domestic-EU linkage. For example, in the Slovenian case,

> despite the *formally* crucial role assigned to the Government Office for European Affairs in managing EU issues . . . *in practice* a relatively *polycentric model* developed. . . . In the vertical co-ordination, the *Prime Minister* played the key co-ordinating role in cases of politically sensitive questions. The *Negotiating Team* as an expert group ensured the prevalence of expertise over political and factional interests in the negotiating process, and the *Council of Ministers* played the role of the ultimate national executive unit for EU affairs. (Fink Hafner and Lajh 2003, 166; emphases in the original)

By contrast, in Poland, after a prolonged period during the 1990s, when "the Polish core executive lacked sufficient resources to effectively direct, coordinate and advise line ministries in the transposition process" (Zubek 2002, 6), there was a shift toward a much more centralized approach in 2000, which included "strong leadership from the prime minister and the minister for European affairs" and "reinforced central and hierarchical coordination mechanisms" (11).

It has been suggested that the creation of specialized executive units dealing with accession, transposition, and preaccession funds has fostered fragmentation at the level of central government, as such units constitute organizational "islands of excellence" or "enclaves" (Goetz 2001b; Nunberg 2000); certainly, dealing with EU business has, on the whole, tended to increase the autonomy of executive actors. For example, a recent study of Czech civil servants concerned with EU accession has found that involvement in EU business brings a "significant degree of institutional autonomy towards domestic politics since civil servants tend to be more sensitive to signals from the EU institutions than those from their political leadership. This sensitivity is most pronounced with those who are most exposed to the EU" (Drulák, Česal, and Hampl 2003, 651).

There are several reasons that help explain why there has been a pronounced tendency for the emergence of distinct "EU core executives," which are, to a greater or lesser extent, separated from the rest of the administration. Negotiating entry and ensuring legal transposition of the entire *acquis* posed challenges of a different quality and magnitude from those associated with everyday EU business in long-standing member states. It was much more akin to the "high politics" of shaping member states' basic relationships with the EU than it was to the "low politics" surrounding individual policy decisions. The EU itself insisted on dealing with a small range of authoritative interlocutors, stressing the need for an effective lead from the center. It commissioned the SIGMA unit at the Organization for Economic Co-operation and Development to develop "baselines" for the effective interministerial coordination, and the progress reports regularly commented on this issue. Perhaps most crucially, centralization has been a less-challenging form of coordination than have network-based solutions.

As regards the evolution of the EU's approach, it has been noted that there was an increasing concentration on linkage institutions, while initiatives aimed at wider governmental and administrative reform were marginalized. As accession turned from an almost universally shared aspiration to an imminent reality, "readiness for Europe" became progressively more narrowly defined to mean the creation of effective domestic interlocutors for the EU institutions and ensuring the institutional prerequisites for compliance with the *acquis*. In the EU's approach, broader concerns with democratic governance in CEE became subordinated to the functional requirements associated with EU membership.

This narrowing of the reform agenda as defined by Brussels—from creating democratic governance to ensuring effective linkage and compliance— has been attributed to several reasons. Thus, the EU Commission in particular found itself under considerable pressure by existing member states to ensure that preaccession funds made available to the accession countries would be used as intended. This implied efforts to increase the absorptive capacity of the future members (i.e., create an institutional infrastructure through which the funds could be channeled to worthwhile projects) and to guarantee financial probity (i.e., avoid financial mismanagement and irregularities). The evident need to create specialized domestic administrations for the implementation of key EU policies—perhaps, most notably, the highly complex EU agriculture policy—further reinforced the concentration on an accession-driven reform agenda. As Verheijen (2002, 255) puts it, "horizontal" reforms were increasingly overshadowed by a "sectoral" approach, and "the virtual imposition of the Accession Partnerships on the candidate countries provides an illustration of the fundamental change in approach in the provision of EU assistance, from a demand-driven approach to an accession-driven approach."

The exigencies of imminent accession are only part of the explanation for the gradual retreat on the part of EU from attempts to foster broader governance reforms in CEE. Equally influential have been the difficulties involved in formulating the details of such an approach and the critical evaluations of its results. Thus, it has been suggested that the diversity of administrative practices in the member states meant that there were few, if any, concrete institutional templates or ready-made models that would have commanded universal support among the fifteen EU members. As Grabbe (2003, 313) has pointed out, "the European Union often lacks a single model to export . . . and its own diversity can undermine its effort to export a single model of governance."

Practical exigencies favoring a narrow focus on linkage, combined with a lack of broadly accepted Western templates, have been identified as key obstacles to EU initiatives aimed at civil service development and regionalization. As noted in chapter 7, students of civil service policy in the region have generally assumed that the EU itself has only minimal treaty-based competences in this field (Dimitrova 2002; Fournier 1998; Scherpereel 2003; Verheijen 2002), although, as Bossaert and Demmke (2003, 74) argue, "the fact that the Community does not have powers to regulate the civil service does not mean that European integration has no effect on national civil services." Despite this, major efforts were made in the mid-1990s to promote civil service reform, not least through the formulation of "baselines" for civil service development, carried out by SIGMA on behalf of the EU, which were informed by the principles of a Weberian career civil service (Fournier 1998). Assistance was made available to the applicant states to develop civil service systems through both the SIGMA program and the PHARE projects aimed at individual countries; thus, the need for the adoption of a comprehensive set of civil service legislation, and its effective implementation, was a regular refrain in the annual accession progress reports. Nonetheless, the results of this type of horizontal reform initiative, in terms of creating nonpoliticized civil service systems, seem to have been, at best, modest (Meyer-Sahling 2004). This was especially the case in the Czech Republic, the last to adopt a civil service law in 2003, the coming into force of which has been delayed until 2005, despite repeated interventions by EU actors (for an analysis, see Scherpereel 2003). Even this law, in the view of SIGMA, falls far short of what is desirable. Thus, SIGMA's *Public Service and Administrative Framework Assessment* for the Czech Republic (2003, 5) noted that although the law was

> a positive step towards bringing the Czech civil service system closer to those of the EU Member States, . . . the law has many shortcomings, inconsistencies, and confused wording and structure, which may multiply interpretation issues and implementation problems. . . . It is . . . unlikely that civil servants as defined by this law will be in place before 2008. . . . The positive effects of this law, if any, will begin to be seen only in five to eight years, which represents an unforeseeable future.

Of course, the EU is not alone in having found that cross-sectoral reforms in the public sector are exceedingly difficult to guide from the outside. Thus, the World Bank (1999), in a review of its own civil service reform policies that was carried out at the end of the 1990s, concluded that bank-supported civil service reforms "were largely ineffective in achieving sustainable results in downsizing, capacity building, and institutional reform. This was, in part, due to significant political difficulties in implementing [civil service reforms]" (iii). "Rather than engaging [civil services] as dynamic systems that are influenced by multiple stakeholders, Bank operations relied in a small group of interlocutors within core ministries to design and implement one-size-fits-all [civil service reform] blueprints in diverse country settings" (ii).

Against this background, the shift in the EU's approach to public sector reform did not imply a "return to basics." On the contrary, because the fundamentals of public sector organization are difficult to influence from the outside, sectoral approaches that focused on measures directly linked to the *acquis communautaire* came to dominate, whereas horizontal measures were increasingly sidelined.

This dynamic has also been observed in the EU's approach to decentralization and regionalization in CEE. Thus, for the first few years after it became involved in postcommunist institution building, the EU sought to promote effective decentralization of the administrative systems of the postcommunist states and was generally in favor of strengthening subnational governments at local and regional levels. To be sure, "the perception that the European Commission required the establishment of political regions is as false in central and eastern Europe as in the west" (Keating 2003, 57); but "the Phare programmes and the early phases of adaptation to the EU involved an expectation that there would be widespread regionalization in candidate countries" (58). Yet, recent work on administrative and political decentralization and regionalization in CEE notes "how divergent endogenous interests and pressures triumphed over external convergence pressures, and resulted in a diversity of institutional outcomes" (Hughes 2003, 190). More important, as preaccession funding increased and preparations were made for the postaccession distribution of funds under the EU's structural and cohesion policies, the general preference for decentralization was overshadowed by a concern with maintaining and reinforcing centralized controls over funding streams. Thus, the EU's insistence on central controls in the new member states as a result of sectoral concerns about the correct use of EU funding at least partially undermined the horizontal preference for the strengthening of subnational governance (Ágh 2004).

How do our findings and approach chime with such arguments about CEE countries' "readiness for Europe"? Three points deserve highlighting. First, recent analyses highlight the centralizing effects associated with attempts to make CEE institutions "ready for Europe," whether they take the form of "EU-related core executives" or the recentralization of subnational competences at the level of central ministries. As in the cases investigated in this book, centralization seems to be the most readily available response to addressing performance problems. "Getting ready for Europe" would thus appear to have reinforced domestic dynamics of executive development. It has also fostered disjunctures and incongruence in institutional development similar to the loose coupling between type of government, type of core executive, and type of center of government that our study has found.

Second, wider diffusion effects of integration appear, as yet, limited, and efforts aimed at stimulating horizontal reforms from outside have met with little success. Our analysis of budgetary policy (chapter 8) in particular has highlighted the importance of "crises of performance" in engendering far-reaching domestic reforms; where such a sense of crisis is not shared by domestic policymakers, external calls for reform are extremely unlikely to be heeded. Civil service policy in the region provides a vivid illustration of this point.

Third, the European Union at least initially underestimated the capacity of domestic political and administrative institutions in CEE to resist change of the type demanded by the European authorities in the absence of strong domestic reform coalitions. It subsequently narrowed its own institutional policies in the region to trying to ensure the effective and efficient downloading of EU policies into the domestic contexts of new and prospective members.

EUROPEANIZATION EASTERN STYLE?

The discussion about EU-related institutional capacity has been closely linked to arguments about Europeanization, which have inquired, in particular, into the mechanisms by which European integration produces effects in the political systems of the new and prospective member states.[1] The discussion of Europeanization "Eastern style" has tended, thus far, to stress "hierarchical" aspects of "adaptation" to real or imaged EU requirements and has paid special attention to the impact of EU "conditionality" (Grabbe 2003). Drawing on the insights of the Europeanization literature that focuses on Western Europe, a strong case can be made that both the institutional and the policy effects of accession should have been more immediate than in other parts of the EU (Goetz 2005; Grabbe 2001). Oft-cited reasons include, inter alia, the weakness of institutional "cores" in the post-Communist states— notably, those that only came into being after the fall of Communism— which are less likely to offer resistance to "adaptive pressures" than are the deeply embedded state institutions of Western European countries; evident crises of performance and legitimacy of domestic institutions, which encourage policy transfer and learning from foreign experiences; and the existence of institutional and policy "voids," so that Europeanization involves not so much adaptation but rather the *ab ovo* creation of new actors, institutions, and policies.

Yet, there is a danger of overemphasizing both the hierarchical dimension of Europeanization and the intensity of effects. The focus on "adaptive pressures" should not obscure the "usage" of EU integration (Jacquot and Woll 2003) by domestic actors for their own purposes. More recent work on Europeanization in Western European countries has emphasized "the use that domestic actors make of the EU in order to legitimate policy reforms, to develop new policy solutions, and to alter policy beliefs" (Dyson and Goetz 2003b, 18), and while research from this perspective in CEE is still in the beginning, such usage is likely to have been widespread. At the same time, there are good arguments to suggest that as far as EU adaptation prior to accession is concerned, patterns of "institutionalisation for reversibility" prevailed (Goetz 2004a). Thus, the new members had little incentive to invest in "deep" Europeanization that would "lock in" specific institutional and policy arrangements prior to full membership because of their weak uploading capacity as *demandeurs* prior to accession. They could hope that, as full members, they would be able to challenge, or escape altogether, some of the constrictions that a negotiation process, one that was structured to favor the existing members, had imposed on them. "Rationalist" arguments suggesting a pattern of wide-ranging but relatively shallow effects are underscored by more constructivist understandings of Europeanization, which stress the importance of learning and socialization and note that institutions are constructed around not just interests but norms and values. In the new member states, such learning and socialization effects are likely to be, up to now, less deep because of their shorter period of intensive engagement with the EU and, for most of the time, an "outsider" status, and less extensive, since, as discussed later, active engagement with the integration process has, up to now, been restricted to a fairly narrow group of political and administrative elites.

Our own findings do not challenge the tentative conclusions of Europeanization research; its empirical basis is, as far as CEE is concerned, still slim. But it does complement, and perhaps also help to clarify, how Europeanization and its dynamics are best conceived in the CEE context. Thus, our study, by focusing on domestic actor constellations and the domestic political conditioning of executive development, provides an antidote to explanations that see the process of institutional and policy change primarily as one of adapting to, or resisting, external pressures and incentives. It directs attention to the power of domestic "intervening variables" (Radaelli 2003) or "facilitating factors" (Börzel and Risse 2003), including domestic institutional and political legacies and, as chapter 2 highlights, developments in decisive actor constellations, most notably, in the party system.

GOVERNING AFTER COMMUNISM AND EUROPEAN GOVERNANCE

Research and reflection on developments in European governance are still overwhelmingly concerned with Western Europe, although the next decade is set to see an upsurge of work on the governance systems of CEE. The major themes and concepts are, without exception, drawing on the Western European experience. For example, the notion of governance itself, with its suggestion of porous boundaries between state and society and the participation of private and societal actors in public policymaking and delivery, gained prominence in the Western context, as did the theme of Europeanization. Our research intersects with debates on European governance in two ways. First, it helps to address the question to what extent Western European experiences of government and public policy are being replicated in CEE. This theme—of convergence and divergence—in European governance underlies much contemporary comparative work. It informs, for example, recent attempts to define a "European administrative space," "understood as convergence on a common European model" (Olsen 2003, 506; see also Siedentopf and Speer 2003). Second, our findings contain some pointers as to likely future emphases in the European governance debate.

The notion of the "European administrative space" has been associated with efforts by practitioners and academics to map commonalities in the governance practices of European countries and, more ambitiously, to encourage the search for best practices and their diffusion. As we noted in several places, sound, theoretically grounded reasons have been advanced both for expecting the approximation of the CEE to Western European governance norms and for resistance to change. In substantive terms, our research indicates certain commonalities with developmental trends oft noted in Western European contexts, such as prime ministerialization—the formal and informal strengthening of the office and person of the prime minister in the executive system; the strengthening of finance ministries as key parts of the core executive; and the clear limitations of reform strategies aimed at the depoliticization of the public personnel system, notably when it comes to senior civil servants. However, our research also indicates that—with the exception of Hungary—the emerging configurations remain fluid and characterized by considerable tensions: types of government, core executive, and center of government are often incongruent, and formal regulations and informal practice are in conflict rather than mutual reinforcement. Disjunctures of this type are part of a broader pattern of tension "between technocratic enclaves and patronage administration; between political appointees, small cores of civil servants, and the mass of ordinary employees; between Europeanized and non-Europeanized parts of the executive; between formal legal frameworks and shadow institutions" (Goetz 2001b, 1046). In contrast to earlier predictions (Hesse 1993), the transformation of governance in large parts of CEE thus appears still "at the end of the beginning" (Wollmann, Wiesenthal, and Bönker 1995). Normative and teleological arguments that foresaw the rapid transformation of postcommunist public administration toward "rational-legal bureaucratic structures" (Linz and Stepan 1996, 3ff.) or a "classical European administration" (König 1992) are, accordingly, giving way to analyses that stress the ongoing transformation of administrative and governmental institutional structures as an open and indeterminate process that may "conserve these disjunctures for the longer term or lead to their resolution" (Goetz 2001b, 1046–47).

Where we find greater evidence of convergence is in the procedural characteristics of executive development and, perhaps more controversially, in the "loose coupling between formal organization and behaviour" and "loose coupling between formal organization and substantive results" that Olsen (2003, 524) has recently highlighted in his survey of European administrative development. As regards the procedural characteristics, our analysis underscores that, some "grand" reform designs notwithstanding, an eclectic, pragmatic, tentative, and experimenting approach to executive institution building prevailed. In this process, external reform stimuli, such as EU accession, certainly mattered, as did foreign "models"—but, as noted, domestic actors, institutions, and events shaped the processes and outcomes of reform initiatives. Such a finding is in line with recent studies of administrative and governmental Europeanization in Western Europe. For example, Kassim (2003), while stressing the "important organizational consequences for government" that membership of the EU has entailed (104), notes that "the most salient features of the political opportunity structure, such as the territorial organization of the state, the nature of the party system, the structure of the executive, the role of parliament, and the dominant form of interest intermediation, are perhaps the most important determinant" (103).

Given what we say about the nature of institutions and institutionalization in chapter 1, Olsen's "two puzzles for students of formally organized institutions" (2003, 524) generated by his survey of European developments will occasion little surprise for students of government and administration in CEE; rather, what is notable is that the type of decoupling that is often found in CEE also appears to take place in the more highly institutionalized settings of Western Europe. Thus, the often still "shallow" formal institutions found in CEE are, by necessity, less able to structure individual behavior than "deep" institutions are. Moreover, to the extent that domestic institutional arrangements reflect external pressures, "deviant" behavior is to be understood as a reaction to the discrepancy between external requirements and domestic preferences. Similarly, when it comes to institutions and effects, institutional theory would lead us to expect that the higher the degree of institutionalization, the stronger the institutional effects. Conversely, "institutionalization for reversibility" and the low resource endowments that are often noted in respect of CEE state institutions should make for a much less clear-cut link between organization and outcome.

Do the latter remarks suggest that the CEE experience provides pointers for the likely future of European governance beyond the confines of the postcommunist region? It is certainly interesting to note that "deinstitutionalization" and, as its flipside, "personalization" are increasingly prominent themes in analyses of Western European governments and bureaucracies. These themes have not just animated the discussion of the "hollowing crown" that we introduce in chapter 1; they also feature prominently in a diverse range of studies exploring different features of executive development. For example, in the conclusion of a comparative inquiry into Western European senior officials, Page and Wright (1999, 277) have highlighted comparative evidence of a "*deinstitutionalization or personalization of political trust*" (emphasis in the original). The relationship between senior officials and executive politicians is, they argue, subtly changing as trust in the institution of the civil service is progressively replaced in many countries by an emphasis on personal trust. The latter "does not have to be defined strictly in party-political terms. . . . The central point is that increasing political influence in senior appointments suggests the possibility that membership of a 'neutral' civil service is decreasing as a guide to trust among political elites"

(278). Similarly, if from a different angle, popular arguments about prime ministerialization, if not presidentialization, in West European politics are based on observations about the growing concentration of political power in the person of the chief executive, which does not appear to require formal constitutional change.

Looking toward the future of debates about European governance, the CEE experiences are then likely to bring about a partial shift of emphasis in analyses of European governance. Three key aspects of such a reorientation may be summed up as "personalities matter"; "resources matter"; and "temporality matters." As regards the first aspect, recent years have seen a growing convergence of neoinstitutionalist perspectives in the study of European governance (see Aspinwall and Schneider 2001; Jupille, Caporaso, and Checkel 2003), which have laid to rest the dichotomy between actor-centred versus institution-centred approaches. The question is no longer whether institutions or actors matter but how best to conceptualize institutions and understand behavior within them. Indications of institutional fluidity and of deinstitutionalization and personalization suggest that there is a greater likelihood that individual qualities and motivations matter in highly institutionalized settings where the properties of the office weigh more heavily on the officeholder. This implies that in the study of post-communist governance, but increasingly also in Western European settings, special attention needs to be paid not just to "actors" but identifiable individuals. Accordingly, studies of leadership and biographical approaches in particular are likely to gain in prominence.

"Resources matter" is a second key theme that is set to become stronger. Recent writing on European governance has been inclusive when it comes to defining institutions but has tended to be neglectful of the socioeconomic conditioning of institutional and policy choices and of the consequences of socioeconomic differences for how institutions work. Work on the Europeanization of public institutions and public policies, for example, has paid little attention to how differences in national socioeconomic endowments influence patterns of Europeanization in public institutions and public policies. The CEE cases provide ample justification for reconsidering how such differences in resource endowments influence the "differential impact" of Europe.

Finally, "temporality matters." It has been argued some time ago that paying systematic attention to temporal categories in Europeanization research could decisively advance our understanding of processes and outcomes (Goetz 2000), and this suggestion has since been taken up by several authors (Dyson 2002; Grabbe 2003). Likewise, writing on postcommunist institutional and policy change often refers to temporal categories of time, timing, and tempo, but, again, systematic accounts are rare (but see recently

Ekiert and Hanson 2003). The next decade is set to witness more systematic work on the temporality of governance, as the importance of temporal factors in conditioning governance is increasingly recognized.

NOTE

1. This section draws on Goetz (2004a).

References

Ágh, A. 1997. Parliaments as policy-making bodies in East Central Europe: The case of Hungary. *International Political Science Review* 18 (4): 417–32.

———. 1999. Europeanization of policy-making in East Central Europe: The Hungarian approach to EU accession. *Journal of European Public Policy* 6 (5): 839–54.

———. 2001. Early consolidation and performance crisis: The majoritarian-consensus democracy debate in Hungary. *West European Politics* 24 (3): 89–112.

———. 2002. *The accession management and Europeanization in Hungary.* Budapest Papers on Europeanization 7. Budapest: Hungarian Centre for Democracy Studies Foundation.

———. 2003. *Anticipatory and adaptive Europeanization in Hungary.* Budapest: Hungarian Centre for Democracy Studies.

———, ed. 2004. *Europeanization and regionalization: Hungary's accession.* Budapest: Hungarian Centre for Democracy Studies.

Allen, R., and D. Tommasi, eds. 2001. *Managing public expenditure: A reference book for transition countries.* Paris: Organization for Economic Co-operation and Development.

Andeweg, R. B. 2000. Party government, state and society: Mapping boundaries and interrelations. In *The nature of party government: A comparative European perspective,* ed. J. Blondel and M. Cotta, 38–55. Basingstoke, Eng.: Palgrave.

Antoszewski, A. 2002. Ewolucja polskiego systemu partyjnego [The evolution of the Polish party system]. In *Demokratyzacja w III Rzeczpospolitej* [Democratization in the Third Polish Republic], ed. A. Antoszewski. Wrocław, Pol.: Wydawnictwo Uniwersytetu Wrocławskiego.

Aspinwall, M., and G. Schneider, eds. 2001. *The rules of integration: The institutionalist approach to European studies.* Manchester: Manchester University Press.

Bahro, H. 1998. Duverger's concept: Semi-presidential government revisited. *European Journal of Political Research* 34:201–24.

Balázs, I. 1993. The transformation of Hungarian public administration. *Public Administration* 71 (1–2): 75–88.

Bánsági, Z. 1996. A kormány munkája, döntéshozatali rendszere 1995-ben [The work and decision-making system of the government in 1995]. In *Magyarország politikai évkönyve* [Political yearbook of Hungary for 1995], ed. S. Kurtán, P. Sándor, and L. Vass. Budapest: Demokrácia Kutatások Magyar Központja Alapítvány.

Bartók, J. 1997. Hungary moves forward in developing a senior civil service. *Public Management Forum* 3 (2).

Batt, J. 1991. *East Central Europe from reform to transformation.* London: Pinter.

Bekke, A., and F. van der Meer, eds. 2000. *Civil service systems in Western Europe.* Cheltenham, Eng.: Edward Elgar.

Ben-Gera, M., and S. James. 2000. *Review of the central machinery for policy-making and coordination of the Czech Republic.* Paris: SIGMA.

Blondel, J. 1997. Introduction. In *Cabinets in Western Europe,* ed. J. Blondel and F. Müller-Rommel. Basingstoke, Eng.: Macmillan.

Blondel, J., and M. Cotta, eds. 1996. *Party and government.* Basingstoke, Eng.: Macmillan.

———. 2000. *The nature of party government: A comparative European perspective.* Basingstoke, Eng.: Palgrave.

Blondel, J., and F. Müller-Rommel, eds. 1997. *Cabinets in Western Europe.* Basingstoke, Eng.: Macmillan.

———. 2001. *Cabinets in Eastern Europe.* Basingstoke, Eng.: Palgrave.

Borók, G., L. Fekete, and V. Horváth, eds. 2000. *A Miniszterelnöki Hivatal évkönyve 1999* [Yearbook of the Prime Minister's Office 1999]. Budapest: Magyar Hivatalos Közlönykiadó (publisher of the *Hungarian State Gazette*).

Börzel, T. A., and T. Risse. 2003. Conceptualizing the domestic impact of Europe. In *The politics of Europeanization,* ed. K. Featherstone and C. Radaelli, 57–80. Oxford: Oxford University Press.

Bossaert, D., and C. Demmke, C. 2003. Civil services in the accession states: New trends and the impact of the integration process. Maastricht, Neth.: European Institute of Public Administration.

Bozhidarova, V., V. Kolcheva, and R. Velinova. 1999. *Politico-administrative relations in Bulgaria at central government level.* Paper presented at Network of Institutes and Schools of Public Administration in Central and Eastern Europe annual conference, Sofia, Bulg., 25–27 March 1999.

Brixi, H. P., A. Papp, and A. Schick. 1999. *Fiscal risks and the quality of fiscal adjustment in Hungary.* Washington, D.C.: World Bank.

Brusis, M. 1999. Residuales oder europäisches Wohlfahrtsmodell? Die EU und die sozialpolitischen Reformen in Mittel- und Osteuropa. *Prokla* 29 (1): 73–94.

———. 2002. Between EU requirements, competitive politics, and national traditions: Re-creating regions in the accession countries of Central and Eastern Europe. *Governance* 15 (4): 531–59.

Brusis, M., and V. Dimitrov. 2001. Executive configuration and fiscal performance in post-communist Central and Eastern Europe. *Journal of European Public Policy* 8 (6): 888–910.

Brzezinski, M. 1998. *The struggle for constitutionalism in Poland.* Basingstoke, Eng.: Macmillan.

Cepl, V., and M. Gillis. 1994. A survey of presidential powers: Formal and informal— the Czech Republic. *East European Constitutional Review* 3 (1): 66–67.

Checkel, J. 1999. Social construction and integration. *Journal of European Public Policy* 6 (4): 545–60.

Cotta, M. 2000a. Conclusion: From the simple world of party government to a more complex view of party-government relations. In *The nature of party government: A comparative European perspective*, ed. J. Blondel and M. Cotta, 196–222. Basingstoke, Eng.: Palgrave.

———. 2000b. Defining party and government. In *The nature of party government: A comparative European perspective*, ed. J. Blondel and M. Cotta, 56–95. Basingstoke, Eng.: Palgrave.

Derlien, H. U. 1993. Integration der Staatsfunktionäre der DDR in das Berufsbeamtentum: Professionalisierung und Säuberung. In *Verwaltungsreform und Verwaltungspolitik im Prozeß der deutschen Vereinigung*, ed. W. Seibel, A. Benz, and H. Mäding, 190–206. Baden-Baden, Ger.: Nomos Verlagsgesellschaft.

Dimitrov, V. 2001. *Bulgaria: The uneven transition.* London: Routledge.

———. 2005. Ready for European Economic and Monetary Union? Party composition of government, budgeting institutions and fiscal deficit in Central and Eastern Europe. *International Journal of Organization Theory and Behavior* 8 (1): 40–66.

Dimitrov, V. T., and K. H. Goetz. 2000. Executive capacity and executive performance in post-communist Europe: Towards an analytical framework. Paper prepared for the European Consortium for Political Research Joint Sessions of Workshops, Copenhagen, Denmark, 14–19 April 2000.

Dimitrova, A. 2002. Enlargement, institution-building and the EU's administrative capacity requirement. *West European Politics* 25 (4): 171–90.

Döring, H. 1995. *Parliaments and majority rule in Western Europe.* Mannheim, Ger.: Mannheim Centre for European Social Research.

Drulák, P, J. Česal, and S. Hampl. 2003. Interactions and identities of Czech civil servants on their way to the EU. *Journal of European Public Policy* 10 (4): 637–54.

Dunleavy, P. 1991. *Democracy, bureaucracy and public choice.* Hemel Hempstead, Eng.: Harvester Wheatsheaf.

Dunleavy, P., and R. A. Rhodes. 1990. Core executive studies in Britain. *Public Administration* 68:3–28.

Dyson, K. 2002. Conclusions: European states and Euro economic governance. In *European states and the Euro: Europeanization, variation, and convergence*, ed. K Dyson, 335–66. Oxford: Oxford University Press.

Dyson, K., and K. H. Goetz. 2003a. Europeanization compared: The shrinking core and the decline of "soft" power. In *Germany, Europe, and the politics of constraint*, ed. K. Dyson and K. H. Goetz, 349–76. Oxford: Oxford University Press.

———. 2003b. Living with Europe: Power, constraint, and contestation. In *Germany, Europe, and the politics of constraint*, ed. K. Dyson and K. H. Goetz, 3–35. Oxford: Oxford University Press.

Egeberg, M. 1999. The impact of bureaucratic structure on policymaking. *Public Administration* 77 (1): 155–70.

Elster, J., C. Offe, and U. K. Preuss. 1998. *Institutional design in post-communist societies: Rebuilding the ship at sea, theories of institutional design.* Cambridge: Cambridge University Press.

Ekiert, G., and S. E. Hanson. 2003. Time, space, and institutional change in Central and Eastern Europe. In *Capitalism and democracy in Central and Eastern Europe: Assessing the legacy of communist rule*, ed. G. Ekiert and S. E. Hanson, 15–48. Cambridge: Cambridge University Press.

European Commission. 1997. *Commission opinion on Bulgaria's application for membership in the European Union*. DOC/97/11. Brussels: European Commission.

———. 1999a. *Regular report 1999 on Bulgaria's progress towards accession.* Brussels: European Commission.

———. 1999b. *Regular report 1999 on Hungary's progress towards accession.* Brussels: European Commission.

———. 2000. *Regular report 2000 on Poland's progress towards accession.* Brussels: European Commission.

———. 2001a. *Regular report 2001 on Bulgaria's progress towards accession.* Brussels: European Commission.

———. 2001b. *Regular report 2001 on Poland's progress towards accession.* Brussels: European Commission.

———. 2002a. *Regular report 2002 on Bulgaria's progress towards accession.* Brussels: European Commission.

———. 2002b. *Regular report 2002 on Czech Republic's progress towards accession.* Brussels: European Commission.

Evans, A., and G. Evans. 2001. Improving government decision-making systems in Lithuania and Latvia. *Journal of European Public Policy* 8 (6): 933–59.

Featherstone, K., and G. Kazamias. 2001. Introduction: Southern Europe and the process of Europeanization. In *Europeanisation and the Southern periphery*, ed. K. Featherstone and G. Kazamias, 1–22. London: Cass.

Fidien, J. 1996. Poland implements ambitious reform plan. *Public Management Forum*, 2 (4): 10–11.

Financial Times. 2001. Czech Republic country survey. 12 December.

Fink Hafner, D., and D. Lajh. 2003. *Managing Europe from home: The Europeanisation of the Slovenian core executive.* Ljubljana, Slovenia: Faculty of Social Sciences.

Fournier, J. 1998. Governance and European integration: Reliable public administration. In *Preparing public administrations for the European administrative space*, 119–36. SIGMA Papers 23. Paris: SIGMA.

Fricz, T. 2000. The Orbán government: An experiment in regime stabilization. In *From totalitarian to democratic Hungary: Evolution and transformation 1990–2000*, ed. M. Schmidt and L. G. Tóth, 520–70. Boulder, Col.: Social Science Monographs.

Gdulewicz, E., and R. Mojak. 1997. Rola Ustrojowa i Strukura Organizacyjna Rady Ministrów. In *Ustrój i Struktura Aparatu Państwowego i Samorządu Terytorialnego*, ed. W. Skrzydło. Warsaw: Wydawnictwo Sejmowe.

Georgiev, Blagovest. 1999. *Civil Services and State Administration (CSSA), country report: Bulgaria.* Paris: SIGMA.

Göhler, G. 1994. Politische Institutionen und ihr Kontext. In *Die Eigenart der Institutionen: Zum Profil politischer Institutionentheorie*, G. Goehler. Baden-Baden, Ger.: Nomos Verlagsgesellschaft.

Goetz, K. H. 1997. Acquiring political craft: Training grounds for top officials in the German core executive. *Public Administration* 75 (4): 753–75.

————. 2000. European integration and national executives: A cause in search of an effect? *West European Politics* 23 (4): 211–31.

————., ed. 2001a. Executive governance in Central and Eastern Europe. Special issue, *Journal of European Public Policy* 8 (6).

————. 2001b. Making sense of post-communist central administration: Modernization, Europeanization or Latinization. *Journal of European Public Policy* 8 (6): 1032–51.

————. 2003. Executives in comparative context. In *Governing Europe: Memorial volume for Vincent Wright*, ed. J. Hayward and A. Menon. Oxford: Oxford University Press.

————. 2005. The new member states and the EU. In *Member states and the European Union*, ed. S. Bulmer and C. Lequesne, 254–80. Oxford: Oxford University Press.

Goetz, K. H., and H. Margetts. 1999. The solitary center: The core executive in Central and Eastern Europe. *Governance* 12 (4): 425–53.

Goetz, K. H., F. Panizza, and G. Philip. 2004. *Transferring 'Good Governance' to Emergent Democracies: Ideas and Institutional Change*. Report of research activities and results. www.esrcsocietytoday.ac.uk (accessed September 2005).

Goetz, K. H., and H. Wollmann. 2001. Governmentalizing central executives in post-communist Europe: A four-country comparison. *Journal of European Public Policy* 8 (6): 864–87.

Grabbe, H. 2001. How does Europeanization affect CEE governance? Conditionality, diffusion and diversity. *Journal of European Public Policy* 8 (6): 1013–31.

————. 2003. Europeanization goes East: Power and uncertainty in the EU accession process. In *The politics of Europeanization*, ed. K. Featherstone and C. Radaelli, 303–27. Oxford: Oxford University Press.

Gray, P., and P. t'Hart, eds. 1998. *Public policy disasters in Western Europe*. London: Routledge.

Greskovits, B. 2001. Brothers-in-arms or rivals in politics? Top politicians and top policy makers in the Hungarian transformation. In *Reforming the state: Fiscal and welfare reform in post-socialist countries*, ed. J. Kornai, S. Haggard, and R. Kaufman, 111–41. Cambridge: Cambridge University Press.

György, J. 1999. *Country report: Hungary, Civil Services and State Administration (CSSA)*. Paris: SIGMA.

Hall, A. 1999. Gdzie jest władza? [Where does power reside?]. *Rzeczpospolita*, 13 January.

Hallerberg, M. 2000. *The importance of domestic political institutions: Why and how Belgium and Italy qualified for EMU*. ZEI Working Paper B10. Bonn, Ger.: Zentrum fur Europäische Integrationsforschung, Rheinische Friedrich-Wilhelms-Universität.

Hallerberg, M., and J. von Hagen. 1999. Electoral institutions, cabinet negotiations, and budget deficits within the European Union. In *Fiscal institutions and fiscal performance*, ed. J. Poterba and J. von Hagen, 209–32. Chicago: Chicago University Press.

Hay, C., and D. Wincott. 1998. Structure, agency and historical institutionalism. *Political Studies* 46 (5): 951–57.

Hayward, J. 2002. *Government from the centre: Core executive co-ordination in France*. Oxford: Oxford University Press.

Hazafi, Z., and Z. Czoma. 1999. Civil service reform in Hungary. *Public Management Forum* 5 (2): 6–7.

Hesse, J. J. 1993. From transition to modernisation: Administrative change in Central and Eastern Europe. *Public Administration* 71 (1–2): 219–57.

Hesse, J. J., and K. H. Goetz. 1993a. Public sector reform in Central and Eastern Europe I: The case of Poland. *Jahrbuch zur Staats- und Verwaltungswissenschaft* 6:237–82.

———. 1993b. Public sector reform in Central and Eastern Europe II: The case of Czechoslovakia. *Jahrbuch zur Staats- und Verwaltungswissenschaft* 6:283–323.

———. 1993c. Public sector reform in Central and Eastern Europe III: The case of Hungary. *Jahrbuch zur Staats- und Verwaltungswissenschaft* 6:325–64.

Hughes, J. 2003. Regional convergence and divergence in an enlarged EU. In *The regional challenge in Central and Eastern Europe: Territorial restructuring and European integration*, ed. M. Keating and J. Hughes, 183–91. Brussels: Lang.

International Monetary Fund. 1998. *Czech Republic: Statistical appendix*. IMF staff country report 98/37. Washington, D.C.: International Monetary Fund.

———. 1999. *Czech Republic: Statistical appendix*. IMF staff country report 99/91. Washington, D.C.: International Monetary Fund.

———. 2000. *Czech Republic: Statistical appendix*. IMF staff country report 00/119. Washington, D.C.: International Monetary Fund.

———. 2001. *Czech Republic: Selected issues and statistical appendix*. IMF staff country report 01/112. Washington, D.C.: International Monetary Fund.

Izdebski, H. 1993. *Funkcjonowanie i Aparat Rady Ministrów i Prezesa Rady Ministrów* [The operation and organizational support of the Council of Ministers and the president of the Council of Ministers]. Warsaw: Urząd Rady Ministrów, Pełnomocnik Rządu ds. Reformy Administracji Publicznej.

———. 1994. Reforma administracji publicznej w Polsce [Public administration reform in Poland]. *Państwo i Prawo* (September): 50–61.

Izdebski, H., and M. Kulesza. 1999. *Administracja publiczna: zagadnienia ogólne* [Public administration: An introduction]. Warsaw: Liber.

Jacquot, S., and C. Woll, eds. 2003. *Les usages de l'Europe. Acteurs et transformations européennes*. Paris: L'Harmattan.

Janicki, M., and P. Pytlakowski. 1998. Pieluchy Władzy: Grupa Wiesława Walendziaka [New power: The Wiesław Walendziak's entourage]. *Polityka*, 4 April.

Jasiewicz, K. 1997. Poland: Wałęsa's legacy to the presidency. In *Postcommunist presidents*, ed. R. Taras, 130–67. Cambridge: Cambridge University Press.

Jupille, J., J. Caporaso, and J. Checkel. 2003. Integrating institutions: Rationalism, constructivism, and the study of the European Union. *Comparative Political Studies* 36 (1–2): 7–40.

Kabele, J., and L. Linek. 2004. *Decision-making of the Czech cabinet: EU accession and legislative planning between 1998 and 2004*. Paper prepared for the European Consortium for Political Research Joint Sessions of Workshops, Uppsala, Sweden, 13–18 April 2004.

Kassim, H. 2000. The national co-ordination of EU policy: Confronting the challenge. In *The national co-ordination of EU policy: The domestic level*, ed. H. Kassim, B. G. Peters, and V. Wright, 235–64. Oxford: Oxford University Press.

———. 2003. Meeting the demands of EU membership: The Europeanization of national administrative systems. In *The politics of Europeanization*, ed. K. Featherstone and C. Radaelli, 83–111. Oxford: Oxford University Press.

Kassim, H., B. G. Peters, and V. Wright, eds. 2000. *The national co-ordination of EU policy: The domestic level*. Oxford: Oxford University Press.

Keating, M. 2003. Regionalization in Central and Eastern Europe: The diffusion of a Western model? In *The regional challenge in Central and Eastern Europe: Territorial restructuring and European integration*, ed. M. Keating and J. Hughes, 51–67. Brussels: Lang.

King, G., R. O. Keohane, S. Verba. 1994. *Designing social enquiry: Scientific inference in qualitative research*. Princeton, N.J.: Princeton University Press.

Kodela, L., and G. Szilvásy. 1997. A Magyar Köztársaság kormányzati rendszerének szervei és szervezetei az 1996. decemberi állapot szerint [Organs and organizations of the government system of the Hungarian Republic, situation as of December 1996]. In *Magyarország politikai évkönyve* [Hungarian political yearbook], ed. S. Kurtán, P. Sándor, and L. Vass. Budapest: Demokrácia Kutatások Magyar Központja Alapítvány.

König, K. 1992. The transformation of a "real socialist" administrative system into a conventional West European system. *International Review of Administrative Sciences* 58:147–61.

Kopecký, P. 1996. The organization and behaviour of political parties in the Czech Parliament: From transformative towards arena type of legislature. In *Party structure and organization in East-Central Europe*, ed. P. G. Lewis, 66–88. Aldershot, Eng.: Edward Elgar.

———. 2001. *Parliaments in the Czech and Slovak republics: Party competition and parliamentary institutionalization*. Aldershot, Eng.: Ashgate.

Kormány. 1996. A közigazgatás reformjának programja [Programme for the reform of public administration]. *Magyar Közigazgatás* 46 (11): 641–71.

Körösényi, A. 1996. Demokrácia és patronázs [Democracy and patronage]. *Politikatudományi Szemle*, no. 4:35–62.

———. 1999. *Government and politics in Hungary*. Budapest: Central European University Press.

KPRM. 1998. *Informacje o Działalności Komitetów Rady Ministrów w Latach 1993–1997* [A databook on the operation of the committees of the Council of Ministers in 1993–1997]. Warsaw, KPRM.

Kreppel, A. 2002. *Old dog new tricks: Understanding the role of the Sejm since democratization*. Paper presented at the meeting of the American Political Science Association, 29 August–1 September 2002.

Kritz, N., ed. 1995. *Transitional justice: How emerging democracies reckon with former regimes, country studies*. Vol. 2. Washington, D.C.: United States Institute of Peace Press.

Krok-Paszkowska, A. 2001. Divided government in Poland. In *Divided government in comparative perspective*, ed. R. Elgie. Oxford: Oxford University Press.

Kublik, A., and D. Wielowieyska. 1997. Moc Walendziaka [Walendziak's clout]. *Gazeta Wyborcza*, 13 November.

Kulesza, M., and A. Barbasiewicz. 1999. *Administracja na Rzecz Rządzenia* [Administrative capacity for governing]. Warsaw: Kancelaria Prezesa Rady Ministrów.

————. 2000. Funkcje gabinetów politycznych [The functions of the political cabinets]. *Służba cywilna* 1(1): 50–72.

Laffan, B. 2003. Managing Europe from home: Impact of the EU on executive government; A comparative analysis. Research project report, EU Fifth Framework Programme, Dublin, European Institute, University College Dublin.

Laver, M., and I. Budge, eds. 1992. *Party policy and coalition government*. London: Macmillan.

Laver, M., and N. Schofield. 1990. *Multiparty government*. Oxford: Oxford University Press.

Laver, M., and K. Shepsle. 1996. *Making and breaking governments: Cabinets and legislatures in parliamentary democracies*. Cambridge: Cambridge University Press.

Lengyel, L. 1993. *Útfélen* [Mid-way]. Budapest: Századvég Kiadó és 2000-ért Alapítvány.

Lepsius, M. R. 1997. Institutionalisierung und Deinstitutionalisierung von Rationalitätskriterien. In *Institutionenwandel*, ed. G. Göhler. Opladen, Ger.: Westdeutscher Verlag.

Lijphart, A., ed. 1992. *Parliamentary versus presidential government*. Oxford: Oxford University Press.

Linz, J., and A. Stepan. 1996. *Problems of democratic transition and consolidation: Southern Europe, South America and post-communist Europe*. Baltimore: Johns Hopkins University Press.

Lippert, B., and G. Umbach. 2005. *The pressure of Europeanisation: From post-communist state administrations to normal players in the EU system*. Baden-Baden, Ger.: Nomos Verlagsgesellschaft.

Lippert, B., G. Umbach, and W. Wessels. 2001. Europeanization of CEE executives: EU membership negotiations as a shaping power. *Journal of European Public Policy* 8 (6): 980–1012.

Lipski, J. 2003. *Analiza ilościowa projektów ustaw wniesionych do Sejmu IV kadencji w toku pierwszego roku jego działalności* [A quantitative analysis of draft legislation submitted to the 4th Sejm in the first year of its operation]. Warsaw: Biuro Studiow i Ekspertyz Kancelarii Sejmu.

Meyer-Sahling, J. H. 2001. Getting on track: Civil service reform in post-communist Hungary. *Journal of European Public Policy* 8 (6): 960–79.

————. 2003. Governance by discretion: Civil service reform in post-communist Hungary. PhD thesis, London School of Economics and Political Science, University of London.

————. 2004. Civil service reform in post-communist Europe: The bumpy road to depoliticisation. *West European Politics* 27 (1): 71–103.

Mikule, V. 1998. Zdokonalovani Verejne Spravy. *Narodni vzdelavaci fond*. Prague.

Millard, F. 2000. Presidents and democratization in Poland: The roles of Lech Walesa and Aleksander Kwasniewski in building a new polity. *Journal of Communist Studies and Transition Politics* 16 (3): 39–62.

Mittag, J., and W. Wessels. 2003. The "one" and the "fifteen"? The member states between procedural adaptation and structural revolution. In *Fifteen into one? The European Union and its member states*, ed. W. Wessels, A. Maurer, and J. Mittag, 413–53. Manchester: Manchester University Press.

Müller, W., and K. Strom, eds. 2000. *Coalition governments in Western Europe.* Oxford: Oxford University Press.

Nakrosis, V. 2003. Assessing governmental capacities to manage European affairs: The case of Lithuania. In *The road to the European Union.* Vol. 2, *Estonia, Latvia and Lithuania,* ed. V. Pettai and J. Zilonka, 104–39. Manchester: Manchester University Press.

National Training Fund. 1998. *An analysis of public administration of the Czech Republic: Summary Report.* PHARE project report. Prague: National Training Fund.

Nielsen, K., Jessop B., and J. Hausner. 1995. Institutional change in post-socialism. In *Strategic choice and path-dependency in post-socialism,* ed. J. Hausner, B. Jessop, and K. Nielsen, 3–44. Aldershot, Eng.: Elgar.

Niskanen, W. A. 1971. *Bureaucracy and representative government.* Chicago: Altine Atherton.

Nunberg, B. 1997. *Leading the horse to water.* Paper presented at the Conference on Comparative Civil Service Systems, University of Indiana, Bloomington.

———. 1999. Breaking administrative deadlock in Poland: Internal obstacles and external incentives. In *The state after communism: Administrative transitions in Central and Eastern Europe,* ed. B. Nunberg, L. Barbone, and H.-U. Derlien, 7–51. Washington, D.C.: World Bank.

———. 2000. *Ready for Europe: Public administration reform and European accession in Central and Eastern Europe.* Washington, D.C.: World Bank.

Nunberg, B., L. Barbone, and H.-U. Derlien. 1999. *The state after communism: Administrative transitions in Central and Eastern Europe.* Washington, D.C.: World Bank.

Offe, C. 1996. Designing institutions in East European transitions. In *The theory of institutional design,* ed. R. Goodin, 199–226. Cambridge: Cambridge University Press.

Olczyk, E., and M. Subotić. 2002. Wszyscy ludzie premiera [All the prime minister's men]. *Rzeczpospolita,* 24 January.

Olsen, J. P. 2003. Towards a European Administrative Space. *Journal of European Public Policy* 10 (4): 506–31.

Olson, D. M. 1997. Paradoxes of institutional development: The new democratic parliaments of Central Europe. *International Political Science Review* 18 (4): 401–16.

Olson, D. M., and P. Norton, eds. 1996. *The new parliaments of Central and Eastern Europe.* London: Frank Cass.

Orenstein, M. 1998. Vaclav Klaus: Revolutionary and parliamentarian. *East European Constitutional Review* 7 (1): 46–55.

Organization for Economic Co-operation and Development. 2000. *Public management developments in the Czech Republic: The 2000 update.* www1.oecd.org/puma/focus/compend/cz.htm (accessed May 2002).

Page, E. C., and V. Wright. 1999. Conclusion: Senior officials in Western Europe. In *Bureaucratic elites in Western European states: A comparative analysis of top officials,* ed. E. C. Page and V. Wright, 266–79. Oxford: Oxford University Press.

Paradowska, J. 1998. Służba czy drużba: raport o urzędnikach państwowych [Whose servants: A report on state officials]. *Polityka,* 14 March.

————. 2001. Tuczarnia Lewiatana: O Miękkim Państwie Raz Jeszcze [Leviathan's farm: The soft state revisited]. *Polityka*, February.

————. 2002. Miło już było. Aleksander Kwaśniewski i Leszek Miller: Konflikt, Spór, Różnica Zdań? [Good old times are over. Aleksander Kwaśniewski and Leszek Miller: Conflict, dispute or difference of opinion?]. *Polityka*, 23 February.

Pedersen, K., and R. Zubek. 2004. *State of the state in Poland.* DEMSTAR research report 17. Aarhus, Den.: DEMSTAR.

Pełczynski, Z. 1993. Rządzić to znaczy sterować [Governing means steering]. *Rzecz-pospolita*, 10 December.

Pennings, P., H. Keman, and J. Kleinnijenhuis. 1999. *Doing research in political science: An introduction to comparative methods and statistics.* Thousand Oaks, Calif.: Sage.

Peters, G., R. Rhodes, and V. Wright, eds. 2000. *Administering the summit: Administration of the core executive in developed countries.* Basingstoke, Eng.: Macmillan.

Pilczynski, J. 2001. Tak, jak chciał Miller [Just like Miller wanted it]. *Rzeczpospolita*, 19 December.

Pomahac, R. 1993. Administrative modernization in Czechoslovakia between constitutional and economic reform. *Public Administration* 71 (1–2): 55–63.

Proksa, A. 2002. Rządowy proces legislacyjny [The intra-executive legislative process]. Unpublished manuscript, Warsaw.

Radaelli, C. 2003. The Europeanization of public policy. In *The politics of Europeanization*, ed. K. Featherstone and C. Radaelli, 27–56. Oxford: Oxford University Press.

Reschova, J., and J. Syllova. 1996. The legislature of the Czech Republic. In *The new parliaments of Central and Eastern Europe*, ed. D. M. Olson and P. Norton, 82–107. London: Frank Cass.

Rhodes, R. A. 1994. The hollowing out of the state: The changing nature of the public service in Britain. *Political Quarterly* 65: 138–51.

————. 2003. What is new about governance and why does it matter? In *Governing Europe: Memorial volume for Vincent Wright*, ed. J. Hayward and A. Menon, 61–73. Oxford: Oxford University Press.

Rhodes, R. A. W., and P. Dunleavy, eds. 1995. *Prime minister, cabinet, and core executive.* Basingstoke, Eng.: Macmillan.

Riker, W. T. 1962. *The theory of political coalitions.* New Haven, Conn.: Yale University Press.

Rokita, J. M. 1998. Batalia o rząd [The struggle for a new government]. In *O Naprawę Rzeczpospolitej* [Reforming Poland], ed. A. Nelicki. Krakow: Platan/Instytut Spraw Publicznych.

Rybak, A. 2003. Kogo słucha premier [Who does the prime minister listen to?]. *Polityka*, 31 May.

Rybicki, M. 1985. *Studia nad Rządem PRL w Latach 1952–1980* [Studies on the government of the Polish People's Republic]. Warsaw: PAN.

Rydlewski, G. 2000. *Rządzenie Koalicyjne w Polsce* [Coalition governance in Poland]. Warsaw: Elipsa.

————. 2002. *Rządowy system decyzyjny w Polsce: studium politologiczne okresu transformacji* [The governmental decision-making system: A political science enquiry into the transformation period]. Warsaw: Elipsa.

Rzeczpospolita. 1999. Premier Wielkiej Poczciwości [A prime minister of great decency]. *Rzeczpospolita*, 25 February.

Sárközy, T. 1995. A kormány kezdeti müködése és az államapparatus [The initial functioning of the government and the state apparatus]. In *Kérdöjelek: a magyar kormány 1994–1995*, ed. Csaba Gombár. Budapest: Korridor Politikai Kutatások Központja.

————. 1996. *A hatékonyabb kormányzásért* [For a more effective government]. Budapest: Magvetô.

————. 1999. Az Orbán-kormány szervezeti felépítése. A politikai racionalitás kormányzati struktúrája? [The organizational set-up of the Orbán government. The government structure of political rationality?]. In *Magyarország politikai évkönyve* [Hungarian political yearbook], ed. S. Kurtán, P. Sándor, and L. Vass. Budapest: Demokrácia Kutatások Magyar Központja Alapítvány.

Sartori, G. 1994. *Comparative constitutional engineering*. Basingstoke, Eng.: Macmillan.

Saward, M. 1997. In search of the hollow crown. In *The hollow crown: Countervailing trends in core executives*, ed. P. Weller, H. Bakvis, and R. A. Rhodes, 16–36. London: Macmillan.

Scherpereel, J. A. 2003. Appreciating the third player: The European Union and the politics of civil service reform in East-Central Europe. Paper presented at the annual meeting of the American Political Science Association, Philadelphia, August 2003.

Schick, A. 1993. Governments versus budget deficits. In *Do institutions matter? Government capabilities in the United States and abroad*, ed. A. K. Weaver and B. Rockman, 187–236. Washington, D.C.: Brookings Institution.

Schopflin, G. 1993. *Politics in Eastern Europe: 1945–1992*. Oxford: Blackwell.

Siedentopf, H., and B. Speer. 2003. The European Administrative Space from a German administrative science perspective. *International Review of Administrative Sciences* 69:9–28.

SIGMA. 1999. *Public management profile: Bulgaria*. Paris: SIGMA.

————. 2003. *Czech Republic: Public service and the administrative framework assessment 2003*. http://www1.oecd.org/sigmaweb/PDF/assessments/Candidates 2003/CzechCivServ200603.pdf (accessed May 2004).

Spasov, B. 1977. *Konstitutsia i narodnoe predstavitel'stvo v Narodnoi Respublike Bolgarii* [Constitution and parliamentary representation in the People's Republic of Bulgaria]. Moscow.

Staniszkis, J. 1995. Polityka Postkomunistycznej Instytucjonalizacji w Perspektywie Historycznej [The politics of post-communist institutionalization in a historical perspective]. *Studia Polityczne*, no. 4:39–60.

————. 2000. The post-communist state: In search of a paradigm. *Polish Sociological Review*, no. 2:193–214.

Stembrowicz, J. 1985. O Koncepcji i Roli Rządu [On the concept and role of the executive]. In *Studia nad Rządem PRL w Latach 1952–1980* [Studies on the government of the Polish People's Republic 1952–1980], ed. M. Rybicki. Warsaw: PAN.

Strecková, Y. 1998. Public administration reform and the civil service: Interview with the Czech deputy minister of the interior. *Public Management Forum* 4 (6): 8–9.

Strom, K., I. Budge, and M. Laver. 1994. Constraints on cabinet formation in parliamentary democracies. *American Journal of Political Science* 38:303–35.

Stumpf, I. 1999. Kormányzásváltás 1998-ban [Change of governing in 1998]. In *Magyarország politikai évkönyve* [Hungarian political yearbook], ed. S. Kurtán, P. Sándor, and L. Vass. Budapest: Demokrácia Kutatások Magyar Központja Alapítvány.

Subotić, M. 1994. Bliżej służby cywilnej, dalej od reformy centrum [Getting closer to civil service, dragging feet on reform of centre of government]. *Rzeczpospolita*, 31 August.

———. 1996. Narodziny decyzji [The birth of decision]. *Rzeczpospolita*, 24 July.

———. 1997. Rząd pod świetlikiem [Inside the cabinet]. *Rzeczpospolita*, 7 March.

———. 1998. Co dzieje się w Kancelarii Premiera [What is going on in the prime minister's chancellery]. *Rzeczpospolita*, 24 February.

———. 1999. Spory o klocki władzy [Quarrels over the building blocks of power]. *Rzeczpospolita*, 17 May.

Szablowski, G. J. 1997. Division or cohesion in the Polish executive and the democratic order. In *Institutions and Democratic Statecraft*, ed. M. Heper, A. Kazancigil, and B. A. Rockman. Boulder, Colo.: Westview.

Szántó, A. 1992. Államháztartás a Dirigizmus Jegyében [Public finances under the influence of dirigisme]. *Társadalmi Szemle* 47 (1): 3–11.

Szczerbiak, A. 1998. Electoral politics in Poland: The parliamentary elections of 1997. *Journal of Communist Studies and Transition Politics* 14 (3): 58–83.

———. 2002. Poland's unexpected political earthquake: The September 2001 parliamentary elections. *Journal of Communist Studies and Transition Politics* 18 (3): 41–76.

———. 2003. Old and new divisions in Polish politics: Polish parties' electoral strategies and bases of support. *Europe-Asia Studies* 55 (5): 729–46.

Szente, Z. 1999. Közigazgatás és politika metszéspontján: a miniszterek és az államtitkárok rekrutációja Magyarországon [On the interface of public administration and politics: The recruitment of ministers and state secretaries in Hungary]. *Századvég*, no. 13:3–51.

Szilvásy, G. 1994. A Miniszterelnöki Hivatal négy éve [Four years of the Prime Minister's Office]. In *Magyarország politikai évkönyve* [Hungarian political yearbook], ed. S. Kurtán, P. Sándor, and L. Vass, 455–77. Budapest: Demokrácia Kutatások Magyar Központja Alapítvány.

———. 1995. A kormányváltás technikája [The technique of the change of government]. In *Magyarország politikai évkönyve* [Hungarian political yearbook], ed. S. Kurtán, P. Sándor, and L. Vass. Budapest: Demokrácia Kutatások Magyar Központja Alapítvány.

———. 1998. A közigazgatás szakmai vezetése, 1988–1998 [The professional governance of public administration]. In *Magyarország politikai évtizedkönyve. A rendszerváltás 1988–98* [Hungarian political decadebook. The change of system 1988–98], ed. S. Kurtán, P. Sándor, and L. Vass. Budapest: Demokrácia Kutatások Magyar Központja Alapítvány.

Taylor, M., and M. Laver. 1973. Government coalitions in Western Europe. *European Journal of Political Research* 1: 205–48.

Thuma, J., H. Polackova, and C. Ferreira. 1998. Reforms in public finance management. In *Public finance reform during the transition: The experience of Hungary*, ed. L. Bokros and J.-J. Dethier, 377–97. Washington, D.C.: World Bank.

Torres-Bartyzel, C., and G. Kacprowicz. 1999. The national civil service system in Poland. In *Civil service systems in Central and Eastern Europe*, ed. T. Verheijen, 159–83. Cheltenham, Eng.: Edward Elgar.

Ulicka, G. 1997. Reforma Centrum Rządu: Potrzeba i Zakres Politycznego Konsensusu [The reform of the centre of government: The need for and the scope of political consensus]. In *The reform of the government centre in Poland in light of European standards: The final report from the PHARE/OMEGA programme PL9208-01-01*, by the Warsaw University Faculty of Journalism and Political Science. Warsaw: Warsaw University Faculty of Journalism and Political Science.

URM. 1991. *Raport o stanie prac* [Progress report]. Warsaw: Urząd Rady Ministrow, Zespół do Opracowania Koncepcji Zmian w Organizacji Terytorialnej Państwa.

———. 1992. *Wstępne Założenia Przebudowy Administracji Publicznej* [The initial proposal for public administration reform]. Warsaw: Urząd Rady Ministrów, Zespółdo Spraw Reorganizacji Administracji Publicznej.

———. 1993. *Założenia i Kierunki Reformy Administracji Publicznej* [The principles and direction of the public administration reform]. Warsaw: Urząd Rady Ministrów, Pełnomocnik Rządu do Spraw Reformy Administracji Publicznej. Reprinted in *Samorząd Terytorialny*, January–February 1995.

———. 1995. *Założenia reformy Centrum Gospodarczego Rzadu* [The proposal for the economic centre of government reform]. Warsaw: Pełnomocnik Rady Ministrów do Spraw Reformy Centrum Gospodarczego Rządu.

Urząd Służby Cywilnej. 1999. *Sprawozdanie Szefa Urzędu Służby Cywilnej za rok 1999* [The annual report of the head of the civil service in 1999]. Warsaw: Urząd Służby Cywilnej.

———. 2000. *Sprawozdanie Szefa Urzędu Służby Cywilnej za rok 2000* [The annual report of the head of the civil service in 2000]. Warsaw: Urząd Służby Cywilnej.

———. 2001. *Sprawozdanie Szefa Urzędu Służby Cywilnej za rok 2001* [The annual report of the head of the civil service in 2001]. Warsaw: Urząd Służby Cywilnej.

———. 2002. *Sprawozdanie Szefa Urzędu Służby Cywilnej za rok 2002* [The annual report of the head of the civil service in 2002]. Warsaw: Urząd Służby Cywilnej.

Van der Meer Krok-Paszkowska, A. 1999. Poland. In *Semi-presidentialism in Europe*, ed. R. Elgie, 170–92. Oxford: Oxford University Press.

Van Stolk, C. C. 2005. Europeanization of regional and agricultural policy in the Czech Republic and Poland. PhD Thesis, London School of Economics and Political Science, University of London.

Vass, L. 1999. *Hungarian public administration reform and EU accession*. Budapest.

———. 2001. Civil service development and politico-administrative relations in Hungary. In *Politico-administrative relations: Who rules?* ed. T. Verheijen, 147–74. Bratislava: Network of Institutes and Schools of Public Administration in Central and Eastern Europe.

Verebélyi, I. 1996. A kormányzás és a közigazgatás reformjának tervezete [Plan for the reform of governing and public administration]. *Magyar Közigazgatás* 46 (4): 193–229.

———. 1998. Összefoglaló a közigazgatási reformfolyamat elsô szakaszáról és soron
következô feladatairól [Summary of the first stage of the public administration
reform and the tasks ahead]. *Magyar Közigazgatás* 48 (6): 321–36.

Verheijen, T. 1999a. *Civil service systems in Central and Eastern Europe.* Cheltenham,
Eng.: Edward Elgar.

———, ed. 1999b. Conclusions. In *Civil service systems in Central and Eastern
Europe,* ed. T. Verheijen, 327–38. Cheltenham, Eng.: Edward Elgar.

———, ed. 2001. *Politico-administrative relations: Who rules?* Bratislava, Slovakia:
Network of Institutes and Schools of Public Administration in Central and Eastern
Europe.

———. 2002. The European Union and public administration development in Central and Eastern Europe. In *Transitions from authoritarianism: The role of bureaucracy,* ed. R. Baker, 245–59. Westport, Conn.: Praeger.

Vidláková, O. 1999. *Civil services and state administrations. Country report: Czech
Republic.* Paris: SIGMA.

von Hagen, J. 1998. *Budgeting institutions for aggregate fiscal discipline.* ZEI Working
Paper B01. Bonn, Ger.: Zentrum fur Europäische Integrationsforschung, Rheinische Friedrich-Wilhelms-Universität.

von Hagen, J., and I. Harden. 1994. National budget processes and fiscal performance. *European Economy: Reports and Studies* 3:315–418.

Warsaw University Faculty of Journalism and Political Science. 1997. *The reform of
the government centre in Poland in light of European standards: The final report
from the PHARE/OMEGA programme PL9208-01-01.* Warsaw: Warsaw University
Faculty of Journalism and Political Science.

Wasilewski, J. 1990. The patterns of bureaucratic elite recruitment in Poland in the
1970s and 1980s. *Soviet Studies* 42 (4): 743–57.

Waszkielewicz, B., and M. D. Dort. 1999. Bitwa o Buzka: Intryga polityczna czy
problem charakterologiczny premiera [The batttle for Buzek: Political intrigue or
problem with premier's personality]. *Rzeczpospolita,* 4 March.

Weller, P. 1991. Support for prime ministers: A comparative perspective. In *Executive
leadership in Anglo-American systems,* ed. C. Campbell and M. J. Wyszomirski,
361–79. Pittsburgh, Pa.: University of Pittsburgh Press.

Weller, P., and H. Bakvis. 1997. The hollow crown: Coherence and capacity in central
government. In *The hollow crown: Countervailing trends in core executives,* ed.
P. Weller, H. Bakvis, and R. A. Rhodes, 1–15. Basingstoke, Eng.: Macmillan.

Weller, P., H. Bakvis, and R. A. Rhodes, eds. 1997. *The hollow crown: Countervailing
trends in core executives.* Basingstoke, Eng.: Macmillan.

Wiesenthal, H. 2001. Einleitung: Systemtransformation als Theorientest. In *Gele-
genheit und Entscheidung: Policies und Politics erfolgreicher Transformations-
steuerung,* ed. H. Wiesenthal, 9–31. Wiesbaden, Ger.: Westdeutscher Verlag.

Wildavsky, A. 1964. *The politics of the budgetary process.* Boston: Little, Brown.

———. 1986. *Budgeting: A comparative theory of the budgetary process.* Rev. ed.
New Brunswick, N.J.: Transaction.

Wolchik, S. L. 1997. The Czech Republic: Havel and the evolution of the presidency since 1989. In *Post-communist presidents,* ed. R. Taras, 168–94. Cambridge:
Cambridge University Press.

Wollmann, H. 1997. Institution building and decentralization in formerly socialist countries. The cases of Poland, Hungary, and East Germany. *Government & Policy* 15:463–80.

Wollmann, H., and T. Lankina. 2003. Local government in Poland and Hungary. From post-communist reform towards EU accession. In *Local democracy in post-communist Europe*, ed. H. Baldersheim, M. Illner, H. Wollmann, 96ff. Opladen, Ger.: Leske & Budrich.

Wollmann, H., H. Wiesenthal, and F. Bönker, eds. 1995. *Transformation sozialistischer Gesellschaften: Am Ende des Anfangs*. Opladen, Ger.: Westdeutscher Verlag.

World Bank. 1998. *Towards EU-accession: The Czech Republic*. Washington, D.C.: World Bank.

———. 1999. *Civil service reform: A review of World Bank assistance*. Report no. 19599. Washington, D.C.: World Bank.

———. 2000. *Progress toward the unification of Europe*. Washington, D.C.: World Bank.

Wright, V. 1996. The national co-ordination of European policy-making: Negotiating the quagmire. In *European Union: Power and policy-making*, ed. J. Richardson, 148–69. London: Routledge.

Wright, V., and J. Hayward. 2000. Governing from the centre: Policy co-ordination in six European core executives. In *Transforming British government*. Vol. 2,*Changing roles and relationships*, ed. R. A. W. Rhodes, 27–46. Basingstoke, Eng.: Macmillan.

Zasuń, R. 2000. Zero koalicji [Bogus coalition]. *Gazeta Wyborcza*, 13 May.

Zubek, R. 2001. A core in check: The transformation of the Polish core executive. *Journal of European Public Policy* 8 (6): 911–32.

———. 2005a. Complying with transposition commitments in Poland: Collective dilemmas, core executive and legislative outcomes. *West European Politics* 28 (3): 592–619.

———. 2005b. Europeanizing from the centre: Core executive institutions and transposition of the European Community legislation in Poland. PhD thesis, London School of Economics and Political Science, University of London.

List of Interviewees

Unless otherwise indicated, positions current at the time of interviews.

BULGARIA

Center of Government

Secretary-general, Council of Ministers' Administration
Head, Prime Minister's Cabinet
Head, Economic Policy Directorate, Council of Ministers' Administration

Ministry of Finance

Minister of finance, Atanasov and Lukanov governments
Minister of finance, Indzhova government
Minister of finance, Videnov government
Deputy minister of finance
Director, External Finance Directorate
Head of Division for European Integration and International Agreements, External Finance Directorate
Head of Division, Budget, and Treasury Directorate
Head of Strategic Policy Division, Budget, and Treasury Directorate
Research analysts, Budget, and Social Policy Department, Agency for Economic Forecasts

Other Institutions

Deputy chairman, Trade Union (Podkrepa)
Executive director, National Association of Municipalities
Head, Fiscal Services Department, Bulgarian National Bank
Official, Confederation of Independent Trade Unions
Research analyst, World Bank Resident Representation, Bulgaria
Research fellows, Centre for the Study of Democracy

CZECH REPUBLIC

Center of Government

Deputy minister for specialist agenda, Government Office
Head, Government Agenda Department, Government Office
Head, Secretariat of the Deputy Prime Minister for Economic Policy, Government Office
Head, Secretariat of the Tripartite Council, Government Office
Head, Secretariat of the Council for Social and Economic Strategy, Government Office
Permanent secretary, Legislative Council, Government Office
Official, Secretariat of the Council for Social and Economic Strategy, Government Office
Advisor, Deputy Prime Minister for Economic Policy, Government Office

Ministry of Finance

Minister of finance, Klaus governments
Deputy minister of finance, responsible for the budget
Director, State Budget Department
Head, Financial Organizations Unit, Department of International Organizations
Deputy director, Department for Financial Policies

Other Institutions

Governor, Czech National Bank
Deputy governor, Czech National Bank
Director, Supreme Audit Office
Deputy minister, Ministry of the Interior, responsible for public administration reform
Permanent secretary, Budget Committee, House of Deputies

Researchers

Director, Institute of State and Law, Czech Academy of Sciences
Professor, Faculty of Economics, Charles University, Prague
Professor, Faculty of Sociology, Charles University, Prague

HUNGARY

Center of Government

Minister heading the Prime Minister's Office
Administrative state secretary heading the Prime Minister's Office, Antall
government; currently responsible for parliamentary relations, Hungarian
National Bank
Administrative state secretary heading the Prime Minister's Office, Horn Gov-
ernment and prior to 1990 head of group, Economic and Financial Affairs
Ministry Desk, Prime Minister's Office

Ministry of Finance

Deputy minister of finance and advisor to the prime minister, Németh gov-
ernment
Political state secretary, Ministry of Finance, Antall government
Political state secretary and secretary of the Cabinet Economic Committee,
Horn government
Administrative state secretary; formerly deputy state secretary, 1990–1994
Deputy state secretary, responsible for macroeconomic forecasts, financial
affairs, and operational negotiations with the International Monetary Fund,
1990–1993; head of division, Hungarian National Bank
Head, Budget Planning Department
Deputy head, Department of Budget and Financial Policy

Other Institutions

Administrative state secretary (former), Ministry of Transport, Telecommu-
nication, and Water Management
Deputy state secretary, Ministry of Agriculture and Rural Development
Head of division, Ministry of Social and Family Affairs
Deputy chairman, Parliamentary Budget and Financial Affairs Committee;
member of the Budget Committee since 1990
Member of parliament and budget expert of the Alliance of Free Democrats
(SZDSZ)
Advisor to the president, State Treasury

Head of the International Monetary Fund Delegation to Hungary, 1990–1993, currently advisor to the president of the Hungarian National Bank
Political advisor, EU Delegation, Hungary
Economic advisor, EU Delegation, Hungary
Economic journalists, *Hungarian Economic Weekly* (*HVG*)

Researchers

Director, Hungarian Institute of Public Administration; former government commissioner for the modernization of public administration
Professor of economic law, Budapest University of Economics
Professor of political science, Budapest University of Economics
Professor of political science, Budapest University of Economics
Professor, Central European University
Researcher, Hungarian Institute of Public Administration
Researcher, Hungarian Institute of Public Administration

POLAND

Center of Government

Minister heading the Office of the Council of Ministers, Mazowiecki government
Head, Office of the Council of Ministers
Head, Prime Minister's Chancellery
Government commissioner for the reform of the center of government, 1995–1996
Government commissioner for the reform of public administration, 1992–1994, 1997–1999
Acting director-general, Prime Minister's Chancellery
Secretary-general, Council of Ministers
Head, Prime Minister's Political Cabinet, 1997–1999
Head, Prime Minister's Political Cabinet, 1999–2000
Head, Prime Minister's Political Cabinet, 2000–2001
Head of secretariat, Prime Minister's Political Cabinet, Prime Minister's Chancellery
Chief economic advisor to the prime minister, Buzek government; formerly advisor to the prime minister, Mazowiecki government
Director, Parliamentary Affairs Department, Prime Minister's Chancellery
Director, Policy Analysis Department, Prime Minister's Chancellery
Deputy director, Policy Analysis Department, Prime Minister's Chancellery
Director, Social Affairs Department, Prime Minister's Chancellery

Director, Government Agenda Department, Prime Minister's Chancellery
Director, Economic Affairs Department, Prime Minister's Chancellery

Ministry of Finance

Minister of finance and deputy prime minister (former)
Deputy minister of finance, responsible for the budget, 1995–2000
Deputy minister of finance, responsible for the budget, 1989–1994
Director, Budget Department
Director, Financial Policy and Analysis Department, 1991–2000

Other Institutions

Deputy prime minister, Suchocka government and chairman of the Public Finance Committee, 1991–1992 and 1997–1999
Member, Monetary Policy Council, National Bank of Poland
Head of Economic Section, Delegation of the European Commission to Poland
President of the Foundation for the Development of Local Democracy, Warsaw

Researchers

Director, Institute of Political Science, Warsaw University
Professor, Institute of Political Science, Warsaw University
Professor, Institute of Sociology, Warsaw University
Professor, Department of Economics, London School of Economics, advisor to the finance minister
Professor, Stefan Wyszynski University, Warsaw

Index

About the Authors

Martin Brusis is a research fellow at the Center for Applied Policy Research, Munich. **Vesselin Dimitrov** is senior lecturer, Department of Government, London School of Economics and Political Science. **Klaus H. Goetz** is reader in government, Department of Government, London School of Economics and Political Science. **Hellmut Wollmann** is professor emeritus of public administration, Humboldt University Berlin. **Radoslaw Zubek** holds a PhD in government from the London School of Economics and Political Science.